Including People *with*

DISABILITIES

in Faith Communities

Including People *with*
DISABILITIES
in Faith Communities

A GUIDE FOR SERVICE PROVIDERS, FAMILIES, & CONGREGATIONS

by

Erik W. Carter, Ph.D.
University of Wisconsin–Madison

·P·A·U·L·H·
BROOKES
PUBLISHING C⁰ ®

Baltimore • London • Sydney

Paul H. Brookes Publishing Co.
Post Office Box 10624
Baltimore, Maryland 21285-0624

www.brookespublishing.com

Typeset by Spearhead Global, Inc., Bear, Delaware.
Manufactured in the United States of America by Versa Press,
Inc., East Peoria, Illinois.

Most individuals described in this book are composites, pseudo-
nyms, or fictional accounts based on the author's actual experiences. Individuals' names have been changed and identifying
details have been altered to protect confidentiality.

Scripture quoted on page 17 taken from *The Message.* Copyright
© 1993, 1994, 1995, 1996, 2000, 2001, 2002. Used by permission
of NavPress Publishing Group.

The quote on page 86 is an excerpt from a statement commended for study, comment and action by the World Council of
Churches (2003).

Second printing, July 2010.

Library of Congress Cataloging-in-Publication Data

Carter, Erik W.
  Including people with disabilities in faith communities : a
guide for service providers, families, and congregations / by
Erik W. Carter. — 1st ed.
       p.   cm.
Includes bibliographical references and index.
ISBN-13: 978-1-55766-743-4 (pbk.)
ISBN-10: 1-55766-743-8
1. Church work with people with disabilities.   I. Title.

BV4460.C37 2007
259'.44—dc22   2007008484

British Library Cataloguing in Publication data are available
from the British Library.

Contents

1677

124945

About the Author

Erik W. Carter, Ph.D., Assistant Professor, Department of Rehabilitation Psychology and Special Education, University of Wisconsin–Madison, 432 North Murray Street, Madison, Wisconsin 53706-1496

Dr. Carter received his doctorate in special education from Vanderbilt University in Nashville. His research and writing focuses on effective strategies for including children and youth with developmental disabilities more fully and meaningfully in schools and communities. With Dr. Carolyn Hughes, Dr. Carter co-wrote *The Transition Handbook: Strategies High School Teachers Use that Work* (Paul H. Brookes Publishing Co., 2000) and *Success for All Students: Promoting Inclusion in Secondary Schools Through Peer Buddy Programs* (Allyn & Bacon, 2006).

Foreword

Signs and Invitations

Several years ago, the Bethsaida Task Force, a committee working on accessibility and inclusion issues for Episcopal congregations in the Diocese of Newark, New Jersey, brought a resolution to the annual meeting of the Diocese. The resolution proposed that any church that had a sign on its front lawn stating the name of the church and the phrase "Everyone's Welcome" should have to take the welcome phrase off by a certain date if the building was not accessible to everyone, especially people with disabilities. The resolution did not pass, but it generated a great deal of discussion, leading to creative initiatives and actions in many parishes in the diocese.

Signs of hospitality and real invitations, not just announcements or proclamations of inclusiveness…those are two of the many themes that are important to the central message of *Including People with Disabilities in Faith Communities: A Guide for Service Providers, Families, and Congregations*, by Erik Carter. I would propose that the book itself is a sign and an invitation. It is a sign that captures some of the multitude of creative inclusive ministries and religious supports happening around the country. It is an invitation to clergy and laity in faith communities on the one side, and special educators and service providers on the other, to work together in new and creative ways to tap the real and potential power of congregations to support children and adults with disabilities and their families. The vision of congregations is one in which inclusion is expected, contributions are possible, and communities are strengthened.

This book is a sign in a number of other ways, as well. It is the first book published by Paul H. Brookes Publishing Co. that focuses entirely on building inclusive faith communities and spiritual supports. Brookes Publishing Co. is justifiably known and recognized as a premier publisher of books for professionals and parents but is not known to many clergy and congregations. The book is also one of the first by a professor of special education working within a public university that addresses the important role of spirituality and congregational supports in the lives of many children, adults, and families. One of the long-awaited gifts of this book, then, is having someone immersed in the field of special education bring some of the tools and lessons learned in inclusive schools around behavioral supports, inclusive education, and strategies for learning and teaching into the world of religious education in language that is accessible and usable by religious educators and laity. Just as important, the book invites congregations and clergy to think about special educators and other professionals in their communities as resources.

These signs point to an emerging interest on the part of researchers and practitioners from the secular sciences and disciplines in the importance of inclusive congregational supports as a way to address both spiritual and religious needs as well as many other areas that contribute to quality of life (e.g., social inclusion, friendship and connection, recreation, lifelong learning, cooperative caregiving, and opportunities for service and contribution), or as Dr. Carter says in Chapter 5, how they can offer support "the other six days."

Thus, while the book is an invitation to faith communities to "practice what they preach" about inclusion and welcoming everyone, it offers the same invitation to educators, advocates, and service providers to do the same regarding individual choice, quality of life, collaboration, and community inclusion. With both groups, Dr. Carter practices what he preaches in a wonderful message in the book—that an invitation that is not known and received is more of an announcement or decree than a real invitation. The real importance of this book is that it is a tool that can be used by congregations, families, teachers, service providers, and advocates to move beyond pronouncements or prescriptions about what congregations or agencies *should* be doing to act as a resource that empowers people on both "sides" of the congregation with the tools to turn vision into reality.

This book is a treasure trove of tools. It includes comprehensive reviews of the literature addressing spirituality, disability, and inclusive faith supports. Dr. Carter summarizes and outlines many of the barriers that hinder effective response without getting bogged down in them, preferring to provide a number of pathways and planning strategies that congregations and agencies can use to address particular concerns. For example, he provides or points to assessment and planning tools for congregations that are reflecting on what they need to do, samples of individual assessments and plans that can be used to support individual children or to develop an individual religious education plan, several types of spiritual assessments that can be used by agencies and service providers, and lots of examples and strategies throughout for specific kinds of action.

Planning strategies, partnerships, and tools—all of these are ways to help realize the promise inherent in inclusive congregations and communities. Dr. Carter has provided us with a resource so that congregations who, as he says, are compelled "by deep love and sacred call," will never let their invitation, welcome, and hospitality be diminished by the fact of disability. But the power of this book is that he also invites service providers and educators—who are also compelled by deep commitment—to embrace the importance of spirituality and inclusive congregational supports rather than avoiding them because of a lack of professional vision or just because these individuals have never done it that way before. The book is also a resource that parents and families can use to bring these worlds—those of congregations, service providers, educators, and their own loved ones—together.

Two of my favorite stories from my own experience point to the power of invitation for the sake of the families with children and adult family members whom congregations, schools, and agencies support. One came from the mother of a child with Down syndrome who responded to my invitation to the audience to share some of their "church stories." She said, "We took our minister with us to the IEP [individualized education program] at the school. It was wonderful. We got everything we wanted.... They thought he was our lawyer." That story always gets a laugh in a world of professional–parent relationships in which collaborative planning too often becomes adversarial. But think about the possibilities. A minister, priest, or rabbi offers to go with a family to an IEP meeting, thereby communicating the message, "We know that this is an anxious time. Can we support you? And we would like to know what they are doing at school (or through an agency's IHP [individualized habilitation plan] or person-centered plan) so we know better how to support your son/daughter." And think what it would do for professionals from schools or agencies to realize that there was, indeed, a generic community organization or natural support that was lined up, ready to work on many kinds of supports, and also willing to advocate for and with the family.

In just such another story, a religious educator attended the IEP meeting of a child with autism in which the religious leader heard that a major issue was the child's refusal to speak at school. The religious educator was able to offer that the boy had, in fact, just sung in the Christmas pageant at the church.

Twenty years ago, as adults with developmental disabilities were moving out of the facility where I was chaplain and coordinator of religious services, a local pastor once said to me, "Bill, I saw eight of your people at the mall yesterday." "Your people." The truth was that more than half of that group lived in a group home near his church, and they had been telling me about the importance of the welcome and hospitality they had felt there. As one woman said, "You know, they treat us just like we were one of them."

The real gift and power of inclusive congregations and collaborative partnerships between congregations, schools, and agencies is that people with intellectual, developmental, and other disabilities and their families will indeed feel like they belong, not in a particular place apart from others, but in places such as churches and schools that are the hearts of our communities. They will know that belonging is real, and, we, both in faith communities and public services, will know that we have contributed to helping build that sense of belonging and purpose. Or, to paraphrase one version of sacred scripture, "You who were once strangers and felt like no people are now our people. The dividing walls of partition have indeed been broken down," and we are learning, together, about the richness of inclusive community. Enjoy and use this book as just such an invitation to that kind of community and as a sign of things partially present and more to come. You may indeed experience what Dr. Carter describes in his acknowledgments as "an unexpected invitation—the one I tried so many different ways to refuse," which becomes a form of revelation and transformation.

Bill Gaventa, M.Div.
Associate Professor, Pediatrics
The Elizabeth M. Boggs Center on Developmental Disabilities
Robert Wood Johnson Medical School
University of Medicine and Dentistry of New Jersey
Editor
Journal of Religion, Disability, & Health

Foreword

Belonging, Believing, and Becoming

Erik Carter's book title presages two key concepts: *inclusion* and *faith communities*. The first concept—inclusion (belonging)—implies a welcoming posture, something beyond simply being *in*, more like being *of* and being eagerly taken in. The second—faith communities—asks us to consider what *community* means beyond a coming-together, a conjoining of people, and it also asks us to inquire into the meaning of *faith* (believing and becoming). Both inclusion and faith communities challenge us to look at what they mean in terms of people with intellectual and related disabilities. These individuals, along with people without disabilities, are the objects of inclusion into communities that are brought together by a shared faith. What does it mean to belong, to believe, and to become in the context of a distinction that makes a difference—cognitive limitations? Taking for granted that inclusion and belonging are parts of another journey, the one toward faith, the one toward believing and becoming faithful, Dr. Carter's book challenges its readers to ask, "What has been?" and then "What might be?" and to answer those questions at two levels, the personal and the congregational.

Having highlighted these questions, we must approach (and perhaps answer) them in our capacities as parents of a 39-year-old son, JT, who experiences an intellectual disability, autism, and bipolar disorder. Our responses echo our own concerns as well as those of our nation about secular segregation, but we ground them in pastoral—that is, congregational—environments. Our answers also mitigate those concerns by acknowledging that full participation in a community of worship entails more than physical integration. *Being in* is not the same as *belonging to*.

We were raised in and still participate in the liberal Protestant sects—Rud as a High Church Episcopalian and Ann as a Methodist originally, and now we are both members of the United Church of Christ. During the 26 years we have lived in our present community, we (along with JT; his sister Amy, now 31; and his sister Kate, now 28) have attended our church for a variety of reasons: to be guided in the way of the faithful; to be challenged to be more faithful; to know how to act in Christian ways; to raise our three children to know the nature of faithfulness and then seek their own faithfulness; to confess our shortcomings; to receive the undeserved assurance of grace and forgiveness; and, truth be told, to have respite from being constant advocates for JT's full citizenship in his community. Being in church, then, is a place for both our hearts and our souls—our spirits— to be informed, and for our family as a whole and each of its members to connect intellectually and spiritually with the Lord.

Dr. Carter's book addresses these reasons—these rationales for participation in communities of worship—as they apply to people with intellectual and related disabilities. It is appropriate to preface the book, then, in terms relevant to JT; not that our son is an ideal exemplar of people with his disabilities, but because his experiences are comparable enough to many of them that his narrative may speak to other readers even as a parable teaches large lessons in diminutive terms.

JT conforms readily to expectations about proper "church behavior," dressed in a blazer, button-down shirt and tie, eager to greet and be greeted, and glad to open his wallet to make his offering. He nonetheless is unable to participate fully in the "head" or intellectual aspect of the services. The readings from the Old Testament, Gospel, and bulletins, the recitations of births and deaths, and the message of the sermon—all these pass over him, being just so many words spoken at levels incomprehensible to him. The reasons that we and other people attend church—to be guided, challenged, and instructed on how to act in faith-witnessing ways—are nearly completely irrelevant to him. That is always so because of his intellectual disability and especially so when JT is in his place in a pew and aspects of his bipolarity are acute and affect his behavior: Depression causes sleepiness and mania causes restlessness.

Congregational tolerance is requisite, and, because we sit in the same pew nearly every time we attend, as do our "neighbors" in their pews, it is forthcoming—a manifestation of Christian behavior in a Christian setting. We have appreciated those silent gestures of acceptance, the refusal to stare or give disapproving looks, to say "shush" or "quiet, please," or to shift uncomfortably and even change pews.

Yet something else happens when JT attends church, something beyond tolerance. It is something less desirable: It is segregation, of a sort. True, the ushers and ministers know JT and go out of their way to greet him. Those are personal gestures. Congregationally, the community is welcoming. Corporately, however, the church does not yet know how to include JT. For all of its aspirations for openness and inclusion, our church (like others) remains primarily accessible to those who do not have intellectual (and other) disabilities, and JT remains on the outside of much of its being. Disability and shut doors are uneasy companions.

When JT was of Sunday-school age, staff and teachers simply did not know how to accommodate their activities, curricula, and methods to JT in church-school classes or confirmation. Now that he is an adult, potentially a lifelong learner of Christian doctrine, JT is still not involved in church activities beyond the worship service. It is not that staff and lay workers are unwilling; it is that they simply have not had the occasion to learn what to do in order to genuinely invite his participation.

Nor have we taken on church-based advocacy to instruct or prod these individuals. Church attendance is a time for many benefits for us as his parents and (when they lived in our community) his sisters. Advocacy interferes with the reasons why we attend church. It diminishes the benefits of attendance. Like nearly every family affected by disability, we seek times to untether ourselves from that single aspect—not from our son, but from that particular trait and its manifold demands. Like those other families, we knowingly make trade-offs, asking forgiveness if our decisions are unacceptable in the eyes of the Lord. In a peculiar way, JT's attendance in church—his very presence in the sight of God and the congregation—prompts us to ask ourselves about our own shortcomings (Could we do more? Should we?) and to turn, yet again, to the ultimate donor of forgiveness.

This church's staff and lay volunteers' behavior is equally rife with lessons. Their non-deliberate segregation might seem intolerable, but we do not find it so. It is not motivated by animus toward disability and those who experience it. It originates from secular segregation and lack of know-how. It is the byproduct of our secular lives, an emblem of our culture. Fortunately, this type of segregation is overcome by a form of integration that JT brings to his attendance on his own. By himself and for himself, he conquers institutional, congregational separateness as well as our own fatigue as advocates and our own needs to be in the moment, to open our heads and hearts to lessons and liturgy. And in so conquering, he becomes a lesson in and of himself.

How does JT do this? JT's head—his intellect—is the only barrier; his heart—his spirit—is the conquering force. When the minister or congregation or both raise up prayers of confession, assurance, and grace, JT either speaks the same prayers, quietly mumbling words or semi-words, or is silent, head bowed, eyes shut, and, in that way—his way—he is fully participating in those corporate and individual moments of speaking with God. He has a sense of "surroundedness"—of being embedded in something quite beyond himself, beyond his understanding.

When the musical preludes, offertories, and postludes fill the sanctuary—the organ with all throttles open, the bell choirs in plenary ringing, the vocal choirs in full throat—then JT connects with God. No parishioner is more moved than he by the High Season music—the traditional Advent and Christmas hymns, the soul-raising alleluias of Easter day, the pilgrim hymn of Thanksgiving, the martial power of *Onward, Christian Soldiers*, the inner peace-giving of *Abide with Us*, and the closing chant that asks God to smite death's sting. Music is a channel to God. JT takes a full journey in that channel.

And then there is the Lord's Prayer. When it declares, "Thine is the Kingdom, the Power, and the Glory," JT places special emphasis on "the Power." He stiffens his back and fills his chest with air, and then enunciates "Power" with more vigor than he speaks any other word in any other sentence at any other time. He pushes out the "P" as though it were a sour lemon. In nearby pews, parishioners cannot fail to hear; they nod in agreement, or, when the service is over, they tilt their heads in respectful silent greeting to JT—their acknowledgment that he is singularly different and perhaps singularly blessed. Nearly 30 pews away and across the aisle in front of the altar, our minister looks up, spots JT, fails to control a satisfied grin, and knows that, whatever efficacy he had in reaching others in the congregation that day, he—as God's minister—has touched JT.

Is that the end of the mystery? We think not. Turn the matter upside down and ask about JT's role as an actor, not as a recipient of the Holy Spirit. Is it that JT has touched the minister and the whole congregation? Their responses speak yes. But there is more to this narrative.

"Power," spoken so potently by one who is seemingly so powerless because of his disability, takes on different meaning. It is no longer an ordinary, well-memorized, rote-recited attribute of God; it is a trait manifest at that very moment in this one person, and through him, made accessible to all of us in the congregation. JT vitalizes God's power—he makes it rejuvenating, life-giving—by proclaiming it potently. He is a powerful agent of the omnipotent. And in that way he no longer is separate and segregated. He is as fully included as any one of us. What he and others lack in their heads, they supplant by what they have in their hearts. Spirit is recompense for intellectual disability.

Belong? No, JT does not in every way, such as the way of the head or physical participation, but, in the most important way, that of the spirit. Believe? Yes, JT does, and he offers that belief to others, proclaiming that, even as he believes, so can we all. Become? Yes, JT becomes another person when speaking the ultimate prayer and, in being particularly empowered and powerful, he evidences the transformation that comes with faith.

Dr. Carter's two key concepts—inclusion (belonging), and communities of faith (believing and becoming)—describe Christian journeying, pilgrimages of faith. They tell us how we can take people as they are, how we can come to the naturally spiritual person. Moreover, Dr. Carter challenges us to find the way to hear lessons about Samaritans and lepers, blind men and those at death's door, wrestlers like Jacob who struggled with his Jehovah—about those who, in parables, teach us what we, in our congregations, can do and, indeed, must do. JT calls us—as do others with differences and disabilities—to confront our congregations and ourselves, and to seek to know God and walk in His ways by knowing about differences and their significance.

It is not as though JT and his peers were in the temple, overturning all of our mores; it is more the case that they ask us "What kind of temple do you have, and is it faithful enough?" That is a question this book asks, and it is one that it helps us answer.

Rud Turnbull
Marianna and Ross Beach Professor of
Special Education and Life Span Studies
Co-founder and Co-director, Beach Center on Disability
The University of Kansas, Lawrence

Ann Turnbull
Marianna and Ross Beach Professor of
Special Education and Life Span Studies
Co-founder and Co-director, Beach Center on Disability
The University of Kansas, Lawrence

Preface

Across the country, congregations are beginning to discover their incredible capacity to welcome and weave people with developmental disabilities and their families into the life of their faith community. These congregations often speak poignantly and passionately of how their communities have been enriched by the presence, gifts, and contributions of people with disabilities. At the same time, service and support providers are exploring new avenues for partnering with congregations to expand the opportunities that people with disabilities have to assume more valued roles within their faith communities. They readily speak of how supporting people's spiritual aspirations—just like supporting other aspirations—can be instrumental in enhancing individuals' quality of life, promoting self-determination, and increasing community inclusion. Growing networks of caring and committed people are bridging these movements, gathering regularly to develop new opportunities and supports that enable people with disabilities to participate more fully throughout their communities. Together, they are learning how communities can work collaboratively to increase their own capacity to invite, include, and support their neighbors with disabilities.

This book is an invitation for you to join in these efforts.

Despite many encouraging signs of progress, however, there is still much work to do. The promise and possibilities of full inclusion remain unfulfilled. Most congregations continue to struggle with how to meaningfully support people with developmental disabilities in various aspects of congregational life. Too many service and support providers express uncertainty and reluctance regarding how to address the spiritual and religious needs of those whom they serve, instead deferring responsibility for meeting these needs to someone else or overlooking them altogether. And efforts to initiate broad changes across entire communities sometimes remain narrow, uneven, or stagnant. These challenges can create great frustration. They also can offer up an incredible opportunity for congregations, service providers, and other community members to make a real and lasting impact in the lives of people with disabilities.

The fact that you are reading this preface suggests that you may be ready to embark on this journey. If so, this book will equip you with practical strategies and helpful resources to guide you along the way. It is a book about *hospitality*—written to show congregations how to extend sincere invitations and a genuine welcome to people with disabilities and their families. It is a book about *belonging*—encouraging congregations to strive for more than just shared presence and challenging them to move toward a place where people with disabilities truly are recognized as integral members of the congregation. It is a book about *community*—affirming that when people with disabilities are not worshipping, learning, living, and serving among us, our communities are less then they could be, ought to be, and were intended to be. It is a book about *natural supports*—calling on service providers to seek out and draw on the rich reservoirs of support and relationships that already exist in their communities. And it is a book about *reciprocity*—reminding all of us that we have as much to gain as we have to give from our relationships with people with disabilities.

May this book be a source of encouragement and guidance as you begin this journey.

Acknowledgments

It has been almost 15 years since a man named Bob Cagle extended an unexpected invitation—the one I tried so many different ways to refuse—to spend my summers in the company of people with developmental disabilities. This certainly was not on my agenda; indeed, such encounters would have never before crossed my mind. Bob introduced me to John Ray, Michael, Margaret, Wayne, and many other men and women whose friendship and faith, grace and gifts I found so attractive. My long-held notions about the roles of giver and receiver, guide and traveler, and counselor and camper were turned upside down through these new relationships. The seeds of this book were first planted there at that camp along the edges of Cane Creek in Georgia.

I have had the opportunity to learn alongside many fine people in the years since, including Jennifer Aitken, Marsha Baggett, Judd Brannon, Patty Brubaker, Liz Cloaninger, Kip Conner, Lyle Dorsett, Keith Gerecitano, Steve Grant, Hope Hallsworth, Pat Kilgo, April Lewandowski, David Light, Brooke McLaughlin, Joe Metzker, Susan Owens, Andy Peabody, Robbie Quinn, Jeanette Randall, Jenny Rogers, Stephanie Spencer, and Susan Summerour. I am grateful to Traci Dutter, Lisa Pugh, Tom and Shari Purnell, Beth Swedeen, Pam Stoika, and Diane Thomas for so generously sharing their time and thoughts with me. Thank you to Lynn Au, Laura Blakeslee, Dana Brickham, Danielle Pelsue, and Matthew Pesko for their assistance in tracking down many, many resources.

A special word of appreciation goes to the wonderful team at Paul H. Brookes Publishing Co. who partnered with me on this project. I am especially grateful to Rebecca Lazo, whose vision and enthusiasm have been a source of great encouragement. I also thank Leslie Eckard, Jen Lillis, Steve Peterson, Jessica Reighard, and other members of the Brookes staff for their professionalism, expertise, and persistence.

I am especially thrilled that Bill Gaventa, Rud Turnbull, and Ann Turnbull have so eloquently introduced this book with their forewords. Bill is a true pioneer in this important work. His writings, trainings, and conversations have been a source of inspiration, encouragement, and support for countless congregations, families, service providers, and communities. He shares his many gifts so generously and so effectively. The contributions of Rud and Ann to improving the quality of life of people with disabilities and their families truly are inspirational. Each has left a deep and indelible mark on our field.

Finally, I thank three people who inspire me each day with their love and grace—Sharon, Mason, and Madeleine.

To
Bob
for the invitation
and to
Michael, Margaret, John Ray, and Wayne
for sharing your gifts

Chapter 1

Lives of Faith

Moving Toward Full Participation

For as long as he can remember, Ethan has felt certain of his call to serve and minister to others. His outgoing personality, engaging smile, and seemingly endless compassion have been a source of great encouragement to others in his congregation. The congregation has surrounded him and sought out ways for Ethan to share and cultivate his gifts, nurturing him as he seeks God's direction for his life.

Rebecca cannot wait for weekends to arrive. The weekly services and other congregational activities offer a chance to refresh her spirit, to enjoy fellowship with friends, and to grow in her faith. As a volunteer in the youth program, Rebecca also finds that her synagogue is one of the few places where she really feels recognized as having something important to contribute. Occasionally, she and some of the other youth workers will get together during the week for a meal or to catch a movie.

For the Castillos, attending church together is an important aspect of family life. Knowing that their children love going to Sunday school, Carmen and Elias look forward to attending Mass as a couple. Indeed, it is one of the few times during the busyness of the week when they can slow down, reconnect with God, find encouragement for the challenges of everyday life, and be fed spiritually. Confident that their children are learning important life lessons and are well taken care of by their teachers, the Castillos are grateful for their church home.

Faith, community, relationships—each are important in the lives of Ethan, Rebecca, and the Castillo family. Indeed, millions of Americans affirm the importance of faith in their lives, most associate themselves with a particular community of faith, and substantial numbers gather together each week with others to worship, enjoy fellowship, learn,

1

and serve (Ammerman, 2005; Chaves, 2004). Within the life of a congregational community, faith is formed, shared, and strengthened; relationships are forged and deepened; and gifts are discovered, developed, and dispensed. It should come as little surprise that congregational life plays such an important role in the lives of so many people.

Unfortunately, too many people with disabilities do not experience the same opportunities as others to grow spiritually, enjoy community, and experience relationships. Conversations with faith community leaders, congregational members, families, and service providers often reveal an uncertainty about how to address the spiritual needs of children and adults with developmental disabilities. Parents struggle to find a faith community that will embrace their child; congregations express uncertainty with how to extend a meaningful welcome; and service providers wrestle with how best to support people with disabilities and their families in this important dimension of life. In fact, simply introducing a disability into the opening vignettes might alter the story lines substantially.

Because he has Down syndrome, Ethan's many gifts simply went unrecognized.

Living in a large group home, Rebecca lacked the staff support and transportation she needed to stay involved in her synagogue, leaving her disconnected from others in her community.

Carmen and Elias were unable to find a church willing to accept their daughter with autism into Sunday school. Tired of alternating who would attend worship services and who would stay home, the Castillos eventually stopped attending church altogether.

WHAT ARE DEVELOPMENTAL DISABILITIES?

Between 4 and 6 million children and adults in the United States have developmental disabilities (e.g., Braddock et al., 2005; Steinmetz, 2006). *Developmental disability* is a label shared by an incredibly diverse group of people who often experience substantial difficulties in several major life activities—such as mobility, self-care, language, socialization, learning, or independent living. For these individuals, their disabilities affect them cognitively and/or physically, and their need for support is expected to last throughout their lifetimes. As a result, children and adults with developmental disabilities often require a constellation of services and supports to participate fully and meaningfully in the life of their communities. The specific conditions they experience may sound familiar to you, including autism, cerebral palsy, Down syndrome, mental retardation (often called intellectual disability), or traumatic brain injury. Other conditions may be less familiar, such as Angelman syndrome, deaf-blindness, fetal alcohol syndrome, Fragile X syndrome, Prader-Willi syndrome, or Williams syndrome.

Although labels usually highlight differences, people with and without developmental disabilities share almost everything in common. *Like everyone else*, people with developmental disabilities need support to live a good life. However, this support sometimes must be a bit more intensive, deliberate, or lasting. *Like everyone else*, people with developmental disabilities have wonderful strengths and gifts that exist alongside their limitations. Yet, these incredible capacities too frequently are overlooked. *Like everyone else*, people with developmental disabilities will struggle in some contexts and shine in others. Unfortunately, they usually are viewed only in terms of what they cannot do. And *like everyone else*, people with developmental disabilities want to express their spirituality and belong to a community. But these needs and connections are regularly overlooked.

PROGRESS TOWARD FULL PARTICIPATION

The last few decades have been a time of great change for children and adults with developmental disabilities. Remarkable progress has been made toward engaging people with disabilities more fully in their communities, both as active participants and meaningful contributors. Although people with developmental disabilities once resided largely on the peripheries, increasingly they are being woven into the fabric of community life. Schools, businesses, and communities are discovering their capacity to welcome, include, and support students, employees, and neighbors with disabilities. It is against this backdrop that we will first consider efforts to weave children and adults with developmental disabilities into congregational life. This progress should serve as a challenge to faith communities, raising expectations for what congregations should be accomplishing and pushing them to do more, to travel further, and to respond more profoundly. As you read on, ask yourself: *What is our congregation doing to welcome people with disabilities and their families? What is our agency or organization doing to support people to participate in all aspects of community life, including communities of faith?*

Inclusive Schools

Prior to 1975, public education was inaccessible or wholly unavailable to most children and youth with developmental disabilities. Spurred by parent advocacy, litigation, legislation, and research, the growth and development of special education services has progressed at a rapid pace. Today, under legislation such as the Individuals with Disabilities Education Improvement Act of 2004 (PL 108-446), every child with a disability is entitled to a free and appropriate public education alongside their peers without disabilities. Schools are mandated to support full participation, and no child can be excluded. In fact, the burden has since shifted to schools to explain why a child with disabilities should not participate in the same classes and activities as his or her peers.

Inclusive education is becoming a reality for increasing numbers of students with developmental disabilities (Williamson, McLeskey, Hoppey, & Rentz, 2006). These developments have been accompanied by improvements in attitudes toward students with disabilities and a broadening of expectations for all that these students might contribute (Krajewski & Hyde, 2000). Classmates speak vividly about the positive impact of learning alongside their peers with disabilities, often reporting personal growth, meaningful friendships, greater appreciation of diversity, and more accepting attitudes (e.g., Copeland et al., 2004). Teachers may wonder at first how to involve students with disabilities in their classrooms, but they often come to share how inclusion enhances the educational experiences of every student.

Inclusive Workplaces

A meaningful job was not always considered a realistic outcome for people with developmental disabilities, particularly those with more extensive support needs. To many people with disabilities, sheltered workshops (i.e., segregated workplaces only employing workers with disabilities) once were the only employment option available. Increasingly, the doors to real job opportunities are being opened and people with disabilities are making exciting contributions to the workforce. Almost one-third of youth and adults with developmental disabilities are working competitively or with support in their communities (Rusch & Braddock, 2004). With support from co-workers or a job coach (i.e., a paid staff person who assists someone on the job), people with disabilities are enjoying opportunities to earn money, cultivate meaningful social relationships, expand their skills, realize personal goals, and contribute back to their communities.

As with public education, legislation has played an important role in increasing access to meaningful employment for people with developmental disabilities. Vocational rehabilitation services have been funded to support people with disabilities to enter the workforce, whereas work incentives have been offered to encourage employers to hire people with disabilities. As employers gain experience working with people with disabilities and discover their contributions to workplace culture, they are expressing greater willingness to hire employees with disabilities in the future (Morgan & Alexander, 2005). In fact, customers may be more likely to support businesses that make this kind of commitment (Siperstein, Romano, Mohler, & Parker, 2006).

Inclusive Neighborhoods

Until recently, community living was an uncommon experience for people with developmental disabilities. Many parents were encouraged to place their children in state-supported institutions. Legislation and advocacy efforts since the 1990s, however, have been reshaping how society thinks about community living for people with disabilities. Public policy is shifting away from supporting institutional living toward greater support for more typical residential situations. States are being challenged to shut down institutions and create opportunities and supports that enable adults with developmental disabilities to live more independently in real communities (Prouty, Smith, & Lakin, 2004). People with disabilities also are enjoying greater involvement in their communities. Laws such as the Americans with Disabilities Act (ADA) of 1990 (PL 101-336) mandate that everyone be given equal opportunities and access to public transportation, accommodations, and community services.

Great strides have been made toward including people with developmental disabilities in the mainstream of everyday community life. These movements toward full participation in school, work, and community settings echo several themes. First, inclusion progressively is becoming the expectation, rather than the exception. As Americans attend school, go to work, and interact in their communities, they increasingly can expect to meet their fellow neighbors with disabilities. Second, when given basic opportunities and some additional support, people with developmental disabilities repeatedly demonstrate their incredible capacity to contribute to the life of their community. Third, communities are strengthened by the presence and participation of people with disabilities. Over and over, people share how everyone benefits when people with and without disabilities get to know one another. Even with these strides, however, there is still much left to do. Although greater numbers of people with developmental disabilities are *participating* in school, work, and community life, the vision of true *membership* remains yet unrealized for too many.

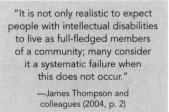

"It is not only realistic to expect people with intellectual disabilities to live as full-fledged members of a community; many consider it a systematic failure when this does not occur."

—James Thompson and colleagues (2004, p. 2)

MEANINGFUL PARTICIPATION IN COMMUNITIES OF FAITH

Many congregations can boast of a long and sustained history of welcoming people with developmental disabilities and their families into their faith communities. Unfortunately, the history of faith communities, as with the history of all institutions, has been uneven—sometimes stellar, but other times lacking (see Covey, 2004; Merrick, Gabbay, & Lifshitz, 2001; Miles, 1995; Morad, Nasri, & Merrick, 2001). Taken together, the responsiveness of faith communities has been less than resounding; the call to be more inclusive remains largely unanswered. Many people with developmental disabilities and their families simply are not being welcomed into congregational life.

Most Americans associate themselves with a congregational community (Dudley & Roozen, 2001). One might expect similar involvement among people with disabilities and their families. However, a series of national surveys conducted by the National Organization on Disability and Harris Interactive offers revealing insight into the religious participation of adults with a wide range of disabilities. A recurring theme of the past five surveys—conducted between 1986 and 2004—is that the presence of a disability affects congregational participation. Adults with disabilities are involved in faith communities substantially less often than are adults without disabilities. In their 2004 survey, 44% of adults with severe disabilities reported attending a church, synagogue, or other place of worship at least once a month, compared with 57% of people without disabilities. This 13 percentage-point discrepancy, which stood at 20 percentage points in 2000, is often dubbed the "participation gap."

Other research projects focusing specifically on children and adults with developmental disabilities have echoed similar findings:

- According to their parents, fewer than one-half of children and youth with autism, deaf-blindness, intellectual disabilities, or multiple disabilities participated in religious group activities *at any point* during the previous year (Wagner, Cadwallader, & Marder, 2003; Wagner et al., 2002)

- When more than 200 parents of adolescents and young adults with autism were asked about their children's attendance at religious services, less than one-third reported that their child attended religious services on a weekly basis. Furthermore, only 11% of youth and adults with autism attended social events at religious settings more than once or twice a month (Orsmond, Krauss, & Seltzer, 2004).

- Kregel, Wehman, Seyfarth, and Marshall (1986) found that although almost half of young adults with intellectual disabilities attended church services, only 14% participated in other congregational activities, such as youth groups and choirs.

- Hayden and colleagues (1992) reported that almost one-third of children and adults with intellectual disabilities living in small foster or group homes "practically never" attended religious services; only about one-fourth "sometimes" attended religious services.

- Slightly more than half of the adults with developmental disabilities interviewed by McNair and Smith (2000) reported having attended church during the previous week. Most often, however, these adults attended church with family members or other housemates with disabilities.

The likelihood that people with disabilities and their families attend a congregation certainly is influenced by the extent to which they are welcomed and supported. Several research projects have looked at the ways in which congregations are responding to the needs of people with disabilities and their families.

- LaRocque and Eigenbrood (2005) surveyed 91 Christian, Jewish, and Muslim congregations about how accessible they were for people with disabilities. Most reported being only in the very early states of increasing their accessibility. For example, although 71% of congregations said general awareness of barriers to the participation of children and adults existed in their faith community, 69% of congregations reported that they had not yet started or were only getting started at transforming their community "into a place where children and adults with disabilities are welcomed, fully included, and treated with respect" (p. 60). Furthermore, only 53% of congregations said that they were well on their way to increasing the participation of people with disabilities in their congregation and only 28% had explored partnerships with community agencies and organizations serving people with disabilities.

- The U.S. Congregational Life Survey revealed that only 10% of congregations provided some form of care (e.g., respite care, home care, skills training) to people with disabilities attending their congregation or living in the broader community (Woolever & Bruce, 2002).

- In focus groups involving family members of children with intellectual and developmental disabilities, Poston and Turnbull found that although some parents reported their congregations were places of wonderful acceptance, other families "felt that their children were not accepted or that they did not have the support to participate fully" (2004, p. 103).

- Even for children and adults with disabilities who attend worship services, many aspects of congregational life may remain inaccessible. In a survey by Riordan and Vasa (1991), 44% of clergy reported that religious education was not available to people with developmental disabilities in their congregation.

- A national survey of Presbyterian pastors revealed that almost one-third knew of people in their congregation who did not participate in worship services or other church activities because the church's facilities were not easily accessible (Presbyterian Panel, 2004). An annual survey of congregations within the Christian Reformed Church of North America (2004) indicated that 43% of congregations were barrier-free, whereas the remainder were only partially accessible.

Collectively, these findings suggest that while some people with developmental disabilities and their families are welcomed into the life of their congregations, many more are not. Even among those individuals who do attend congregational activities, many feel overlooked and are present only at the margins. What stands in the way of people with and without disabilities worshipping, finding fellowship, learning, and serving alongside each other in meaningful ways?

BARRIERS TO FULL PARTICIPATION

The participation gap documented in the National Organization on Disability and Harris Interactive surveys can be attributed to a variety of factors, but the importance of one's religious faith does not appear to offer an adequate explanation. In fact, the same surveys consistently show that religious faith is as important to people with disabilities as it is to the rest of society. In 2004, 84% of adults with disabilities and 84% of adults without disabilities considered their religious faith to be "somewhat important" or "very important" to them. Indeed, numerous studies have explored the depth of faith and richness of spirituality among people with developmental disabilities (see Shogren & Rye, 2005; Swinton & Powrie, 2004; Zhang & Rusch, 2005). Clearly, lack of interest is not what is preventing people with disabilities from participating in congregational life.

If people with and without disabilities affirm the same degree of importance to their religious faith, what accounts for such discrepant levels of congregational participation? Children and adults with developmental disabilities who want to be part of a community of faith encounter a variety of barriers to full participation (e.g., Stookey, 2003; Vogel, Polloway, & Smith, 2006). Sometimes, barriers related to architecture, attitude, communication, programming, and liturgy within a congregation have the effect of pushing people to the margins or away altogether. For individuals or families visiting a congregation, these barriers—often subtle, but sometimes quite striking—may leave them feeling unwelcome and may prevent them from returning. Other barriers, however, prevent people with disabilities from ever coming to your congregation in the first place. Perhaps they were never extended an invitation, they lack reliable transportation, residential staff members have not supported their involvement, or they have never been guided in exploring their own spirituality and desired level of congregational participation. Although you may have very good intentions, you simply cannot welcome people if they never come through your doors. At the same time, it is not enough invite your neighbors through your doors, only to turn them away with your words and actions. A meaningful response will require that these barriers be addressed from *both* sides of the congregational door.

> "If bars are more accessible than altars, if theaters are more welcoming than churches, if the producers of PBS are more sophisticated about communication access than our liturgists, if the managers of department stores know better how to appeal to those with disabilities than our church leadership, if the publishers of popular magazines are more knowledgeable about alternative formats than those who produce religious materials, then we have failed to meet Christ's challenge to us all."
>
> —Mary Jane Owen (1993, p. 19)

Pushing People away from Community

How might your buildings, words, and actions facilitate or impede the participation of people with disabilities? As you read on, consider how barriers in each of these areas may hinder the involvement of anyone in your community, not just people with disabilities.

Architectural Barriers Can people enter through the doors of your congregation's building(s)? Once inside, can they navigate the worship space, classrooms, hallways, and restrooms? Can they navigate all of its features? Your building offers one of the first pronouncements of your congregation's theology. What do your facilities communicate about the commitments and values you hold? What messages do they convey about the importance of people with disabilities in your community?

> "I will never forget a church that had a sign in front of its sanctuary that declared that the building was 'handicap accessible.' A ramp led up the side of the step to the sanctuary, and then one step remained to enter the church. For many people with disabilities, that one step serves as an apt metaphor for how the church has welcomed them."
>
> —Trace Haythorn (2003, p. 344)

Efforts toward improving physical accessibility must extend beyond the worship space to all aspects of shared congregational life, as will be discussed in Chapters 3, 4, and 5. Consider the many other locations in which ministries, fellowships, celebrations, and other activities occur, including classrooms, gymnasiums, community centers, summer camps, retreat centers, and members' homes. People who can participate in only a small fraction of congregational activities are unlikely to ever feel like full members of the community, nor are they likely to continue returning for very long.

Architectural issues often receive the most attention in conversations about accessibility. Such an emphasis certainly makes sense, as presence is necessary for participation. Inaccessibility also affects many people in a congregation, including senior citizens and parents of small children. Furthermore, remedies for architectural barriers often seem more straightforward to address than those involving other types of barriers. But structural inaccessibility is not the only, or even perhaps the primary, obstacle encountered by people with disabilities other than physical disabilities—such as people with developmental disabilities— and their families. Efforts that begin and end with ramps, pew cuts, automatic doors, and designated parking spots will fall far short of what is needed to communicate welcome.

> "If people in your community are going to Wal-Mart in their wheelchairs but not coming to your church, a lot of times the church community calls them shut-ins. They're not shut in; they're just shut out of the church."
>
> —Ned Stoller, as cited in *Making Churches Accessible to Disabled* (1998)

Attitudinal Barriers   Accessibility extends far beyond the physical features of a place; steep stairs represent one type of barrier, penetrating stares comprise quite another (Govig, 1989). Unfortunately, people of faith have not always transcended the attitudinal barriers that persist throughout society; they often share many of the same prejudices and fears. Most barriers of attitude are inadvertent, rather than overt; subtle, but sometimes deeply entrenched (see Table 1.1).

> "Sometimes these attitudinal and institutional barriers are the result of deep-seated prejudice. At times, these barriers result from decisions to follow the 'old paradigm' of considering people with disabilities as 'defective' and in need of 'fixing.' At other times, these barriers are the result of thoughtlessness, indifference, or lack of understanding. It is often difficult, if not impossible, to ascertain precisely why the barriers exist."
>
> —Robert Silverstein (2000, p. 1695)

After encountering unwelcoming attitudes, most people will move on to another congregation; others will decide to give up on congregations altogether. Think about your own congregation: *Is there evidence of the following attitudinal barriers?*

- When invitations are infrequently extended, activities are designed without people with disabilities in mind, or members of the congrega-

Table 1.1. Comments reflecting attitudinal barriers

"It seems like a lot of energy and effort when we can't really be sure that Louise will actually get anything out of being in Sunday school with the other children."

"We have a special class for children just like your son."

"These renovations seem a bit much. After all, we don't have any people with disabilities in our congregation."

"I'd love to invite my neighbor to attend our church, but we just don't have a program for people with disabilities."

"Maybe your family would feel more comfortable at Temple Beth-El—I believe they do disability ministry."

"If Abel can't read, how will he get anything out of the class?"

"She has autism? None of us are trained to work with *those* children."

"Some members of the congregation are finding your group to be distracting. Perhaps you and your clients would be more comfortable sitting in the balcony."

"Our church just isn't big enough to have a disability ministry."

"Sandy really doesn't understand the meaning of communion. I'm not sure we can really allow her to participate."

"I'm so sorry to hear about your child. You must be devastated."

"I know he is a little old, but he would probably still best be cared for in the nursery."

"Will Samuel always be like this? Will he ever grow out of these behaviors?"

---

tion appear reluctant to extend greetings or to engage in conversation, people with developmental disabilities and their families will feel overlooked, invisible, or ignored. When people with disabilities are not already involved in their congregation, members might mistakenly hold the attitude that striving to become more hospitable is not an urgent need.

- People with disabilities and their families sometimes encounter words and actions—most likely well-intentioned—that they perceive to be demeaning, condescending, or paternalistic. People with disabilities often are attributed exceptional faith, described only as inspirational or a divine blessing, offered excessive attention or praise, extended charity in place of justice, or viewed primarily as the objects of ministry. Such responses fail to affirm the individuality, gifts, needs, and contributions that every person has to offer and to receive from the community of believers.

> "The community of faith has failed to honestly engage with people who have disabilities, to seek out and listen to their stories, and instead tends to speak to or about them or does things for them. If they are not ignored altogether, people with disabilities have been talked to or talked about, but not included as key partners in the conversation of faith."
>
> —Deborah Creamer (2003, p. 60)

- Many people with disabilities and their families feel great tension between the messages communicated in their congregation and their own experiences of disability (Eiesland & Saliers, 1998). The teachings and traditions of faith groups have sometimes been mistaken, misunderstood, or misapplied, feeding erroneous and often hurtful conclusions about the cause and implications of disabilities. For example, disability has been linked to parental sin, lack of faith, or divine rejection (Abrams, 1998; Covey, 2004). At other times, the meaning of disability in God's economy is missed; real worth is not determined by one's skills, abilities, IQ scores, or number of diplomas. Recognition of barriers to full inclusion in congregational life should push faith communities to deeper theological reflection and study, calling for better alignment of words, actions, and teachings with scriptures.

- Observing the service system within which most people with developmental disabilities reside, the average member of a faith community might incorrectly presume that professional training or an advanced degree is required to support and include a person with disabilities. After all, apart from family members, most of the people observed surrounding individuals with developmental disabilities are paid support staff. Members may hold the attitude that gestures of welcome are best left to those in the congregation—or other congregations—who have received specialized training.

  > "Susan joined a faith-sharing group at a local church. She participated for several sessions, and the people in the group made room for her and accepted her eccentricities. But one day she became sick at a group session. One of the group leaders then insisted that she just didn't belong in the group, that the real place for her was in a special religious education program for disabled people offered by the Archdiocese. The group asked her not to come back."
  >
  > —Mary O'Connell (1990, p. 24)

- Faith and cognitive ability are equated in the minds of many Americans (Gaventa, 2005). When considering people with intellectual disabilities, people often wonder, "Is faith really important to them?" or "Can they really understand?" or "Would they really get anything out of participating?" To assume that spirituality is irrelevant to a person simply on the basis of a label of intellectual disability or autism is among the deepest forms of prejudice. Someone's ability to thoroughly grasp complex theological doctrines or to express

  > "Faith or religion should not be equated with knowledge, though it's partly that, of course. Faith also involves the elements of trust, loyalty and commitment to someone or something. It is a matter of both head and heart. It is part idea, part feeling, part commitment, and part action. It is something known, and it is also something experienced."
  >
  > —Tom Hoeksema (1995, p. 290)

his or her beliefs in the same way as everyone else neither negates nor diminishes his or her faith.

Communication Barriers   Barriers to participation may also emerge in the areas of sight and sound, language and listening. The avenues through which worship is presented and information is shared may be inaccessible for individuals with visual or hearing impairments. For example, congregations might lack large print or braille materials (e.g., bulletins, hymnals, prayer books, Bibles and other sacred texts), assisted listening systems, sign language interpreters, or alternative communication formats. The level at which information is presented also may be intellectually and experientially inaccessible to members, including those with cognitive disabilities. Many congregations wrestle with how to communicate the doctrines, beliefs, and traditions of their faith effectively to people from an increasingly wide range of backgrounds, including those who come from different cultures, speak different languages, learn in very different ways, or are unable to read. Congregations are challenged to discover new ways of communicating that "transcend words, that invite new insights, and that make room for all worshippers" (Haythorn, 2003, p. 345). Finally, faith communities must do a better job of listening to people with disabilities (Swinton, 2002a). Although many congregations do an exceptional job of marketing all of the services, ministries, and supports that they have to offer, they rarely invest time to discover what people with developmental disabilities might have to offer to them. Such listening, of course, takes both time and a willingness to invest deeply in the lives of people.

Programmatic Barriers   Most congregations offer numerous ways for members to connect with others, use their gifts, and grow spiritually through involvement in activities beyond weekly worship services. For some children and adults with developmental disabilities, a personal invitation to participate and an assurance of welcome are all that are missing. Others, however, may require additional assistance to participate. For example, a child with autism may need extra support from an adult or peer, and may need adapted materials, curricula, or equipment (see Chapter 4). Families may choose to leave a congregation in favor of one that offers occasional respite care, a supportive group for parents, or inclusive programs for children and youth.

Liturgical Barriers   Some sacramental practices and rituals may exclude people with developmental disabilities. When someone is unable to participate in the usual ways, congregational leaders sometimes are unwilling to make adaptations or alterations to long-held practices. As a

"Ray, a young man who has been educated in an inclusive environment, wanted to be baptized in his church as other teenagers and church members are. The initial pastoral response was that Ray did not need to be baptized because his special needs made him already one of 'God's elect.' It took both individual and family persistence, in addition to some outside consulting and encouragement, to help the clergy move beyond a cognitive interpretation of a sacrament to recognition of its importance as a coming-of-age ritual and transition."

—Bill Gaventa and Roger Peters (2001, p. 306)

result, a child with autism is denied participation in communion, a youth with multiple disabilities is refused participation in a Bar Mitzvah program, a couple with intellectual disabilities is not permitted to marry in the congregation, or an adult with severe disabilities is not granted the space and support to grieve the death of a parent.

Failing to Bring People Into Community

As congregations seek to improve their welcome to people with disabilities already within their community, they often focus on removing architectural, attitudinal, communication, programmatic, and liturgical obstacles to full participation. Such efforts are important and essential. But many adults with developmental and other disabilities never arrive at their local congregation in the first place. Indeed, barriers within communities and the existing service system have often failed to bring people with disabilities up to—and into—the doors of a local church, mosque, synagogue, temple, or other place of worship.

Limited Transportation   Many adults with disabilities do not attend worship services, small groups, potlucks, and other congregational activities simply because they cannot get there. Unless someone commits to arranging or providing transportation, those activities will remain out of reach to anyone who cannot drive. Staffing patterns within some group homes and other residential programs also make it difficult to ensure that residents have rides to worship services and other activities, especially when housemates each wish to attend different congregations.

Past Experience   A history of exclusion or inhospitable attitudes can have a wounding effect on people with developmental disabilities and their families. After repeatedly encountering fear, rejection, isolation, or neglect, these individuals may no longer want to make the effort to become involved in a faith community. Given their past experiences, it is not surprising when a parent wonders if a congregation's latest invitation "to all" really includes everybody.

Unreceived Invitations   Unaware of the presence or needs of people with developmental disabilities in their neighborhoods and cities, many congregations fail to extend invitations to this segment of the community.

Traditional approaches for spreading word about programs often do not reach adults with developmental disabilities, leaving them unaware of what congregational offerings and activities are available in their neighborhoods. For individuals who cannot read, have limited involvement in their community, know few of their neighbors, do not control their own transportation, and are surrounded by support staff who are reluctant to arrange for spiritual supports, it should come as no surprise if they never enter through the doors of a local congregation. An invitation can hardly be considered to have been extended if it was never actually received.

Unexplored Preferences Many adults with developmental disabilities are not provided with the opportunities and information they need to make informed choices about the type and avenues of congregational involvement they would like to experience. Service providers report feeling poorly equipped to help people with disabilities explore the spiritual dimensions of their lives (Swinton, 2002b), and so these conversations may never take place. When someone is not aware that participation in a local congregation is among the life choices available to him or her, service providers may misinterpret his or her silence as lack of interest.

Partitioned Professional Roles Professionals often partition the lives of the children and adults they serve into separate domains (e.g., educational, physical, social, vocational). However, such discrete divisions rarely make sense when it comes to spiritual needs. A person's life cannot be neatly partitioned into the sacred and secular; spirituality is inextricably woven throughout every dimension of a person's life. Yet, service providers often compartmentalize a person's spiritual needs, leaving them for someone else to address. When people have few relationships beyond their service providers, no one else may be available to support them in this important aspect of their lives.

Unfamiliarity with a Faith Community Service providers who themselves are not a part of a faith community or who adhere to different faith traditions might conclude that they do not have the knowledge and skills to connect people with developmental disabilities with a congregation. Concerned that they may improperly influence the person they support or that they lack expertise in issues related to congregational inclusion, they may defer responsibility for addressing this participation to someone else. Unfortunately, the belief that "it takes an expert" and the decision to relinquish involvement usually means that this need goes unaddressed.

Uncertain Responses A final barrier is fear of the unexpected. Family members, residential staff, and other support providers may be uncertain of just how a congregation will respond when they arrive. *Will they welcome us? Will we be turned away? Will we feel awkward?* Perhaps past experiences with other congregations have reinforced their concerns. In an effort to protect the feelings of the person with disabilities (and perhaps their own), they may decide not to make the attempt at all.

MOVEMENTS TO INCREASE CONGREGATIONAL INCLUSION

Although these barriers serve as very real challenges, they also offer an incredible opportunity, pushing congregations to reflect deeply on their current practices and compelling them to respond differently. Increasingly, congregations, family members, people with disabilities, and agencies and organizations are demonstrating emphatically that barriers to inclusion need be neither permanent nor insurmountable. A range of initiatives are being undertaken to support children and adults with developmental disabilities, as well as their families, in participating meaningfully in their desired faith communities. What inspires and sustains these efforts?

Commitments of Faith Groups

Congregations are certainly influenced—sometimes substantially, sometimes slightly—by the traditions, policies, and initiatives of the broader denominations and faith groups with which they are formally or informally associated. And so it is worth understanding some of the commitments that these groups have articulated concerning the importance of welcoming children and adults with disabilities. These commitments often make their way into formal policies and resolutions issued by denominations, associations, and other faith groups (see Appendix A). These statements are important to consider not only because of the specific charge they make to congregations but also because they articulate a strong rationale for both why and how congregations should respond differently than they have in the past. Thus, they serve as a challenge to congregations, calling for prayerful reflection on current practices, programs, and policies. Several major themes are apparent in many of these statements.

History of Exclusion   Although religious communities have long played a leadership role in providing care and services *to* people with disabilities throughout history, many congregations currently struggle to welcome people with disabilities *into* congregational life. Numerous faith groups have acknowledged their failure to respond to people with disabilities in ways that reflect their calling to be caring, loving, and responsive communities. The heart of many congregations is the desire to build bridges to those who live at the margins and to go about the business of restoring people to community. Although charged in the scriptures to reach out to people who have been marginalized, silenced, or abandoned by others, the statements of many faith groups acknowledge a pattern of either nonresponse or outright exclusion.

All Are Called Although not always bound by the same legislative mandates as the rest of society to include their neighbors with disabilities, congregations are surely compelled by the mandates of their faith. The statements of most faith groups echo this thesis: God invites *all* people to worship, to fellowship, to learn, and to serve. This invitation is never diminished by disability; it comes without qualifiers or footnotes. Thus, congregations should support this call and gladly receive the gifts and contributions of people with disabilities.

> "After I walked back into the sanctuary, I saw Aaron, right in the middle of all the kids, looking just like one of them—no wheelchair...I suppose I was seeing Aaron at that moment as God sees him all the time—just one of his own children, different in body but not in spirit."
>
> —Twyla Becker, as cited in Smietana, B. (2005)

A Distinctive Response It is not enough for congregations to simply mirror the rest of society when it comes to including people with disabilities. Rather, they are called to be leaders in transforming the culture—to graciously, lovingly, and actively influence their communities. When congregations push toward a higher standard than the rest of society; when they demonstrate leadership, rather than lagging behind; and when their efforts stand in stark contrast to those of others in their community, it sends a powerful message. When a welcome is compelled by deep love and a sacred call, rather than by legal decree, it speaks powerfully to a watching world and provides strong evidence of one's faith commitment.

> "The way God designed our bodies is a model for understanding our lives together as a church: every part dependent on every other part, the parts we mention and the parts we don't, the parts we see and the parts we don't. If one part hurts, every other part is involved in the hurt, and in the healing. If one part flourishes, every other part enters into the exuberance."
>
> —1 Corinthians 12:12, 25–26

Interdependence of Believers Many statements assert the importance—indeed, the necessity—of building community among all believers. The gifts each person possesses are designed to complement the gifts of others, all working in tandem to further God's purposes. Because each person has something essential to offer, it is the collective contributions of many people that lead to wholeness within a faith community. Indeed, communities are strengthened when people with and without developmental disabilities are present together; everyone has a need for each other. This view stands in stark contrast with the high value placed on independence and autonomy in the present culture.

Incomplete Without You   It is more than a "nice idea" to include people with disabilities in your congregation. People of faith are called to view people with disabilities as *integral* to the well-being of their community; every member should be regarded as indispensable. When an entire segment of the population remains absent from the body of believers, that community not only remains less than it *could* be, it remains less than it was *intended* to be. Wholeness will always remain elusive to a community when the gifts and contributions of a whole segment of people are missing. Indeed, it is the community that becomes "handicapped" when people with developmental disabilities and their families are not present.

Image Bearers   Many statements draw on the affirmation that every person bears the image of God. Therefore, every single person is endowed with inestimable worth. People with developmental disabilities are neither exceptions to nor perversions of this image. Thus, people should be treated accordingly and congregational practices should affirm the inherent value and dignity of every person. Words and actions that serve to exclude from congregational life run counter to this recognition.

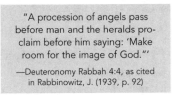

"A procession of angels pass before man and the heralds proclaim before him saying: 'Make room for the image of God.'"

—Deuteronomy Rabbah 4:4, as cited in Rabbinowitz, J. (1939, p. 92)

A Broader Action   Evident across many faith group statements is recognition of the impact that disability can have on family members and caregivers. They call on congregations to rally around family members and caregivers, to offer encouragement and support, and to help bear burdens and celebrate blessings. In addition, several statements attempt to spur action beyond the walls of the congregation and into the wider society. Congregations must do more than passively affirm the rights of people with disabilities, but should also advocate for changes in society to ensure those rights are supported. Such actions might include encouraging passage of favorable laws, standing up against ineffective or oppressive service systems that stifle community participation, or advocating on behalf of people whose voice often is not heard.

"We are sent forth from our communities of worship to help in the transformation of our whole world. We are called to work for a just society. Our ministry in the world is to help overcome injustices by bringing about change in the attitudes and structures of society that are barriers to full participation in our common life by all the people of God."

—Advisory Committee on Social Witness Policy (2001, p. 2)

Intentional Responses   The act of crafting these statements attests to the importance that faith groups are placing on being more intentional. Congregations are called to more than just greater awareness. They must commit themselves fully to increasing their capacity to welcome and include people with disabilities in the life of their communities. Faith groups are urging their member congregations to adopt these resolutions in both principle *and* practice; to couple affirmation of a vision with evidence of action. It is simply not enough to have one without the other. Examples of specific actions recommended by these groups include convening committees to address disability concerns; improving architectural, liturgical, and curricular access; revising congregational policies; training staff; organizing inclusion awareness events; ministering to families; identifying transportation solutions; and making seminaries more accessible and inclusive (see Chapters 3, 4, and 5 for additional potential responses).

> "We believe the human community in all its forms is accountable to God to protect these civil and human rights. God requires the church to give spiritual and moral leadership to society in protecting these rights. The church must exercise its leadership by its public preaching and teaching but even more by its example as an inclusive community of faith, using the gifts of all its members."
> —National Council of Churches (1998)

> "While many mainline denominations have eloquent position papers stating that all people should be welcomed, individual congregations have been scandalously inhospitable to children with disabilities."
> —Brett Webb-Mitchell (1993, p. 981)

Actions of Faith Groups

In addition to articulating these commitments, faith groups are taking additional steps to promote the inclusion of people with disabilities.

* National task forces and advisory committees have been organized to coordinate, guide, and support efforts to include people with disabilities in communities of faith (see Appendix B). Examples include Presbyterians for Disability Concerns (Presbyterian Church-USA), Task Force on Developmental Disabilities (United Methodist Church), National Jewish Council for Disabilities (Orthodox Union), and the National Catholic Partnership on Disability. Some denominations have even established youth task forces, such as the Definitely-Abled Advisory Committee (Evangelical Lutheran Church in America). If such a team is not already in existence within your faith group, consider advocating for a disability office at a regional or national level.

* Some denominations, dioceses, and organizations confer awards to recognize the efforts and leadership of individuals and congregations who

have made significant strides toward creating communities that welcome people with disabilities (see Table 1.2). If you offer such recognition, submit press releases to local newspapers, television stations, and affiliated congregations describing the award, the steps that have been taken to improve welcome, and a contact point for additional information.

- Many groups have established a speakers bureau or resource team by compiling the names of people who have expertise and experience on disability issues. These individuals are available to offer resources, guidance, and encouragement to help congregations become more responsive to the needs of people with disabilities and their families. Individuals chosen for such roles should be people who have a heart for sharing and a gift for igniting passion about this issue in others.

- Some groups earmark funds to support individual congregations and community organizations in their efforts to become more inclusive. Small grants might be awarded to assist congregations to improve the accessibility of their facilities, start respite care or parent support programs, disseminate innovative ministry models, or establish new

Table 1.2.   Examples of recognition efforts by faith communities

Accessibility Award
Evangelical Lutheran Church of America

Accessible Congregations Campaign
National Organization on Disability

Caring Church, Vision, and Aaron Awards
Christian Council on Persons with Disabilities

Individual, Family, Advocacy, Lay Leadership, Congregation, Youth Group, and Clergy Awards
New Jersey Coalition for Inclusive Ministries

Nancy Jennings Award
Presbyterian Church (USA)

Open Hearts Awards
Pathways Awareness Foundation

"Open to All" Campaign
North American Mission Board

Open Roof Award
Association of Brethren Caregivers

Robert M. Pitzer Award
Southeastern United Methodist Agency for Rehabilitation

Churches for All Award
Through the Roof

partnerships in their community. Funds often are collected during an inclusion awareness event, such as an Inclusion or Disability Awareness Sunday (see Chapter 3).

- Many faith groups have organized conferences focused specifically on improving the capacity of congregations and communities to support the religious participation of children and adults with disabilities. Others have woven strands on disability into conferences and trainings addressing children's programming, youth ministry, leadership development, outreach programs, and summer camping (see Chapter 7).

Commitments of Agencies and Organizations

Recognition of the importance of religion and spirituality in the lives of people with developmental disabilities is not unique to faith communities alone. Many service, support, and advocacy programs—from local to national levels—have established policies and practices that reflect the importance of supporting people with disabilities to explore and practice their faith in personally meaningful ways. Although the driving force behind these efforts may emerge from somewhat different sources than those of faith groups, the commitment they express is often the same: Every person with disabilities should be supported in pursuing and attaining outcomes—including spiritual ones—that bring meaning and purpose to their lives. What are the core values that might lead agencies and organizations to support the religious participation of people with developmental disabilities?

Universal Aspirations   Meaningful life in the community ought to be anchored against what other members of the community aspire to—a satisfying job, a home of one's own, close personal relationships, and opportunities to worship freely and in personally significant ways. People with developmental disabilities hold the same desires and dreams as their neighbors without disabilities; a disability label is not a reliable predictor of someone's aspirations. Thus, people with disabilities should be supported in pursuing life experiences similar to those pursued by others in their communities. Among service providers, this idea is called the normalization principle and has been espoused in the United States for more

> "Disability is a natural part of the human experience that does not diminish the right of individuals with developmental disabilities to live independently, to exert control and choice over their own lives, and to fully participate in and contribute to their communities through full integration and inclusion in the economic, political, social, cultural, and educational mainstream of United States society."
>
> —Developmental Disabilities Assistance and Bill of Rights Act (2000)

than 30 years (Wolfensberger, 1972). A commitment to this philosophy does not to mean that everyone should lead identical lives, but rather that the opportunities, activities, and outcomes that others in society pursue should be available to people with developmental disabilities. Every person should have the freedom—and supports—to pursue the life he or she envisions for him- or herself (Nerney & Vining, 2005). Numerous surveys confirm the importance of religious faith in the lives of most Americans; it should come as no surprise that people with developmental disabilities desire similar opportunities for spiritual expression. They should be supported in pursuing these aspirations.

Community Inclusion   For many years, people with developmental disabilities were largely excluded from community life. State institutions, sheltered workshops, and segregated schools characterized the life experiences of too many people. With the normalization principle as one catalyst, service and support providers have come to hold full participation in the community for people with disabilities as the ideal toward which to strive. Thus, one important indicator of the quality of human services is the extent to which people with developmental disabilities are participating actively in the same school, work, and community settings as their classmates, co-workers, and neighbors without disabilities.

> "Every effort should be made to ensure that Americans with disabilities have the opportunity to be integrated into their communities and welcomed into communities of faith."
>
> —New Freedom Initiative, as cited in White House (2001, p. 23)

Natural Supports   The ways in which people are assisted in pursuing their dreams and becoming involved in their communities really does make a difference. Most Americans rely on family members, friends, and other informal supports to help them to participate in community life. Yet, the lives of many people with developmental disabilities are dominated by service providers and other professionals. Recognition of the importance of cultivating and connecting people with disabilities with more natural sources of support to help them participate fully in their communities is growing. That is, it makes good sense to draw on the resources already available within a community to meet a need before creating new services or programs. This gradual shift away from an over-reliance on paid supports is challenging agencies and organizations to seek out new partnerships within communities, including religious congregations. Thus, fellow members of a faith community can serve as critical allies in supporting the full participation of a person with disabilities.

Self-Determination   Historically, people with developmental disabilities have been afforded little opportunity to direct their own lives

(Wehmeyer & Patton, 2000). Professionals tended to make decisions about where and how someone with disabilities would live, learn, work, recreate, and even worship. Increasingly, service and support organizations are recognizing the importance of putting people with disabilities at the *center* of their own life decisions and preparing them to play a more prominent role in their own planning. Increasing the capacity of people with disabilities to live self-determined lives is a key indicator of high-quality services and supports (Council on Quality and Leadership, 2005). To support self determination, people with disabilities must be equipped with the skills and knowledge to make important choices *and* be provided opportunities to act on their decisions in meaningful ways. Although many people with disabilities describe their religious faith as holding an important place in their lives, they are provided few opportunities to express that faith as part of a congregation. Supporting self-determination must include consideration of people's faith commitments, ensuring that they are able to participate fully and actively in a congregation *of their choice,* as well as respecting the decisions of others not to participate in congregational

---

STATEMENT OF PURPOSE

The rights, needs and wants of many individuals with disabilities, including the basic need for freedom of spiritual expression, have been denied consistently. Many people with disabilities experience limited opportunities for spiritual expression. Especially acute is the denial of opportunities and supports related to spiritual exploration and expression for those who live in institutional and other restrictive settings....

RATIONALE

Faith and spirituality may offer positive supports to people with disabilities, as they do for others in our communities. Because we firmly maintain that an individual's spiritual beliefs could be representative of an entire array of beliefs, definitions, expressions, and faith communities, TASH supports a range of expressions of spirituality that communicate value and respect for all individuals. The Spirituality Committee of TASH exists to support various spiritual issues of people with disabilities but does not advance any specific faith or religion. TASH supports opportunities for spiritual expression for individuals with disabilities, both privately and in community.

THEREFORE BE IT RESOLVED THAT TASH, an international advocacy association of people with disabilities, their family members, other advocates and people who work in the disability field, believes that all people with disabilities have the right to spiritual expression including the reflection upon and sharing of spiritual purposes for their lives. TASH further supports the right of individuals with disabilities to participate in spiritual expression or organized religion as they so choose and promotes the provision of any and all supports needed by people with disabilities to so participate.

Figure 1.1. TASH resolution on spirituality. (From TASH. [2003]. *TASH resolution on spirituality.* Baltimore: Author; reprinted by permission.)

life. Indeed, the American Association on Intellectual and Developmental Disabilities (formerly known as the American Association on Mental Retardation), the Arc, and TASH—three prominent organizations committed to advocating for people with disabilities—have issued policy statements articulating the importance of supporting people's choices and preferences in this area (see Figures 1.1 and 1.2).

Quality of Life   The extent to which people are pursuing their aspirations, participating in the community, receiving meaningful supports,

---

POSITION STATEMENT

People with mental retardation and related developmental disabilities have the right to choose their own expressions of spirituality, to practice those beliefs and expressions, and to participate in the religious community of their choice or other spiritual activities. The person also has a right to choose not to participate in religious or spiritual activity.

ISSUES

While many agencies providing services and supports recognize the right to religious freedom, they seldom include spirituality in individual planning. Nor do they often help people participate in the spiritual activities or religious communities of their choice and/or tradition.

Individuals and their families also often face a mixed response from congregations, even though many congregations and faith networks have established model programs and strategies for including people with disabilities. Spiritual resources and congregations are an untapped source of community supports and inclusion, beyond the practice of faith and belief. They offer opportunities to express choice, develop relationships and social networks, respect cultural and family backgrounds, and serve others.

POSITION

Spirituality, spiritual growth, and religious expression that respect a person's history, tradition, and current preference or choice are rights that should be honored by supports from service systems and religious communities, as should the choice not to participate.

- Spirituality is an important part of human experience that may be expressed both through religious practice and through expressions of personal meaning and values. Thus spirituality and religious preference should be part of all assessments of individual and family needs, interests, and strengths.

- Faith communities should receive assistance to build their capacity to support and welcome our constituents and their families, through partnerships with provider agencies and advocacy organizations that respect and honor spiritual needs and religious preferences.

- Agencies and spiritual communities should offer training and education regarding spiritual supports for people with mental retardation and related developmental disabilities.

Figure 1.2.   Excerpt from the American Association on Mental Retardation/Arc Position Statement on Spirituality. (From American Association on Mental Retardation and The Arc. (2002). *AAMR/The Arc position statement on spirituality.* Available online at http://thearc.org/posits/spiritualitypos.htm. Washington, DC: Author; reprinted by permission.)

and acting on their own preferences certainly influences how satisfied they are with their lives. The concept of quality of life has become a guiding principle for service delivery for people with disabilities. Increasingly, agencies and organizations are examining the extent to which the services and supports they deliver truly improve the life satisfaction of those whom they serve. The efforts of agencies and organizations should further people's emotional, material, and physical well-being; enhance their social relationships and inclusion; support their personal development and self-determination; and advance their rights (Schalock et al., 2002). For many people, spirituality is an important dimension of quality of life (Renwick, Schormans, & Zekovic, 2003). Thus, it is essential that service providers ensure that this dimension of consumers' lives is being addressed and supported by someone.

CONCLUSION

Congregations are being called to pledge, renew, and expand their commitment to seek out and welcome people with developmental disabilities and their families. Although some congregations are still perceived as unwelcoming places for people with developmental disabilities and their families, growing numbers of communities are proving that it is possible to break down these barriers. Service and support organizations also are discovering new ways of supporting the spirituality and congregational participation of the people whom they are called to serve. Although faith communities still have a long way to go before these core commitments and values are fully realized, the journey is an essential one. Indeed, a recurring theme is that it will be exceedingly worth your efforts.

Chapter 2

A Welcoming Congregation

Signs of Hospitality

Any given week, millions of people gather together with family, friends, neighbors, and strangers in a local church, synagogue, mosque, temple, or other place of worship. What draws people through the doors of their congregation for the first time? What leads them to keep coming back? Every person can tell their own story. They come to encounter the presence and holiness of God; to worship corporately and share in the sacraments. They come for spiritual nurture and growth; to walk alongside and lean on others as they mature in their faith. They come to satisfy deep longings; to discover who they are, to whom they belong, and what they are called to do. They come for a sense of community and belonging; to enrich and be enriched by the lives and experiences of others. They come bearing burdens and vulnerabilities; seeking an anchor in difficult times and support in the midst of uncertainty. People with developmental disabilities also have stories to tell; they are fellow travelers on the very same journey of life. They hold the same desires for worship, growth, direction, and support; they share the same need for community, connectedness, and belonging.

Mirroring the broader movements among denominations and faith groups, as well as affirming the efforts of service and support organizations to promote community involvement, individual congregations throughout the country are taking steps to improve their capacity to welcome and include people with developmental disabilities and their families. Most congregations, if asked, would probably affirm that they are called to be an inviting home and safe haven for people with disabilities. But knowing exactly how to live out this call might seem unclear to congregations initially. What does it really mean to be a welcoming congregation? What does it look like to meaningfully include people with disabilities? What indicators of hospitality and sanctuary will be recognizable to others in the broader community? This is a journey; with each step moving you closer to becoming the sort of congregation you aspire to be. Fortunately, there are many signposts to guide you as you proceed.

INDICATORS OF A WELCOMING CONGREGATION

Congregations can mean very different things when they assert that they are a welcoming community. For some, evidence for their claim is found in their well-crafted mission statement, a newly installed elevator, or a handful of designated parking spaces. Others point to a special Sunday school class or children's program for people with intellectual disabilities. A few might describe how people with disabilities are helping on the worship team, contributing to small groups, or serving on an outreach committee. What does a welcoming congregation really look like? What features characterize a community in which people with developmental disabilities and their families are participating, contributing, and feel assured that they belong? If inclusion is a journey, how will you know when you have finally arrived? It may be helpful to begin by considering several characteristics of a welcoming congregation, recognizing that these indicators are likely to be evidenced in different ways from one congregation to the next. As you read this chapter, ask yourself the following: *To what extent are these indicators evident in our congregation?*

Presence

Inclusion begins with presence. It is difficult to welcome individuals when they are not actually present among you. What does a glance across the pews, a peek into your programs for children and youth, or a look at your leadership and ministry teams reveal about the extent to which people with disabilities are currently involved in your faith community?

Accessibility

Presence is only a starting point, not a signal to stop. Once they come through your doors, people must be able to participate in the activities and programs you offer, as well as have access to the different locations and facilities in which they take place. When a youth group meets on the second floor of a building without elevators, when raised sections of the sanctuary lack ramps, when recreational areas are designed so that only some children can play together, or when transportation is infrequently available, it is difficult for someone to move from mere presence to true participation. Would visitors describe your congregation as barrier free?

When Brian's parents first visited St. Michael's, they were skeptical that their son's wheelchair would be able to navigate the historic building. Insist-

ing that Brian's participation was as important to them as every other child's, the youth leaders brainstormed a plan. With guidance from a few especially "handy" members, the youth group pitched in to build a small ramp, raise a couple of tables slightly, and partially renovate a bathroom. While waiting for more extensive renovations to be done in the meeting room, the youth leaders decided that the group would gather elsewhere rather than leave Brian out.

Hospitality

Although an accessible building is essential, it is through interactions and relationships with others that welcome is truly communicated. Hospitality can be demonstrated in simple ways: extending a greeting, remembering a name, noticing a new haircut, or asking about someone's week. But an inclusive congregation is known for more than just easy hospitality. Its members invite people to lunch, spend time really getting to know them, celebrate their suc-

> "Hospitality depends on a disposition of love; it has more to do with the resources of a generous and grateful heart than with availability of food or space."
>
> —Christine Pohl (1999, p. 14)

cesses, and stand alongside them in difficult times. Gestures must have authenticity and substance; they must offer much more than just the veneer of welcome. A congregation can *say* all of the right things, but still fail to nurture close relationships and fall short of addressing people's felt needs.

Not one member of the congregation would have to hesitate when asked to share how Pat had touched their lives. So, when Pat was not seen sitting in her usual seat—fourth row, second seat from the aisle—at the 9:00 A.M. service, it was definitely noticed. By mid-afternoon, five people had already called Pat to find out how she was feeling and whether she needed a meal, a visit, or just some encouragement. Pat wasn't simply absent; she was missed.

A Sense of Shared Lives

Sharing lives entails more than just sharing space. A welcoming congregation strives to weave people with and without disabilities into a common community (see Box 2.1). Sometimes, disability ministry efforts originate as separate religious education classes, worship services, or study groups for people with developmental disabilities. However, an

> "Alan was a living lesson in authenticity. He was authentically glad to be in community every time he was at church. It never occurred to him to act pious or perfect. He never worried about being liked or loved by the community or by God. He simply trusted that he was.... Alan was a lesson for each of us in the art of self-acceptance. The gift Alan gave to us was more powerful than anything we gave to him.... What congregation can afford to pass up such gifts?"
>
> —Jim Kasperson, as cited in Carlson (2004, p. 193)

Box 2.1
Proximity versus Participation

Across educational, employment, and community settings, research findings echo an important lesson: Inclusion is about much more than location. It is entirely possible for a person to be physically present in a sanctuary, class-room, or fellowship hall, but completely isolated from all of the interactions, learning opportunities, and relationships that energize that setting. For peo-ple with developmental disabilities, this possibility is too often the reality. Welcoming a person with a disability into a congregation should not be lim-ited to that discrete moment when someone enters through the doorway of your building. Rather, it should be an ongoing process whereby a person was first welcomed, is being welcomed, and will always be welcomed. This is the difference between being present and having a presence (Granzen, 2005).

even closer reflection of true community is evidenced when people wor-ship, fellowship, learn, and serve alongside, rather than parallel to, each other. An inclusive congregation welcomes people with disabilities into every aspect of congregational life, allowing everyone to learn and live amongst each other.

> *Michael was invited to join a small group that met weekly at various homes in the neighborhood. He knew very little about the Bible and had trouble grasping complex theological ideas, not unlike several other members of the group. He could not read, but several others were also shy about reading aloud. He took a long time to put his thoughts into words and he sometimes got distracted, but others in the group knew that their words rarely were very articulate. Still, Michael sure could pray! And everyone recognized that they would all be losing out on something important—something essen-tial—if Michael were not given the chance to be a part of their small group.*

Different Motivation

In inclusive congregations, it is not legislation or policy that compels the welcome. Their desire is not for filling empty pews or seeking public praise; they are neither responding out of pressure nor acting out of pity. Instead, they are motivated by God's clear call on their congregation to be a community that invites, receives, and embraces their brothers and sisters with disabilities. They recognize that they are missing something vital—indeed, they are impoverished—when this segment of their community is not participating.

No one with autism had ever attended Cottage Grove Church. But on hearing that two group homes for adults with developmental disabilities had recently been established in the neighborhood, several members of the church determined that it would no longer be due to the lack of an invitation. After discussing a recent sermon on what it really means to have an impact on their community, members of the young adult class all committed to getting to know the newest residents in their neighborhood.

A Recognition of Contributions

It is next to impossible to enter the sanctuary without a firm, almost knuckle-cracking handshake from Aaron. As a greeter, his confident assurance is always the same: "It is going to be a great day!" It is next to impossible to walk away from Aaron without believing it.

Everyone wants to feel certain that they are valued; that they matter to others. Historically, people with developmental disabilities have been defined by what they cannot do and, by extension, what they cannot contribute. An inclusive congregation recognizes the gifts of everyone in their community—including those members with developmental disabilities—and they seek to discover and unlock the gifts and talents that each person possesses. In addition to asking what their congregation has to offer people with disabilities, they also strive to discover all that people with disabilities have to offer to them.

"She's touched other lives with her smile and her acceptance. I see it in the eyes and smiles of her Sunday school teachers when they welcome her into the children's worship hour. I see it when other parents greet her in the hallway between services. She's reaching out—and others are reaching back. Others who've looked beyond Sarah's disability to see the child that God created."

—Mary Ann McPherson (2004, p. 28)

Proactive Efforts

Welcoming congregations have learned to think ahead about emerging and future needs. They prayerfully anticipate the needs of people in their community who have not yet come through their doors. They recognize that if someone cannot enter in or is not welcomed the very first time, there is unlikely to be a second chance to welcome him or her back. If you wait until a person arrives at your door to begin thinking about how you will welcome him or her, you have simply waited too long. When you never encounter people with disabilities, it is easy to overlook the importance of addressing issues of accessibility. If your congregation is not accessible, you are unlikely to encounter people with disabilities. Congregations must be intentional about breaking this cycle.

"Would we ever plan a new church without providing a children's program? Of course not, even if the people planning the church didn't have children. We'd have a program ready, waiting expectantly for that first family with little ones to walk through the front door. Let's be as zealous in providing for families with special needs. No one should be turned away from God's house; nor should we have to scramble around and offer a quick, inadequate, makeshift program because nothing is in place when the family arrives."

—Louise Tucker Jones (2004, p. 50)

As Temple Beth Or sought out a new and permanent location for their annual retreat, the planning team began discussing factors to consider, including cost, location, amenities, and, for the first time, accessibility. After all, it became clear that their congregation was aging and, in several years, it was quite likely that older adults would appreciate being able to continue the tradition of attending each year. Moreover, an accessible retreat center would open opportunities for extending invitations to new and future members who have physical disabilities.

A Willingness to Learn

Within the vast majority of congregations, the backgrounds and experiences of members are very similar (DeYoung, Emerson, Yancey, & Kim, 2003). Many wrestle with determining exactly what it should look like to welcome strangers—people who have remained unfamiliar and unknown—into the life of their communities. Throwing the doors wide open and extending invitations to new and diverse people can be a very humbling experience. And it is not always clear how to proceed. Inclusive congregations evidence a willingness to learn from others, as well as from their own mistakes. This work is ongoing as congregations strive to do better, to be more responsive, and to live out their call more fully.

To say that Sarah challenged expectations at First Baptist Church would be an understatement. Her "meltdowns" were never subtle and her fondness for throwing hymnals usually shocked the more senior members. No one quite like Sarah had ever wanted to join the church. So, several members agreed to work closely with Sarah's parents and support staff to figure out what triggered these behaviors, as well as to identify ways that the congregation could help Sarah participate "more peacefully" in worship services and membership classes. It took some time and a willingness to develop some new partnerships, but the congregation eventually learned to welcome and support Sarah as their newest member.

Reciprocity

People with developmental disabilities want opportunities to contribute to and make a difference within their congregations. Their gifts are as varied as those of people without disabilities; only perhaps more underutilized, less often nurtured, and more frequently overlooked. An inclusive congregation helps all of its members discover their gifts and equips them to use those gifts on behalf of others. This perspective stands in stark contrast to communities in which certain segments of the population always end up on the receiving end of ministry. Inclusive congregations challenge the presumption that people with disabilities must exclusively assume the position of "designated" or "perpetual" receivers of service (Gaventa, 2003; Van der Klift & Kunc, 2002). People with disabilities need more than just care, more than just to be served; they also need the chance to serve others. The roles of servant and served will not always be perfectly balanced in a person's life, but neither should they remain static.

> "Those who take time to know such people speak eloquently of their gifts: One woman is an excellent baker, another is tender and loving with little children. One man loves to hear gossip but never repeats it; another loves animals and is a willing caretaker for them. And one man is described, simply, as bringing joy and peace into other people's lives."
>
> —Mary O'Connell (1988, p.8)

Benjamin always loved attending Vacation Bible School, especially when members of the youth group spent time helping him out as part of a buddy program. Now that he is older, Benjamin wants to find a way to offer something of himself back to this program. Each day, he is responsible for helping to organize and deliver the craft supplies to each classroom, as well as preparing the morning snacks. But his favorite times are when he gets to help out the kindergarteners as a buddy.

The Journey Toward Inclusion

The work of welcoming and learning to welcome better is ongoing. Congregations should always be seeking ways of becoming more inviting, more intentional, and more hospitable. Including people with developmental disabilities will be new for most congregations; for others, it has long been an important part of who they are as a community. Many congregations find themselves at the beginning of this adventure; others have traveled much further along. It truly is a journey.

> "The question is not how can we help people with disabilities (which is an important question)...a more important question is how can people with disabilities give their spiritual gifts to us and call us to love?"
>
> —Henri Nouwen (1996)

Movement of Relationships

Congregations are learning to enter into new relationships with people with disabilities. Gaventa (1986) offers one description of the stages through which congregations often move as they strive to become more inclusive. This movement of relationships illustrates how congregations are discovering new ways of relating to people with disabilities; shifting away from ministry apart from or exclusively to people with disabilities and toward ministry that is with and by people with disabilities. Eventually, ministry distinctions based on the presence of a disability might vanish altogether.

Apart Much of what takes place in congregations throughout the country happens *apart* from people with disabilities. Whether excluded or overlooked, people with developmental disabilities frequently are missing from the pews, not attending religious education classes, absent from leadership teams, not among those potlucking or partaking in ceremonial meals, nowhere to be found in ministry programs, and untouched by outreach efforts. The first step for many congregations is recognizing that an important part of their community is not actually part of their community. Absent this initial awareness, it is unlikely that congregations will be energized to respond differently.

To As they consider a starting point for ministry, many congregations begin by establishing special religious education classes, worship services, small groups, or other programs and activities designed exclusively for people with developmental disabilities. For example, a Sunday school class might be started for children with intellectual disabilities or a social club might be started for adults with autism. In such cases, ministry efforts are extended *to* people with disabilities; they primarily function one-way. Only a handful of individuals within a congregation—those serving as leaders and helpers—usually have opportunities to develop relationships with participants with disabilities. And while these volunteers would likely be quick to convey the many ways they have benefited from these experiences, the majority of the congregation still remains disconnected from the lives of people with disabilities. Sometimes, the prevailing view is that a person must receive training or possess a "special gift" to work with people with disabilities. Other times, people conclude that the spiritual needs, faith development, or learning styles of people with developmental disabilities diverge so substantially from the rest of the congregation that their needs can only be met within a specialized program. Neither view is accurate.

With Increasingly, congregations are discovering avenues for supporting the full and active participation of people with developmental disabilities in the life of their faith communities. They are realizing the value—indeed the necessity—of worshipping, fellowshipping, learning, and serving *with* people with disabilities. Evidence of shared ministry is found when people with and without disabilities are seen sharing a hymnal, reading scriptures, passing the peace, kneeling together in prayer, catching up over coffee during the social hour, rooming together on a weekend retreat, or serving alongside each other at the food pantry. Such congregations are convinced that relationships are at the heart of community.

By Where intellectual and physical abilities are valued above all else, it can be difficult to imagine how someone with developmental disabilities would have much to contribute. Yet, the powerful testimony of a young man with autism, the faithful help of a teenager with Down syndrome in the nursery, the prayerful encouragement of a woman

> "Those of us who have worked in this field know firsthand that people with developmental disabilities have ministered to us as much as we have ministered to them. Ministry is spirit to spirit. It does not depend on the state of a person's eyesight, hearing, ability to walk, talk or sit still. Nor does it depend on one's intellect. It depends on one's heart."
>
> —Terry Sieck and Rebecca Hartvigsen (2001, p. iii)

with cerebral palsy, and the reassuring smile of a child with multiple disabilities offers abundant evidence of the substantial contributions that can be made *by* people with disabilities. Congregations are slowly learning how to equip people with disabilities to engage their passions and gifts in the service of others, as well as demonstrating a willingness to gratefully receive these new offerings. This willingness to receive the gifts of people with disabilities is new territory for many congregations. Yet, anyone who has allowed a

> "I have learned more about the Gospels from the handicapped people, those on the margins of our society, those who have been crushed and hurt, than I have from the wise and the prudent."
>
> —Jean Vanier (1975, p. 99)

person with developmental disabilities the chance to share his or her gifts will likely testify to the profound impact it has had on his or her life. A congregation that cannot find a home for the gifts of all its members simply is not thinking hard enough.

We What an incredible testimony it would be if the distinction between people with and without disabilities disappeared altogether in communities of faith. It could simply be *we* who engage in ministry, everyone together. When a congregation no longer thinks first and foremost along the lines of disability, it has probably arrived at its destination.

Movement of Responses

The journey toward inclusion also might be thought of as a movement of responses, where congregations endeavor to continuously improve and broaden their efforts to include people with disabilities and their families in the life of their community. Some congregations are still in the planning stages, others have demonstrated a strong and lasting investment in the lives of people with disabilities. The National Organization on Disability's (NOD's) *Journey of a Congregation* offers one approach for considering where along this continuum a congregation finds itself, as well as where it envisions itself going (see Table 2.1). Early efforts often are characterized by growing awareness of barriers present within the congregation, a stirring among members to remove these obstacles, an articulation of the desire to be more welcoming, and initial conversations about proper starting points. As congregations deepen their commitment, plans give way to actions. New invitations to participate are extended, alterations are made to usual practices, attitudes begin to shift, and growth in the number of people with disabilities in the congregation becomes apparent. Eventually, an entire congregation can be transformed. People with disabilities are woven throughout congregational life, new relationships are forged, and passive participation gives way to true membership. Recognizing the impact on their own community, congregations often begin reaching out to guide others interested in undertaking this same journey.

Most congregations are still in the beginning stages of this journey (LaRoque & Eigenbrood, 2005). But, point of entry is probably less important than the direction and pace at which you are moving. More than two thousand congregations have committed to embarking on this journey, as evidenced by their decision to join the NOD's *Accessible Congregations Campaign*. Each participating congregation affirms the inherent worth of all people as created in the image of God, commits to removing barriers that hinder people with disabilities from participating actively in the life of the congregation, and encourages all of its members to share their faith, gifts, and talents fully in the life of the congregation. Where on this journey is your congregation? Are you still waiting to embark? Can you yet catch a glimpse of your destination?

Beginning Your Journey: How Welcoming Is Your Congregation?

Until this point, this chapter has focused on some of the marks of a welcoming congregation and the ways in which one's welcome might evolve. But, how can you determine whether *your* congregation truly is accessible—structurally, attitudinally, theologically, and programmatically? What signs exist that your community is a place that faithfully and continually welcomes people with disabilities? How can you identify areas in which your responses might be strengthened? Hospitality and welcome are hard

Table 2.1. *Journey of a Congregation* self-assessment tool

Level	Examples
Awareness	Recognition exists in some congregation members or the leadership that certain barriers are preventing children or adults with physical, sensory, or mental disabilities from gaining access to a full life of faith.
Internal advocacy	Advocacy is growing within the congregation to welcome people with disabilities as full participants and to remove barriers to this participation.
Discussions	Concerns are raised about the ability of the congregation to meet these challenges and—with input from people with disabilities and other experts—solutions are identified.
Plans	Invitations are extended to people with disabilities to join the congregation as full members, action plans are devised to achieve barrier-removing goals, and formal commitments are made to welcome people with disabilities.
Accommodations	Accommodations are made to improve the participation of people with disabilities.
Welcoming environment	Appreciation is expressed for the changes being made and friendships are extended to people with disabilities and their family members.
Hurdles	Identification of architectural, communication, transportation, financial, or other barriers are made and ways are found to move forward in spite of them.
Inclusion	Increased participation of people with disabilities in worship, study, and service to others is seen, as well as increased comfort levels of members with a more diverse congregation.
Local outreach	Options are explored and action plans formulated for partnership opportunities with local agencies and organizations serving people with disabilities.
Leadership	Lay members with disabilities are recruited for leadership roles within the congregation and willingness to accept and accommodate an ordained leader with a disability is demonstrated.
Transformation	Ongoing transformation of the congregation into a place where children and adults with disabilities are welcomed, fully included, and treated with respect occurs.
External advocacy	An expanded advocacy role is evidenced for congregation members regarding the needs and rights of people with disabilities in the community at large.
Outreach	Successful strategies, insights, and effective practices are compiled and shared with other congregations and communities.
Sharing the story	The story of the transformation of the congregation is publicized through articles, presentations, and/or media events.

From National Organization on Disability. (2001). *The journey of a congregation.* Washington, DC: Author; adapted by permission.

to quantify; two congregations are unlikely to define them in precisely the same way. The presence of people with disabilities in your congregation is one essential indicator, but certainly not the only one. It will take something more.

Many congregations begin by prayerfully examining how people with developmental disabilities and their families are currently participating, the barriers that may hinder their involvement, and the ways that welcome might be more clearly articulated. This process of self-reflection—sometimes called an *accessibility audit, congregational assessment, inclusion inventory*, or *barrier survey*—offers an opportunity to consider what is going well and what steps you might be led to take next. It is designed to answer the following questions: Where is your congregation on this journey? What direction are you heading? How swiftly along are you moving?

Creating a Congregational Team This process often begins with gathering a team of people for the purpose of examining the congregation's buildings, activities, policies, and practices. Who should contribute to this reflection process? Involve members who have experience with different aspects of congregational life—from children's programs to adult religious education to outreach ministries. Bringing together people with varied perspectives ensures that every facet of congregational life is considered, ownership is broadened, and creativity and resources are maximized. For example, consider inviting members of the pastoral staff, children and youth program directors, ministry leaders, parents of children with disabilities, and other interested congregational members.

It is not uncommon for people at first glance to conclude that their congregation is completely accessible. After all, you yourself may encounter little difficulty participating in services and programs. Stepping back and viewing your congregation from the standpoint of a visitor—especially a visitor with developmental disabilities—can be a difficult perspective to adopt. Although you may consider your congregation to be free of barriers and most welcoming, would a stranger? Therefore, two additional invitations are important to extend. First, include at least one person with disabilities on your team who is willing to share his or her own perspective on congregational activities. If no one in your congregation fits this description, consider contacting local service and support organizations to identify someone with disabilities willing to assist with this assessment (see Chapter 3, Table 3.1). It sometimes takes a personal experience with disability to recognize the barriers present in a congregation. Second, it might be beneficial to invite someone from outside of your congregation to provide a fresh perspective on aspects of congregational life that invite or inhibit the participation of people with disabilities and their families. For example, special educators, rehabilitation counselors, therapists, and other service providers who work with people with disabilities have much expertise to share. Moreover, your own denomination (see Appendix B) or a local community resource network (see Chapter 7) may have people willing to contribute to such congregational assessments.

Tools for Reflection Several approaches can be taken to guide your team in reflecting on the facilities and practices of your congregation. For example, numerous organizations and faith groups have developed formal tools to help you know which features of your congregation should receive your attention (see Table 2.2). Some tools include checklists of architectural elements that should be examined, including parking lots, walkways, entrances, restrooms, stairways, and fixtures (also see Chapter 3, Box 3.4). They may prompt you to consider issues related to communication, lighting, transportation, curricula, and attitudes. Other tools list various aspects of congregational life, inviting appraisal of the extent to which people with disabilities are currently involved. These tools can be useful for identifying potential obstacles to the participation of individuals with a broad range of

Table 2.2. Examples of congregational reflection tools

Reflection tool	Organization
The ABCs of Access	Anabaptist Disabilities Network
Accessibilities Mini-Audit	Unitarian Universalist Association
Accessibility Audit for Churches	United Methodist Church
Accessibility Checklist	Joni and Friends Ministries
Accessibility Review	Christian Council on Persons with Disabilities
Accessibility Survey	Pathways Awareness Foundation
An Audit of Barriers	National Organization on Disability
Assessment Tool for Congregations, People Who Have Developmental Disabilities, and Those Who Support Them	Bethesda Lutheran Homes
Churches for All: Access Standards & Questionnaire	Through the Roof
How Accessible is Your Church?	North American Mission Board
Inventory on Parish Attitudes	Evangelical Lutheran Church in America
Journey of a Congregation	National Organization on Disability
Local Church Accessibility Survey	Center on Aging & Older Adult Ministries, United Methodist Church
Parish Accessibility Survey	National Catholic Partnership on Disability
Signs of an Open-Door Parish	National Catholic Partnership on Disability

disabilities, including visual impairments, hearing impairments, and physical disabilities. However, children and adults with developmental disabilities often encounter additional barriers that may require consideration. Figure 2.1 displays a self-reflection guide—called *Indicators of Welcome: A Tool for Congregational Reflection*—for communities particularly interested in improving their capacity to welcome and support people with intellectual disabilities, autism, and other developmental disabilities.

The information needed to complete these tools can be gathered in a variety of ways. An attentive walk around the property and facilities is necessary when assessing architectural issues, but it should be coupled with conversations with individuals who use wheelchairs, walkers, and scooters, as well as users of other forms of specialized equipment. Team members also might visit the various events and activities that occur throughout the congregation each week, looking to see how people with disabilities currently are involved in or precluded from participating. Progress is sometimes exceptional in one area but slow in others, so it is important to look systematically across your congregation. For example, it is not uncommon for teachers of a preschool program to do an outstanding job of including children with disabilities at the same time as youth leaders struggle to welcome teenagers with disabilities into the high school group. Finally, blank copies of the reflection tool might be shared with team members, as well as with other members of the congregation, to be filled out individually. Once returned, responses can be examined to identify commonly held perceptions.

These tools should be used flexibly and adapted to address the specific issues present in your congregation. Consider adding or rewording items so that it is easy for people to share their feedback. Remember that these tools are only guides and should be interpreted carefully. They offer only examples of areas a congregation might consider; some issues may be more relevant than others. Moreover, they do not provide a cutoff score indicating when your congregation is "accessible enough"; neither do they include a standardized score against which to compare your congregation to others. Their purpose is simply to guide you in reflecting more deeply.

As an alternative or supplement to more structured tools, consider these other avenues for assessing your congregational practices.

- *Meet with new members and recent visitors to ask about their experiences and impressions on first visiting your congregation.* Talking with families who visited once or twice but decided not to return may help you to understand subtle barriers that exist within your congregation. Ideas for getting these conversations started are displayed in Table 2.3.

Indicators of Welcome

Perspectives

Whose perspectives were sought as part of this self-reflection process?

☐ Clergy ☐ Person(s) with disabilities ☐ Community members
☐ Children/youth ☐ Family member(s) ☐ Service or support
 program leader providers
☐ Adult program leader ☐ Other congregation members ☐ Other: _____

Presence and Participation

What steps have we taken to identify individuals *within* our congregation affected by disabilities?

What steps have we taken to identify individuals *beyond* our congregation affected by disabilities?

To what extent are children and adults with developmental disabilities, as well as their families, *actively* participating in the following dimensions of congregational life?

	Actively	Some-times	Never	Uncer-tain	Comments
Worship services	☐	☐	☐	☐	
Sacraments and rituals	☐	☐	☐	☐	
Fellowship events	☐	☐	☐	☐	
Adult religious education	☐	☐	☐	☐	
Small groups and Bible studies	☐	☐	☐	☐	
Children's religious education programs	☐	☐	☐	☐	
Youth groups and young adult programs	☐	☐	☐	☐	
Summer programs and camps	☐	☐	☐	☐	
Greeters, ushers, or other worship assistants	☐	☐	☐	☐	
Choir or worship team members	☐	☐	☐	☐	
Congregational committees	☐	☐	☐	☐	
Outreach ministries	☐	☐	☐	☐	
Congregation-sponsored schools	☐	☐	☐	☐	
Leisure, recreation, and social activities	☐	☐	☐	☐	
♦Other: _____	☐	☐	☐	☐	
♦Other: _____	☐	☐	☐	☐	

♦List other activities in which members of your congregation typically participate.

Figure 2.1. Indicators of welcome: A tool for congregational self-reflection.

(continued)

Figure 2.1. *(continued)*

What barriers seem to be hindering their involvement in these areas?

Architectural and Physical Accessibility

Can the following areas of our building and grounds be navigated easily by people using wheelchairs, walkers, and scooters, as well as other adaptive equipment?

	At present, how accessible are we?				
	Completely	Some-what	Not at all	Uncer-tain	Comments
Sanctuaries and other worship spaces	❑	❑	❑	❑	_____
Classrooms and meeting rooms	❑	❑	❑	❑	_____
Fellowship areas	❑	❑	❑	❑	_____
Nursery	❑	❑	❑	❑	_____
Restrooms	❑	❑	❑	❑	_____
Playgrounds and recreation areas	❑	❑	❑	❑	_____
Gymnasium	❑	❑	❑	❑	_____
Parking lots and sidewalks	❑	❑	❑	❑	_____
Doorways and hallways	❑	❑	❑	❑	_____
Congregational offices	❑	❑	❑	❑	_____
Kitchen and eating areas	❑	❑	❑	❑	_____
School building and child care center	❑	❑	❑	❑	_____
Summer camps	❑	❑	❑	❑	_____
♦Other: _____	❑	❑	❑	❑	_____
♦Other: _____	❑	❑	❑	❑	_____

♦List other locations within your congregation that visitors or members might encounter.

Which three architectural barriers are the most pressing?

1.

2.

3.

Read the following statements. To what extent does each statement describe our congregation? If you are not sure, mark *Uncertain*.

Worship services	Absolutely	Some-what	Not at all	Un-certain
Greeters, ushers, and other worship assistants know how to extend welcome and offer assistance to people with disabilities.	❑	❑	❑	❑
People with disabilities are supported to sit with friends, family, or whomever they choose.	❑	❑	❑	❑
Faith partners are available to sit with, befriend, and support people with developmental disabilities, if desired.	❑	❑	❑	❑
Worship experiences are designed to engage multiple senses and allow for participation in various ways.	❑	❑	❑	❑
Congregational leaders are willing to explore alternate ways for participating in worship and the sacraments, as necessary.	❑	❑	❑	❑
People with developmental disabilities are contributing to worship services in varied ways, including as greeters or choir members.	❑	❑	❑	❑
The congregation expresses comfort with people who worship in different ways (e.g., making noises, rocking, flapping their hands).	❑	❑	❑	❑
The congregation is periodically asked about chemical sensitivities, food allergies, or other environmental issues that impact involvement.	❑	❑	❑	❑
Other: _____	❑	❑	❑	❑

(continued)

Figure 2.1. *(continued)*

Religious education	Absolutely	Some-what	Not at all	Uncer-tain
Children with developmental disabilities participate in the same activities and classes as their peers without disabilities.	❑	❑	❑	❑
Activities are adapted and supports are provided so that children with disabilities can participate in activities to the greatest extent possible.	❑	❑	❑	❑
Religious curricula appeals to children who learn, participate, and contribute in a variety of ways.	❑	❑	❑	❑
Basic information, training, and support are provided to lay volunteers who work with children with disabilities.	❑	❑	❑	❑
Teachers and helpers are ready to include children with disabilities in their classes from the moment families first arrive.	❑	❑	❑	❑
Topics related to hospitality, inclusion, disabilities, and community periodically are woven into religious education curricula.	❑	❑	❑	❑
Youth with disabilities participate in preparation classes for membership, confirmation, bar/bat mitzvah, and other rites of passage.	❑	❑	❑	❑
Adults with disabilities are included in religious education programs.	❑	❑	❑	❑
Schools and daycare programs sponsored by our congregation include children with developmental disabilities.	❑	❑	❑	❑
Other: _____	❑	❑	❑	❑

Service	Absolutely	Some-what	Not at all	Uncer-tain
People with disabilities contribute on planning teams and serve in leadership positions.	❑	❑	❑	❑
Efforts are made to discern the gifts of people with developmental disabilities and connect them with opportunities to share their gifts.	❑	❑	❑	❑
People with disabilities are serving in varied capacities *within* the congregation.	❑	❑	❑	❑
People with disabilities are serving in varied capacities *beyond* the congregation.	❑	❑	❑	❑
Other: _____	❑	❑	❑	❑

Outreach	Absolutely	Some-what	Not at all	Uncer-tain
Intentional efforts are made to invite people with developmental disabilities and their families to participate in congregational life.	❑	❑	❑	❑
Accessibility symbols and images of people with disabilities are included in our materials and advertising.	❑	❑	❑	❑
Transportation to congregational activities is provided or arranged for individuals who cannot drive.	❑	❑	❑	❑
Visitation programs are extended to people with disabilities and their families, as well as those who are homebound.	❑	❑	❑	❑
We actively seek out ways to address unmet needs of people with disabilities living in our community.	❑	❑	❑	❑
Members are informed of opportunities to support people with disabilities within and outside of the congregation.	❑	❑	❑	❑
Other: _____	❑	❑	❑	❑

General awareness	Absolutely	Some-what	Not at all	Uncer-tain
Our policies and practices clearly communicate our desire to worship and serve alongside people with disabilities.	❑	❑	❑	❑
Our vision to be inclusive is frequently shared with members and broadcast throughout the community.	❑	❑	❑	❑
Reflection on our accessibility and hospitality is conducted at least annually.	❑	❑	❑	❑
Inclusion awareness events are observed each year.	❑	❑	❑	❑
Basic disability awareness is communicated through sermons, bulletin inserts, newsletters, religious education curricula, and other avenues.	❑	❑	❑	❑
Accessibility and support needs are considered when congregational events are planned.	❑	❑	❑	❑
Our resource library includes books and materials about disabilities, as well as resources for family members.	❑	❑	❑	❑
Our clergy and ministry leaders are familiar with disability issues related to their specific programs, roles, and responsibilities.	❑	❑	❑	❑
Other: _____	❑	❑	❑	❑

(continued)

Figure 2.1.   *(continued)*

Families	Absolutely	Some-what	Not at all	Uncer-tain
Families feel welcomed and included in the congregation.	❑	❑	❑	❑
Families contribute to discussions on congregational accessibility.	❑	❑	❑	❑
Respite care is available to interested parents.	❑	❑	❑	❑
Support groups are available to interested parents, siblings, and others within our congregation.	❑	❑	❑	❑
Financial support is available to people with disabilities and their families, as it is to all members of the congregation.	❑	❑	❑	❑
People with disabilities and their families know who to contact to ask for support and assistance.	❑	❑	❑	❑
Clergy and care ministers feel equipped to provide spiritual care and support to people with developmental disabilities and their families.	❑	❑	❑	❑
Other: _____	❑	❑	❑	❑

Partnerships with community groups	Absolutely	Some-what	Not at all	Uncer-tain
We have developed relationships with agencies and organizations serving people with disabilities in our community.	❑	❑	❑	❑
We have invited people with disabilities and advocacy groups to provide us with feedback about our materials, programs, and activities.	❑	❑	❑	❑
Staff from service and support organizations are helping us to improve our capacity to welcome and support people with disabilities.	❑	❑	❑	❑
We know where to turn when we need more information about specific disability-related issues.	❑	❑	❑	❑
We advocate for laws, policies, and resources that improve the quality of life for people with disabilities and their families.	❑	❑	❑	❑
Other: _____	❑	❑	❑	❑

Other indicators	Absolutely	Some-what	Not at all	Uncer-tain
We have developed a written plan describing how we will improve our accessibility and welcome.	❑	❑	❑	❑
Intentional efforts are made to support people with and without disabilities to develop meaningful social relationships.	❑	❑	❑	❑
A key person or group in our congregation is committed to making sure that the needs of people with disabilities are being addressed.	❑	❑	❑	❑
People with disabilities and/or their family members are involved in visioning and planning for the future of the congregation.	❑	❑	❑	❑
We have a process for identifying the emotional, spiritual, practical, and other support needs of congregation members.	❑	❑	❑	❑
Other: _____	❑	❑	❑	❑

PLAN OF ACTION

List up to five goals for improving our congregation's welcome and accessibility. What specific steps will we need to take to realize those goals? When will we aim to accomplish each goal? Who will be responsible for ensuring that each goal is followed through to completion?

Goals	Next steps	Completion date	Person(s) responsible
1.			
2.			
3.			
4.			
5.			
Comments:			

- *Survey members directly about their impressions of how welcoming the congregation is for people with disabilities, or for anyone.* Over a period of several weeks, greeters might hand out the surveys or include them in the bulletin. Place slotted boxes at the doorways so that surveys can be returned at any time.

- *Hold a listening session with people in your congregation who are affected by disabilities or who have an interest in making your congregation more inviting and responsive.* Provide coffee, snacks, and an open atmosphere for people to share their own stories and experiences. Members might feel more comfortable sharing openly if this conversation is facilitated by someone not affiliated with your congregation.

- *Meet individually with families of children with disabilities to ask about their ideas for how the congregation can better meet the needs of their child.* Their recommendations can be shared with your team without divulging names or information about families that wish to remain confidential.

Table 2.3.   Conversation starters for current members and recent visitors

- How long have you been attending our congregation?
- How did you first hear about our congregation?
- What initially led you to visit for the first time?
- Describe some of your first impressions.
- What specific steps have people taken to make you and your children feel welcome?
- Have there been experiences that have made you feel unwelcome or uncomfortable?
- Was there anything that almost kept you from returning?
- What could we have done to have made you and your children feel *more* welcome?
- How has your involvement in this congregation deepened over time?
- Are you involved in congregational programs and activities to the extent that you would like?
- If not, what stands in the way of this happening?
- How have people helped you identify ways that your gifts could be used within and beyond this congregation? Your children's gifts?
- How well have we done in supporting your faith journey? Your children's journeys?
- What advice do you have for us to be more responsive to the needs of children and adults with disabilities and their families?
- What needs in our congregation are going unrecognized or unmet? In our larger community?
- Do you know of other families that might want to share their experiences and thoughts with us?
- Is there anything else that we should know?

- *Make members of your congregation aware of avenues through which they can share disability-related needs or suggestions with the congregation's leadership or those leading the reflection process.* Ideas might include an anonymous "suggestion box" in the foyer, a form on the congregation's web site, or a note placed in the offering plate.

- *Engage youth or college-age groups in the reflection process.* Invite them to take a deeper look at congregational activities, perhaps as part of a service project.

- *Visit other congregations known for their accessibility and hospitality.* As you observe, ask yourself: What do they do exceptionally well? What looks different about their practices? What ideas can you take back to your own congregation?

- *Invite people with disabilities from your community to visit your worship services, programs, and other congregational activities.* Ask about the ways they felt welcomed and the barriers they encountered.

Reflecting on your congregation's hospitality should not be a one-time endeavor. Some congregations commit to an annual review of their accessibility, offering regular opportunities to reflect on and celebrate the progress that is being made. Often, these more formal efforts are linked to awareness events, such as a Disability Awareness Sunday (see Box 3.2 in Chapter 3). However, congregations should always be taking inventory of potential barriers and making efforts to remove obstacles to participation as they arise.

Reflecting and Responding

The team should meet together to compile and review all of the information that has been gathered. Begin by discussing what already is being done particularly well. Perhaps much or all of your building is accessible, several children with autism or other developmental disabilities currently are participating in elementary programs, families feel comfortable sharing their needs with clergy, and transportation is being provided for several adults with disabilities living in a nearby neighborhood. Celebrate each accomplishment. Then, discuss the barriers that emerged and identify needs that remain partially or wholly unmet. Perhaps your congregation still struggles to welcome young adults with disabilities in fellowship events, teachers remain unsure of how to adapt their curriculum to meet the needs of a child with severe disabilities, or parents express frustration with the leadership's unwillingness to reconsider how children are prepared for confirmation or other rites of passage. At this point, it may be appropriate to share your findings with your congregation's leadership team or governing board. Or, you may decide to first compile a list of recommended next steps before initiating this conversation.

After reviewing your findings, the team can begin prioritizing the steps they will take to make the congregation more welcoming. When there is much to do, knowing exactly where to begin can be a challenge. Consider the following questions as you begin setting priorities.

- *Are there pressing needs already apparent in your congregation?* Maybe an adolescent with autism is not being welcomed into the youth group, an adult living in a nearby group home has no reliable way to get to weekly Mass, a teacher is struggling with how to include a four-year old with Down syndrome in her preschool class, or a mother desperately needs respite from the round-the-clock care she provides to her son with Tay-Sachs disease.

- *Are there barriers that affect a large portion of your congregation?* The absence of a ramp to your education building or lack of accessible transportation may be preventing a large number of people from attending your congregation, including senior citizens and people with temporary injuries or acquired physical disabilities. A poorly planned and unexciting youth program may not be meeting the needs of any middle and high school students in the congregation. Perhaps most people in the congregation find the sermon series to be unengaging and difficult to apply to their lives.

- *Are there important needs not being met within your broader community?* Maybe several other congregations in your city already have banded together to start a respite program, but a support group for parents still does not exist. Perhaps few congregations have made efforts to develop inclusive programs for children with intellectual disabilities, leaving parents with nowhere to go.

Once the team has established its priorities, it should begin developing a plan of action. Decide on the first issues that you will attempt to address. What resources—including people, materials, and finances—do you have available to draw on? What additional resources and relationships will you need to seek out? Who will assume primary responsibility for assuring that each task is followed through to completion? What is the timeline for completing these tasks? At what point will you revisit your progress? Once drafted, share your plan with others in the congregation and solicit their feedback and suggestions for additions or improvements.

CONCLUSION

A welcoming congregation is more than a place where people with disabilities attend, but do not participate; arrive, but are not welcomed; receive, but do not serve. Becoming a congregation that is inclusive of people with developmental disabilities and their families requires an intentional and continuous commitment. The remainder of this book outlines exactly how you can begin breaking down architectural, attitudinal, communication, and programmatic barriers that keep people with disabilities and their families from participating in congregational life. In the next few chapters, you will read about strategies for weaving people with disabilities into worship services and ministry activities (Chapter 3), expanding religious education programs to meet the needs of all children and youth (Chapter 4), and reaching out to have an impact on the lives of people with disabilities beyond the walls of the congregation (Chapter 5).

Chapter 3

Welcoming, Including, and Connecting

Becoming a Responsive Congregation

Is your congregation a place of welcome, belonging, and contributing to children and adults with developmental disabilities and their families? When asked this question, most people would offer a response along the lines of "Of course! At least...I think so." Yet, many congregations do not count people with developmental disabilities and their families among their members. Even when present, people with disabilities are often found only on the peripheries of congregational life. Is your congregation *truly* a place of welcome and belonging? The architectural, attitudinal, programmatic, and other barriers that may push people away from your congregation are not insurmountable, but they will not disappear without intentional efforts. This chapter describes steps that congregations can take to reach out to people with disabilities and their families and weave them into congregational life. It will equip you to become more responsive to the people already associated with your congregation and, as you improve your capacity to welcome people, challenge you to begin reaching out to the broader community.

DISCOVERING PEOPLE WITH DISABILITIES AND THEIR FAMILIES

As your congregation seeks to truly welcome people with developmental disabilities into deeper fellowship, two questions should be considered. First, are there people with disabilities who already are connected to your congregation in some way, even if only at the fringes? Second, how might the supports, resources, and programs that you already have to offer be shared with your neighbors with disabilities and their families who are not yet involved in your congregation? A continual effort to be responsive both within and beyond your congregation should characterize your congregation's reputation.

Looking within Your Congregation

Begin by looking at who is already affiliated in some way with your congregation and the opportunities that already exist right in your midst. Which of your neighbors are already present? Which neighbors seem conspicuously absent? Most Americans are associated with congregations in which 400 or more adults and children regularly participate, although the average congregation is somewhat smaller in size (Chaves, 2004). If your congregation really reflected the demographic makeup of your surrounding community, how many people with developmental disabilities might you expect to be involved in the life of your congregation? Various estimates suggest that almost 20% of the population has some type of disability and between 2%–3% of people in any community have intellectual disabilities, autism spectrum disorders, or other developmental disabilities (e.g., Braddock et al., 2005; President's Committee for People with Intellectual Disabilities, 2004; Steinmetz, 2006). Therefore, in a congregation of 400 people, you might expect as many as 12 children and adults with developmental disabilities to be in attendance. If your congregation is one of the growing numbers of faith communities with over 1,000 people in attendance, you might expect 30 or more people with developmental disabilities to be present. Once all of the parents, siblings, relatives, and friends of people with disabilities are considered, it becomes clear that the opportunity for affecting numerous lives is substantial. It is quite likely that people with developmental disabilities are connected in some way to your congregation, even if you are not aware of it.

As a starting point, congregations often begin by surveying individuals to identify the opportunities already present within their congregation. An informal survey can help determine who in your congregation is affected by any kind of disability—whether physical, emotional, or intellectual. Certain members may come immediately to mind, but what about people who attend infrequently, have hidden or less-apparent disabilities, have family members who no longer attend because it is just too difficult, or have a child with disabilities whom they never bring to worship services? A survey also can gauge how well your congregation has done in meeting the needs of members. Invite members with disabilities and their families to tell you about the specific ways in which they would like to be involved in congregational activities and the supports they would need to make this possible. Finally, a survey offers evidence of your congregation's commitment to become a more welcoming place, and it can assist with identifying people interested in helping to transform this vision into a reality. Figure 3.1 is a sample survey that can be adapted for use in your congregation.

Congregational Outreach Survey

Our congregation is called to have an impact on our community. We desire to be an inviting congregation that is intentional about finding ways to worship among, mutually support, and serve alongside people with disabilities and their families in fellowship. We invite you to help us realize this vision. Do you know people with disabilities who might want to attend our congregation? Are there needs we can help meet or support we could provide? Would you like to help welcome people with disabilities and their families into our faith community? Your answers to this brief questionnaire will help us identify steps we can take to become a congregation known for our hospitality.

1. **How would you describe yourself?** *Check all that apply.*
   - ❏ I have a disability.
   - ❏ I have a child with a disability.
   - ❏ I have a sibling or relative with a disability.
   - ❏ I have a friend or neighbor with a disability.
   - ❏ I interact with people with disabilities at my workplace.
   - ❏ I do not know anyone with a disability.
   - ❏ Other: _____

2. **If you or a family member has a disability, which of the following supports might help you participate more fully in congregational life or meet a personal need?** *Check all that apply.*
   - ❏ Transportation:
     - ❏ To worship services
     - ❏ To other congregational activities throughout the week
     - ❏ To other events in the community
   - ❏ Additional support to participate in
     - ❏ Worship services
     - ❏ Children's programs
     - ❏ Youth programs
     - ❏ Adult programs
   - ❏ Respite care (e.g., offering a periodic break to parents of children with disabilities)
     - ❏ To attend worship services
     - ❏ To participate in other congregational activities
     - ❏ At other times throughout the week
   - ❏ Support group for parents, siblings, and other caregivers
   - ❏ Pastoral counseling
   - ❏ Financial or other material assistance: _____
   - ❏ Accessible scriptural or other study materials
   - ❏ Support in advocating for your needs among agencies, organizations, and schools
   - ❏ Information about faith-based services and programs within our community

In the space below, we encourage you to share with us other needs not already listed:

Figure 3.1. Example of a blank congregational outreach survey.

(continued)

Figure 3.1.   *(continued)*

3. As we consider new ways of welcoming people with developmental and other disabilities into our congregation, would you be interested in learning more about how you might serve in any of the following ways?

❑ Periodically giving someone a ride to services or other congregational activities

❑ Serving as a companion or partner during congregational activities

❑ Inviting someone with disabilities to sit with you during worship services

❑ Inviting someone over for a meal and fellowship periodically

❑ Joining a ministry team to improve our welcome to people with disabilities

❑ Serving as a children's or youth program teacher

❑ Serving as a helper or buddy to a person with disabilities during children's and youth programs

❑ Volunteering to help us provide respite care activities

❑ Attending an informational workshop about disabilities and our congregation's welcome

❑ Serving on the team that reviews and acts on the responses to this survey

❑ Other: _____

4. People often have gifts that they never thought of using to welcome and support people with developmental disabilities—an outgoing personality, a specific hobby or talent, or a knack for making connections among people. Perhaps there are things you care deeply about. List one or two things that you are really good at or have a passion for doing.

5. Will you commit to inviting your friends and neighbors with disabilities to attend services and activities within our congregation?

❑ Yes

❑ No

❑ I'd like to learn more about how to do this

6. If you would like to talk further about the information you provided on this survey, please let us know your name and the best way to contact you?

Name:

❑ Telephone: _____

❑ E-mail: _____

7. Are there any questions, concerns, or comments you would like to share with us?

Please return to _____ by _____.

The purpose of the survey is to identify existing needs and potential partners within your congregation, so invite input from as many members of your congregation as possible. Distribute surveys in bulletins, include them in mailings, and display them in a prominent place in the congregation's foyer, hallways, or fellowship areas. If people believe their feedback will really be heard and acted on, they are much more likely to share their thoughts. Because newcomers will join your congregation, your efforts to keep abreast of needs should be ongoing, rather than limited to a one-time effort.

Several additional approaches may help you to identify needs and opportunities within your congregation and to let people know about the efforts you are taking to become more welcoming. These strategies might serve as the catalyst for new conversations in your congregation, communicating to families that it is both okay and important to talk about disabilities.

- In many congregations, it is the leadership who determines the issues and priorities set before the congregation. A simple acknowledgement from the pulpit—whether through an announcement, prayer, sermon, or special message—that people with disabilities are absolutely integral to the mission of the congregation can have a profound impact, breaking the silence that often exists in congregations around disabilities.

- Include in your weekly bulletin a brief note describing your ongoing (and planned) efforts to welcome and support children and adults with disabilities as well as their families. Write an article for your congregation's newsletter articulating a rationale for ministry with people with disabilities and communicating your congregation's desire to become a more inviting place. Provide a point of contact through which people can obtain additional information about accessing these supports or contributing their time and gifts to these efforts.

- Develop a brochure or flyer that describes the ways in which adults and children with developmental disabilities and their families are already contributing to congregational life. Place this information in key locations throughout your building, such as in the lobby and outside of classrooms used for nursery and children's activities.

- Create a bulletin board or other display that describes some of the needs of people with disabilities in your community and avenues through which congregation members can respond to these needs (see Chapter 5 for ideas).

- Talk with leaders of other ministry and outreach efforts in your congregation to find out about the people they encounter who may be affected by disabilities. For example, congregational care team members may know of families in the congregation who have children with disabilities; Meals on Wheels volunteers may have met individuals who are living somewhat isolated in the community; or a parish nurse might be aware of special health-related needs within the congregation.

"Some members may complain that no one in the congregation currently has need of those supports, but the complaint begs the question as to who has not come because the support wasn't made available."

—Trace Haythorn (2003, p. 345)

If you discover that few, if any, people with developmental disabilities and their families are involved in your congregation, ask yourself why this might be the case. Have they never heard of your congregation? Did they attend your services at one time, but left feeling unwelcome? Perhaps your congregation had little to offer them or was unable to find a way to meet their particular needs?

Reaching Out to Communities

Most congregations engage in outreach to the wider community living beyond the walls of their buildings (Woolever & Bruce, 2002). This emphasis on getting involved in the community is usually evident in the congregation's mission or vision statement. So, what does your congregation really mean when it says *community*? Would a close look at your congregation's programs and membership suggest that you may have been defining community in too limited or narrow a way? *Is there a place for people with developmental disabilities in your community?*

An incredible opportunity awaits congregations that seek to serve their neighbors. Developmental disabilities are present across every demographic group present within a congregation—male and female, rich and poor, rural and urban, old and young, and every nationality and cultural group. Ask yourself, what is 3% of the number of people living in your neighborhood, your city, or your county? Add to this the number of brothers, sisters, mothers, fathers, and grandparents whose lives are somehow touched by their relative with disabilities. The opportunities for meeting real and pressing needs are incredible. If you remain unconvinced, ask your local school district or vocational rehabilitation office how many children and adults with developmental disabilities they serve in your community.

Individuals with developmental disabilities *are* present in your community. Are they present in your congregation? How are you pursuing relationships with individuals who do not yet have a congregational home, but long for such an invitation? What are the indicators that would assure a visitor that he or she is welcome in your congregation? What is your congregation doing that communicates to people with developmental disabilities and their families that you clearly have them in mind? What efforts are you making that will first draw people to your community and then keep them coming back?

Outreach efforts to this segment of your community may have to be more deliberate than those commonly used by congregations to publicize their offerings and activities. Parents are usually the point of entry into a congregation for children. However, passive efforts such as yellow page advertisements, outdoor signs, newspaper articles, and websites often are inaccessible and ineffective avenues for communicating about your congregation's programs and activities to most adults with developmental disabilities. Consider the following ideas for extending invitations.

- *Make it personal.* There is considerable difference between an *announcement* and an *invitation.* Simply announcing the dates and times of congregational activities is likely to evoke a very different response than extending a personal invitation asking someone to come and join you at your congregation. In fact, most people first visit a congregation because someone they knew extended them a personal invitation. Encourage members to personally ask people with disabilities from their neighborhoods and workplaces if they would be interested in visiting your congregation.

- *Be explicit.* Because many people with disabilities and their families have experienced a history of passive nonresponse or overt exclusion, you may need to be much more specific about who your congregations means by *all* (e.g., *Our congregation desires to welcome all members of our community, including people with disabilities and their families*). In all of your outreach efforts, it may be wise to assume that people with disabilities and their families are wondering, "Sure...but do they really mean me?"

- *Contact service, support, and advocacy organizations.* Many agencies and organizations offer resources and supports to people with disabilities in your community. Parents often turn to these groups for information, guidance, and advocacy. Develop relationships with these organizations, making sure they are aware of the efforts your congregation is making. If you are not sure where to start, Table 3.1 includes a list of community groups and agencies that are likely to be present in your community.

- *Inform residential providers.* Make sure that staff members working in group homes and other residential programs are aware of your efforts

Table 3.1. Potential community partners in supporting people with developmental or other disabilities

Organization or association♦	Web site
The Arc	http://www.thearc.org
American Association on Intellectual and Developmental Disabilities	http://www.aaidd.org
Autism Society of America	http://www.autism-society.org
Brain Injury Association of America	http://www.biausa.org
Center for Independent Living	http://www.ilru.org
Councils on Developmental Disabilities	http://www.nacdd.org
Easter Seals	http://www.easterseals.com
Epilepsy Foundation	http://www.epilepsyfoundation.org
Federation of Families for Children's Mental Health	http://www.ffcmh.org
Goodwill Industries International	http://www.goodwill.org
Muscular Dystrophy Association	http://www.mdausa.org
National Association for the Dually Diagnosed	http://www.thenadd.org
National Disability Rights Network	http://www.napas.org
National Down Syndrome Society	http://www.ndss.org
National Muscular Sclerosis Society	http://www.nationalmssociety.org
Parents Helping Parents	http://www.php.com
People First	Local web search or telephone directory
Salvation Army	http://www.salvationarmyusa.org
Spina Bifida Association	http://www.sbaa.org
TASH	http://www.tash.org
United Cerebral Palsy	http://www.ucp.org
United Way	http://www.unitedway.org
County and state social service agencies	Local web search or telephone directory
Local advocacy groups	Local web search or telephone directory
Local school districts	Local web search or telephone directory
Residential service providers	Local web search or telephone directory
Respite/adult day care service providers	Local web search or telephone directory
Supported employment providers	Local web search or telephone directory
Vocational rehabilitation offices	Local web search or telephone directory
Universities with special education, rehabilitation, psychology, social work, and related programs	Local web search or telephone directory

♦Locate your local chapter or affiliate office.

to involve people with disabilities in your community. Provide information about your congregation's programs and activities, as well as the types of support you are able to offer. In addition, include materials that can be shared directly with residents with disabilities interested in finding a congregational home.

- *Design welcoming outreach materials.* Ask self-advocates (i.e., people with developmental disabilities who speak on their own behalf), family members, and advocacy organizations to provide feedback on the extent to which your outreach materials convey welcome. Include information about the supports you offer, as well as images of people with disabilities or accessibility symbols in your newsletters; print, radio, and television ads; and on your congregation's website. Include language (e.g., *disability ministry, special needs ministry,* or *inclusive ministry*) that clearly signals that your congregation desires to be a place of welcome for people with disabilities.

- *Let your denomination know.* If your congregation is affiliated with a larger denomination or faith group, inform your regional and national offices of how you are including people with developmental disabilities and the steps you are taking to deepen and broaden your response. They can then direct families wishing to find a place to worship within their specific faith tradition. In addition, contact local congregational networks to share your efforts (see Chapter 7).

- *Connect with other congregations.* Share your commitment with others in your community. Congregations that are inaccessible or that feel unequipped to support a person in their congregation should, at a minimum, be able to offer connections with another local congregation that is ready to welcome him or her. Perhaps your example may encourage other congregations to undertake a similar commitment; ensuring a broad response from the religious community and multiple worship options for individuals and their families.

- *Rely on current congregational members to spread the word.* As you include individuals with disabilities in your programs and extend support to families, expect word to spread. Too few congregations are responding in this area, and many other families will be attracted to a congregation that is making even small, but intentional efforts. Expect families to be among the most vocal proponents of your efforts.

- *Connect with new families.* How would a family who is new to town know that your congregation wants to welcome them and their child with disabilities? Are you passively waiting, hoping that they will just happen to walk through your doors? Make sure that information about your congregation is included in welcome packet materials distributed by local businesses, neighborhood associations, or chambers of commerce. Many local disability-related organizations and agencies compile informational packs for new families that describe the services and supports available in a community.

- *Hold an outreach event.* Some congregations plan outreach events specifically for people with disabilities and their families, caregivers, and other support providers. Examples might include an open house, spaghetti supper, potluck dinner, monthly social, special worship service, or evening fellowship. These activities are designed to provide a safe, comfortable place for initial connections to be made with a congregation and an avenue through which new relationships might be forged. Such activities should serve as an entry point into the rest of congregational life, rather than as a permanent, separate ministry.

> "Months and years of exile will not disappear simply because someone says, 'You are invited.' Those at the margins will need to feel the sincerity of the invitation. They will need to see the places at the table where they fit. For most people in exile to re-enter the heart of the community of faith, it will take some bridges."
>
> —Paul Leichty (2003, p. 11)

Of course, it is essential that invitations do not extent beyond what your congregation is currently able and willing to offer. As you discover new ways to welcome people with disabilities into your congregation, your outreach efforts can grow accordingly.

CREATING A VISION FOR WELCOMING PEOPLE WITH DISABILITIES

Responding to the needs of people with developmental disabilities is not merely consistent with the core beliefs of most faith communities, it is often explicitly commanded (Abrams, 1998; Block, 2002; Merrick, 1993). Although the particular doctrines and theology that fuel efforts in this area can vary across faith traditions (see Appendix A), it is essential that the call to include people with disabilities be communicated intentionally, clearly, and regularly. Unfortunately, the views about disabilities held by many people—within and beyond the walls of a congregation—are based on uncertain presumptions, incorrect information, and inaccurate stereotypes (see Chapter 1). As a result, the actual practices of too many congregations fail to reflect the very convictions they affirm. Such barriers of attitude and misinformation must be removed.

An important first step involves creating general awareness of the ways in which your congregation can welcome, support, and be served by people with disabilities and their families. What is the culture and atmosphere of your congregation? What perceptions do members hold regarding the role of people with disabilities in their congregation? In the broader community? As you undertake efforts to promote broad awareness in your congregation and cast a vision for welcoming people with disabilities, consider the following suggestions.

First, numbers and statistics may offer a starting point for disability awareness, but such information by itself often is insufficient to sustain people's motivation to respond differently. Help people catch hold of a vision for what your congregation can be and is called to be. Frame conversations about inclusion within the language of theology, scriptures values, purpose, and call so that people understand why this vision is one worth attaching themselves to. Initial hesitation may be overcome when that vision emerges from clear articulation of the call God has on your congregation and

> "It's a matter of putting the challenge out there and looking people straight in the eye and saying, 'This is what God expects of us. This is who God calls us to be and we can't be anything else. And we need your help.'"
>
> —Martha Bess DeWitt, as cited in Haythorn, T. (2003, p. 195)

an affirmation that serving (and being served by) people with disabilities is instrumental to fulfilling the mission of your congregation.

Second, real awareness comes through personal involvement, not just from an informational campaign. You become truly aware when you invest something of yourself in other people's lives, spending time with them, stepping into their world, sharing their burdens, and celebrating their accomplishments (Leichty, 2003). When you experience—even in small part—the challenges people face, you gain a more tangible awareness, rather than one that is strictly intellectual. It is impossible to catch a true glimpse of people's needs and gifts when they always remain at arm's length.

The following approaches may comprise individual components of the broad effort your congregation can take to create an awareness of the needs and contributions of people with disabilities.

- In all of your communication, model respectful ways of talking about disability that affirm the worth and dignity of people. Because no one should be identified solely by their differences, use language that emphasizes one's personhood, rather than his or her disability. For example, use the phrase *people with disabilities*, rather than *disabled people*; *children with autism*, rather than *autistic*; and *adults with intellectual disabilities*, rather than *the mentally retarded*. Metaphors also matter and can inadvertently alienate, so carefully consider whether your point can be made in a different way (see Box 3.1).

- Talk with people with disabilities and their families about their personal experiences within your congregation and the perceptions that other members seem to hold. Ask for their input on how greater awareness of disabilities might be pursued and explore avenues through which their own needs might be communicated more effectively to others.

- Consider holding an inclusion awareness event to recognize and celebrate the gifts and contributions of people with disabilities (see Box 3.2). In addition, general disability awareness information can be incorporated into religious education curricula for children and youth, congregational activities, worship services, and printed materials to

Box 3.1
Interacting with People with Developmental Disabilities

The manner in which you interact with people communicates volumes about their worth and welcome. Too often, people are unsure of how to interact with a person with a developmental disability or his or her family and so they make no attempts to interact at all. The following general tips can help you feel more comfortable in welcoming and getting to know children and adults with developmental disabilities.

- Hospitality begins with a simple "hello." A warm greeting and hearty handshake require no special training and should be dispensed generously.

- Many people are unsure of exactly what terminology to use when talking about people with disabilities. Refer to people as you wish them to refer to you—by name.

- Adults with developmental disabilities are first and foremost *adults*. Do not interact with them as you would with a child. Avoid being condescending in your speech or tone.

- Always look at and speak directly to a person with disabilities, rather than interacting through the family member, caregiver, or companion who is accompanying the person.

- Greet people with disabilities as you would anyone else, even if they are not able to communicate verbally or interact in typical ways. Do not assume that they cannot understand you.

- It may take some individuals with developmental disabilities extra time to say or do certain things. Patiently offer your attention.

- Grant every person the opportunity to do as much for themselves as possible. Ask a person if he or she would like assistance with a task, but wait until your offer is accepted before providing any help.

- If it seems that a person is having difficulty understanding you, try rephrasing your questions or comments in a different way. Similarly, if you are having trouble understanding someone, it is okay to ask him or her to repeat what was said.

- When in the presence of people with disabilities, do not talk about them as if they were not right there.

- Treat every person with respect, even when his or her participation looks a little different. Give bulletins, hymnals, prayer books, Bibles, and other materials to everyone, regardless of whether or not you believe they can read.

- When you observe a person engaging in behavior that is not appropriate, provide feedback that is clear, but nonjudgmental.

(*Sources:* Accessibilities Committee [1999]; Bolduc [2001]; & Cohen [2003]).

Box 3.2
Inclusion Awareness Efforts

A congregation should always communicate hospitality to people with disabilities and their families. Sometimes, congregations also set aside one or more congregational services a year to intentionally recognize and celebrate the contributions of people with disabilities, as well as to highlight the importance of creating a welcoming congregation. Such events can carry different names, usually involving some combination of words from the following two columns:

Access	Celebration
Accessibility	Day
Awareness	Month
Disability Awareness	Sabbath
Disability Ministry	Service
Hospitality	Sunday
Inclusion	Week
Special Needs	

In planning such an event, you do not have to start from scratch. Many faith groups and organizations have already prepared materials that include ideas and suggestions for worship songs, special music, scripture passages, responsive readings/litanies, prayers, sermon/homily topics, benedictions, and other awareness activity ideas (see Appendix B). Moreover, you can borrow and adapt resources developed by other denominations to create an approach that addresses the specific needs of your congregation. Planning an effective awareness event takes time, so begin early. Consider the following creative ideas used by other congregations:

- Form a planning team that includes people with a variety of perspectives, such as worship leaders, parents of children with disabilities, youth group leaders, and other interested members of your congregation.

- As much as possible, involve children and adults with disabilities in planning and participating in the worship service. As throughout the rest of the year, people with disabilities should have opportunities to serve as greeters, ushers, choir members, acolytes, speakers, and prayer leaders.

- A natural place to create awareness is through sermons, homilies, and other special messages from the pulpit. Use this opportunity to articulate a strong theological foundation for hospitality, community, and inclusion. Intentionally, but thoughtfully, include people with disabilities in stories, illustrations, and prayers. Because the way you approach the topic can inadvertently reinforce outdated stereotypes and negative images of people with disabilities (Black, 1996; Eiesland & Saliers, 1998), reflect carefully on the messages that congregants will leave with. Consider hosting a pulpit exchange and inviting another leader from your community to address the impact of disability on his or her own life and congregation.

(continued)

(continued)

- Invite someone from outside of your congregation to deliver the message or offer his or her testimony, such as a ministry leader from another congregation that has taken notable steps to welcome people with disabilities, a parent or sibling of a child with autism, or a young adult with Prader-Willi syndrome who can speak to the importance of community and faith in his life. Sometimes, an outsider's perspective can have a significant impact on the congregation.

- Call on congregational members to make a commitment to respond in some way. Explain how people's seemingly ordinary gifts can make a profound difference in the life of a person with disabilities. Then, highlight specific ways that people can connect their gifts with needs within and beyond the congregation in this area.

- Collect an offering of monies to be earmarked for outreach activities, improvements in physical accessibility (e.g., adding a ramp, pictorial signs, handrails, or accessible furniture), or training opportunities for staff members, lay leaders, and volunteers working in ministries involving people with disabilities.

- Weave awareness activities into other congregational activities leading up to and occurring on the day of the formal event. Develop discussion guides that can be incorporated into existing small groups or religious education classes or distributed as family devotion guides. If your congregation operates a school, consider integrating information on disabilities into relevant parts of the school curriculum.

- An inclusion awareness event may offer an opportune time to first conduct or report the findings from your congregational survey (see Figure 3.1) or to initiate a self-reflection process (see Chapter 2).

- Use this time as a kick-off for your congregation's disability ministry efforts. Cast a vision before the congregation that describes the direction that you would like to head.

- Submit a press release to your local newspaper describing the activities your congregation is planning that will coincide with this event. Consider inviting advocates and leaders from the disability community.

coincide with recognized national awareness months (e.g., *Developmental Disabilities Awareness Month* in March; *Mental Retardation Awareness Month* in March; *Autism Awareness Month* in April; *Mental Health Awareness Month* in May; *Disability Mentoring Day* in October; *National Disability Employment Awareness Month* in October; *National Family Caregiving Month* in November).

- Invite members of your community to speak on issues related to disability, faith, inclusion, and belonging. For example, youth and adults with disabilities might talk about their spiritual journeys; parents could share what they wish everyone knew about how best to support families; members of the congregation could speak to the impact people with developmental disabilities have had on their lives; or educators, advocates, and service providers might articulate how inclusion strengthens communities and contributes to greater wholeness. Invite these individuals to speak during worship services, small group meetings, Sunday/Sabbath school classes, men's and women's breakfasts, and activities for children and youth.

- Gather and retell stories that speak of the impact your congregation has had on people with disabilities and the ways that your congregation has itself been transformed by those same relationships. Such stories will illustrate vividly the powerful impact of inclusion and reinforce the concepts of mutuality and interdependence among people.

- One of the best outcomes of your awareness efforts would be that people would be *less* focused on disability labels. Awareness efforts should help people to understand the importance of hospitality and embolden them to learn more about particular people, not simply increase their knowledge of disability conditions.

- Remind congregants of what they do *not* need training for when welcoming people with disabilities—just about everything. Simple gestures of welcoming and hospitality do not require specialized training, university coursework, or an advanced degree. In most cases you do not need training to invite individuals out for dinner, ask how their week has been, pray with them, invite them to be part of a small group, bring them a meal, or just be their friend. Often, the most important gestures occur outside of formal ministry programs; it is through everyday interactions that you communicate most clearly the worth you attach to someone. In some situations, it may be helpful to talk with a caregiver or support provider about the individual's specific needs, preferences, and situation if you were going to take the person out alone or make your relationship more long-term and regular.

- Collaborate with other congregations and community organizations to offer periodic workshops, panel discussions, or a speaker series on disability issues (see Chapter 7).

- Host a monthly movie night and include films with disability themes. As you discuss the films, facilitate conversations about lessons that can be learned about the needs of people with disabilities and meaningful congregational responses. Similarly, consider hosting a book study or series of informal discussions on disability-related topics.

- Incorporate themes on disabilities into religious education programs for children and adults. Develop your own materials or draw upon existing resources (e.g., *Different Gifts, But the Same Spirit*, Pathways Awareness Foundation; *Hearts in Motion*, Joni and Friends; *Dignity and Disability*, Bureau of Jewish Education of Greater Washington). Contact your congregation's curriculum supplier or other religious publishers for additional resource ideas.

- Within your congregation's bulletins, newsletters, listserve, or website, include a brief column entitled *Knowing Our Community* or something similar. Use this space to keep your congregation informed about ongoing needs in your community or segments of the population who are not being reached. For example, you might include basic statistics on the number of people with disabilities in your community or highlight the common support needs of parents and siblings of children with disabilities. Community organizations can help you discern these needs.

- Always connect informational efforts with opportunities for action. Increasing awareness should serve as a springboard for change, not as an end unto itself. Provide concrete examples of how people can truly welcome someone into their communities and identify existing or emerging opportunities for people to serve (see Chapter 5). In addition, identify formal and informal ways for individuals or groups to become involved in their community beyond the congregation's walls, such as volunteering with an advocacy and social service organization or participating in inclusive recreational and community events (e.g., Unified/Special Olympics, Best Buddies).

These strategies offer an important starting point for creating awareness of disability issues and articulating a commitment to inclusion in congregations. A welcoming atmosphere is an essential aspect of any congregation that desires to worship, fellowship, learn, and serve alongside their neighbors with developmental disabilities. But it is not enough. Congregations must also commit to actively supporting the presence and contributions of children and adults with disabilities in their communities.

MAKING IT HAPPEN: GUIDING PRINCIPLES

As you think through how you will support people with developmental disabilities in your congregation and reach out to those in the wider community, let the following principles to guide your efforts.

Lead with Prayer

Any congregation will tell you that efforts to live out their call must begin with and be surrounded by prayer. Ministry with people with developmental disabilities is no exception. Prayerfully reflect on the opportunities that lie before your congregation, the lay people who will volunteer, the relationships that will emerge, the people with disabilities and families who will be affected, and the congregation that will welcome them. Seek wisdom and guidance as you pursue God's call on your congregation.

Focus on People, Not Programs

Too many congregations are waiting until they can marshal enough resources, space, and volunteers to establish a disability ministry program before inviting people with developmental disabilities into their congregations. Ministry with people with disabilities does not require *new* programs, but rather plans for weaving people with disabilities into *existing* programs (Pierson, 2004). Rather than creating a separate *anything* just for people with developmental disabilities, explore how you can include everyone in existing activities. Focus on one person at a time and devise thoughtful plans for weaving each individual into all your congregation already has to offer.

Learn from Others

In this area of congregational ministry, it is not necessary to reinvent the wheel. Other congregations also are making strides to reach out to and welcome people with disabilities and it is worth understanding the successes and challenges they have encountered along the way. Visit congregations that are further along on their journey toward inclusion. Talk to the lay people who are spearheading these efforts, learn how they worked through the issues with which you are now wrestling, and find out how to avoid the barriers they have encountered. Ask them to come visit your congregation and offer suggestions on how to improve your efforts. If you are unsure of where to find such a congregation, consider contacting one of the following national resources to consult their list of inclusive congregations: Christian Council on Persons with Disabilities, Council for Jews with Special Needs, Joni and Friends, and the National Organization on Disability (see Appendix B).

Reverse the Question

The questions people raise often reveal that their expectations for people with developmental disabilities are quite different from those they hold for others without disabilities. *Will people with developmental disabilities really get anything out of the sermon? Can they fully grasp the meaning of baptism, the significance of communion, or the weight of bar/bat mitzvah? How can we be sure that they will be welcomed by others in our congregation?* Such questions reveal subtle barriers to full participation and expose people's misperceptions. Gaventa (1986, 2005) suggests that learning to "reverse the question" can be an important strategy for building a congregation that embraces people who have not traditionally been part of their gathering community. The challenge is for congregations to learn to ask these same questions of themselves:

How much is anyone else taking away from the sermon? Is it a requirement that everyone firmly grasp all of the intricate points of the message in order to remain in the sanctuary? Is it quite likely that we all take away different things from the sermon or that some elements of the worship experience may resonate more or less with us? Are there steps that clergy should take to ensure that their sermons capture the hearts, minds, and attention of a greater proportion of the congregation?

To what extent do any of us grasp the full significance of certain religious ceremonies? Does everyone really understand these rituals in the same way? Is it okay to acknowledge the existence of an element of mystery and wonder that each person encounters? Are there steps our congregation could take to ensure that a greater number of people understand and appreciate the significance of these rituals?

> "I suspect that if we went around the average church congregation and asked the participants to define the meaning of the Eucharist there would be multiple answers, and many would not have a clue what its 'true' theological meaning is. There is no good reason why we should deem it appropriate to ask questions of people with [intellectual] disabilities that we would not ask of the majority of the people who actually participate in our services of worship."
>
> —John Swinton (2001, p. 56)

How much do any of us really feel welcomed in our congregation? Is our congregation a difficult place for anyone— whether that person is a first-time visitor or a long-time attendee—to fit in? What can we do as a congregation to better equip all of our members to generously dispense hospitality to every newcomer?

Involve the Leadership

To effect systemic and lasting change in a congregation, the senior leadership has to consider efforts to welcome people with disabilities as important and integral to the mission of the congregation. Meet with those in your congregation who cast the visions and make key decisions. Share your passion for supporting people with disabilities and their families, as well as your ideas for steps the congregation might take to respond to the needs you have identified. Pierson (2004) suggested several topics that might make up the agenda for this meeting (see Figure 3.2). The leadership can play an important role in ensuring that efforts are woven throughout all aspects of the congregation rather than creating a separate "disability

---

Agenda

Pray for God's wisdom and direction.

Affirm the value of every person and the call on your congregation to welcome them.

Explain how the leadership of your congregation can be involved.

Share how you will identify people with disabilities within and beyond your congregation.

Communicate your model for weaving people with disabilities into congregational life.

Outline plans for providing training to staff and lay volunteers.

Describe your plan for addressing behavioral concerns.

Describe how you will communicate with both families who have children with disabilities and those who do not.

Identify places for people with disabilities to serve in your congregation and community.

Share your plan for transitioning children through youth and adult programs.

Describe the rewards your congregation will experience because they are in ministry alongside people with developmental disabilities and their families.

Figure 3.2. Agenda for meeting with congregational leadership. (From Pierson, J. [2004]. First steps for launching a children's special needs ministry. In M. Keefer (Ed.), *Special needs, special ministry: For children's ministry* (pp. 51–63). Loveland, CO: Group Publishing; adapted by permission.)

ministry." In addition, this meeting would provide you with an opportunity to share more about ministry with people with disabilities (see Box 3.3).

WELCOMING EVERYONE: PRACTICAL APPROACHES TO BRIDGING BARRIERS

Congregations have explored many creative and ordinary ways of weaving people with disabilities meaningfully into the life of their community. The recurring theme of these efforts is that the primary obstacle limiting the participation of people with disabilities in congregational life is not a disability, but rather a lack of vision and creativity on the part of congregations.

Congregational Guides

In many congregations, it is not lack of desire that hinders people from welcoming their neighbors with developmental disabilities into the life of their faith community, but rather an uncertainty about where to begin and how to proceed. Drawing on the creativity and connections of a congregational guide offers one approach for introducing a person with developmental disabilities into the numerous activities and social networks that

Box 3.3
Resources for Congregational Leaders

Even when congregational leaders recognize the needs surrounding those
with disabilities in their congregation, they often feel unprepared to respond
or unsure of how to proceed. Many seminaries and theological schools are
only just beginning to equip future and current religious leaders to respond
effectively to disability issues and to serve the needs of people with developmental disabilities and their families within their current and future congregations (Anderson, 2003; Birch, 2003). Few have infused issues related to
disability and congregational inclusion into their curricula. It is quite likely
that your minister, pastor, priest, or rabbi did not receive training focused
specifically on how to welcome and serve people with developmental disabilities and their families into their congregation. How, then, might you
support the leadership of your congregation in learning more about this
issue? Here are some ideas:

- The Religion & Spirituality Division of the American Association on Intellectual and Developmental Disabilities offers a certification process for
  professionals involved in ministry with persons with developmental disabilities (see Appendix B).

- Connect your clergy with leaders of other congregations that are
  responding to the needs of people with disabilities and their families.
  In addition, make them aware of existing resource networks and the
  resources they offer (see Chapter 7).

- Refer leaders to print and web resources offered within their denomination or faith group (see Appendix B).

- Identify upcoming conferences and local trainings that will include
  strands or sessions related to congregational inclusion. Seminaries and
  religious colleges may offer symposia or workshops aimed at equipping
  congregational leadership for ministry in this area.

- The National Organization on Disability maintains an updated list of
  ordained clergy and religious leaders with disabilities who are willing
  to share ideas, resources, and support about congregational inclusion
  with others throughout the country.

exist within your congregation. A congregational guide serves as an advocate for the person in the congregation, intentionally seeking ways to build
bridges between the gifts and needs of a person and opportunities for
relationships and involvement within the congregation (Gaventa, 1996;
McKnight, 1992; O'Connell, 1990). Like a job coach in a place of business,
a community connector in a neighborhood, or an inclusion specialist in a
school classroom, the purpose of a congregational guide is to help others

discover just how well-equipped they already are to support one another to participate in community life.

What exactly does a congregational guide do? Consider the following roles that might be assumed by guides, recognizing that these roles could vary from one congregation to the next.

Listening Congregational guides begin by getting to know a person, learning her story, finding out her interests and strengths, and discovering the offerings she might bring to congregational life. They also listen to family members to discern their needs and the part they wish to play in building an inclusive congregation. Many parents are exhausted from having to advocate for their child in so many other arenas; they simply do not want to have to take the lead in their congregation as well. Guides assume this role of advocate and mentor to a congregation in their place.

Connecting Gifts with Opportunities Guides seek out ways of matching a person's gifts with opportunities to share and grow those gifts. Then, they introduce people to others by these gifts and passions, rather than by deficits and disability labels. A guide might ask

> *"Have you met Tyler? He started attending our church last month. He really loves working with children and his enthusiasm is absolutely contagious. I was thinking he might be an excellent helper in the children's program during the Sunday school hour. How can we make this happen?"*

Guides challenge others to see beyond the disability, helping them to recognize the many contributions waiting to be shared.

Connecting Support with Need As guides learn of the needs that a person might have, they also seek out opportunities for others in the congregation to respond to those needs. People with disabilities or their parents may feel uncomfortable always being in the position of asking for help; perhaps they simply do not know whom to ask. Guides make these connections:

> *"Owen, do you still live out in Hidden Meadows? I have a friend who lives just a couple of blocks from you who would love to be involved in church, but he doesn't have a reliable way to get here. How would you like to pick him up on your way in next week?"*

A guide believes fervently "that the community is a reservoir of hospitality that is waiting to be offered" (McKnight, 1992, p. 60). One simply needs to know who and how to ask.

Cultivating Relationships Congregational guides know that relationships are the core of community. Rather than just making introductions with a series of disconnected people, guides seek out ways to plug a person into existing social networks. This might involve introducing the person to members of a small group Bible study, people with shared interests, or even a group of people who sit in the same area of the sanctuary each week. A guide might mention something like the following:

> "If you think you are a Cowboys fan, you ought to meet Jeff! He'll talk your ear off about football. Perhaps you could invite him over next Monday night when the men's group gets together to watch the game. I think he'd really enjoy getting to meet some other men his age."

Offering Suggestions Congregational guides can serve as an important source of information and encouragement for members of the congregation who are unsure of how to include or interact with a person with developmental disabilities. They constantly reinforce the idea that everyone has the ability to demonstrate hospitality and they provide information to help unleash that capacity. Guides do not have to have all (or even most) of the answers, but they believe strongly in inclusion and are willing to seek out creative solutions:

> "You are right—kids can be pretty cliquish at that age! I have a few ideas for how you might get the youth group to open up a bit more and involve Shannon. Pairing her with a couple of buddies might be a good place to start."

Leaving When Connected As a congregation comes to recognize and gain confidence in its existing ability to welcome a person with disabilities, the guide gradually withdraws his or her involvement. Congregational guides sense when it is the right time to step back, fade away their support, and celebrate a community's newly discovered ability to welcome and support one of their members.

Who might serve effectively in the role of congregational guide? Any number of people might assume this role. Ideally, the guide would be someone who knows your congregation well and is willing to share his or her connections with another (O'Connell, 1990). People who are themselves on the edges of congregational life might have difficulty introducing someone else to all of the opportunities and relationships that are available within the congregation. Perhaps you can readily name an individual in your congregation who has a passion for people with disabilities. Maybe you know one of those people who are friends with everybody, have a knack for making connections, love thinking outside the box, or just care deeply about others. Someone may feel called to this opportunity the moment he or she hears about it. Or, you may consider asking someone who attends another congregation or who works with an organization devoted to promoting community inclusion for people with disabilities.

Faith Partners

A less formal approach to supporting the participation of people with developmental disabilities in congregational life simply involves pairing together people with disabilities and other members of the congregation. Such intentional efforts to make personal connections might provide just the support someone needs to feel welcomed and participate more fully in their congregation (e.g., Minton & Dodder, 2003; Perkins, 2001/2002; Vredeveld, 2005). Also known as a companion or mentor, the term *faith partner* probably better reflects the mutual benefits that characterize such relationships.

> *When Samantha first began attending church at St. Mark's, she and Ellen decided to be faith partners. They sat together each week during worship services and Ellen helped Samantha follow along as they sang from the hymnal, recited the responsive reading, and read passages of scripture. Ellen occasionally provided whispered explanations of certain aspects of the worship service so that Samantha knew exactly what to expect. Together, they composed and rehearsed a prayer that Samantha later shared with the congregation. In addition, Ellen always read the bulletin aloud to keep Samantha informed of upcoming church events, asking her about activities in which she might like to participate. When Ellen was sick, Samantha was the first person asking others for prayer.*

Through these partnerships, people with developmental disabilities have an opportunity to learn about the routines and practices of the congregation and teachings of the faith tradition with the support of another person. In addition, they are introduced to others in the congregation and are assisted in finding out about events and activities offered by the congregation. Within these one-to-one relationships, people with *and* without disabilities grow in their faith and friendship.

> *Samantha truly felt welcome at St. Mark's and Ellen learned more than she could express from her partner's deep and steady faith.*

This approach is similar to peer support models being advocated within both educational and employment settings. Think creatively about how you might identify individuals willing to serve as faith partners with people with disabilities. By pairing together people who share common interests, live in the same neighborhood, or are close in age, relationships may be more likely to spill over beyond a weekly worship service. As the partners get to know each other, they will quickly figure out what additional information and support (if any) that they need. Make sure that both partners know to whom they can turn to if they have any questions or need assistance, such as a family member, a congregational guide, a member of the leadership team, or a support provider who works with the person with disabilities.

Several variations to this approach exist. For example, congregations may decide to start a "Faith Family" program through which people with disabilities living away from relatives are matched with a family from the congregation (Rife & Thornburgh, 2001). Families commit themselves to welcoming a person and take intentional steps to include him or her in congregational activities. Others might identify faith partners from beyond the congregation by drawing upon volunteers such as students from local colleges and universities.

Congregational Inclusion Teams

Fostering broad and lasting changes in the culture of some congregations may require more focused efforts. This does not necessarily mean that a separate ministry must be established specifically to serve people with disabilities and their families. It simply means that one or more people are willing to commit to thinking very intentionally about these issues and serving as a voice for inclusion in all aspects of the life of their congregation. In fact, this group might commit to exploring ways of welcoming anyone who has formerly been considered a stranger to the congregation. Hospitality is good for everyone. Creating a congregational inclusion team—whether called an inclusion task force, accessible ministry team, disability awareness committee, advocacy team, welcome team, or hospitality squad—may be the key to ensuring that the information and supports needed to welcome people with disabilities are made available *throughout* the congregation. Such a team can bring both sustained focus and accountability to your congregation's efforts. Moreover, it establishes a visible point of contact to which individuals in the congregation can come with concerns, suggestions, and needs. Of course, forming a committee should never serve as a substitute for taking more personal and direct action.

Your congregational inclusion team can help identify starting points for a meaningful response. *What barriers should be tackled first? Who are the right people to take responsibility for getting things done? What resources are needed to begin making change?* The findings of your self-reflection (see Chapter 2), conversations with families, and observations of everyday congregational activities can guide the team in prioritizing efforts. For example, the team might decide that addressing the inaccessibility of the building is a pressing concern (see Box 3.4). The team then works together

Box 3.4
Making Your Facilities More Accessible

What message would it send if your congregation was among the least accessible places in your city? Although your congregation may, in certain circumstances, be legally exempt from certain accessibility requirements, it is never morally exempt. If you want to welcome people with disabilities into congregational life, you have to make sure they can first get through the door, down the hall, and into the sanctuary. Many people in your congregation would benefit from a building free of unnecessary barriers—senior citizens, parents with small children, people with temporary injuries. To begin addressing issues of physical accessibility, consider the following suggestions.

- *Form an accessibility team.* Identify a group of people willing to commit to this endeavor. Make sure your group is comprised of a variety of members from your congregation, including people with disabilities, caregivers, and someone in a leadership position. In smaller congregations, this group may be comprised of the same people involved on the congregational inclusion team. Enlist the expertise of people such as engineers, contractors, architects, and carpenters from within or outside your congregation who are familiar with universal design and accessibility issues. In addition, contact your congregation's regional or national leadership to find out if they have consultants available to guide your efforts.

- *Conduct a needs assessment.* Physically move through the property and mentally walk through congregational activities, identifying and recording every barrier a person with disabilities or his or her caregivers might encounter. Be sure to examine worship spaces, classrooms, the fellowship hall, nursery, kitchen, restrooms, gymnasium, and hallways. Several existing inventories can be used to structure and guide your observations (see Appendix B and Chapter 2).

- *Consider classrooms.* Being able to enter a classroom is essential, but it also is important that you consider what equipment or modifications people will need to participate fully in ongoing activities. Is there a child in your congregation who needs a modified table that fits her wheelchair, an adaptive switch to participate in crafts, a larger changing table, or a special mat so she can lie on the floor? Many of these items could be donated or borrowed from another organization.

- *Think beyond the property.* Consider all of the locations where activities take place outside the walls of the congregation—homes, community centers, parks, and schools. When planning community activities, youth group trips, social events, or other outreach programs, make sure that locations are selected with everyone in mind, including people with physical limitations.

(continued)

(continued)

- *Prioritize concerns.* Develop a step-by-step plan that begins with tasks that can be accomplished fairly easily and quickly, gradually progressing to addressing bigger tasks. Stookey (2003) suggested categorizing concerns in the following ways: 1) things that can be done at once, and with little or no cost; 2) things that can be done at once, but at some expense; 3) things that can be done during the next major renovation; and 4) things that can only be done upon erecting a new building.

- *Creatively explore funding possibilities.* Of the many ideas discussed in this book, improving the architectural accessibility of an older building is one of the few steps that may require some expenditure of money. However, congregations have demonstrated amazing creativity when raising money to increase their accessibility (see Alban Institute, 2001). Consider pooling resources with other congregations to purchase equipment that might be cost prohibitive for a single congregation to purchase (e.g., a braille maker, an accessible van), holding fundraisers, submitting grant proposals, initiating a capital campaign, soliciting memorial gifts, and making people aware of opportunities to donate specific equipment by sharing specific needs. Enlist help from a local community service organization such as Kiwanis, Knights of Columbus, Lions Club, or Rotary Club.

- *Celebrate your efforts.* Publicly recognize your efforts in this area. Corporately celebrate each small step accomplished as you press forward toward full accessibility.

to define the steps that need to be taken in the congregation. It also remains focused on the big picture, ensuring that hospitality efforts are woven throughout all aspects of congregational life—from children's activities to programming for adults, from outreach efforts to activities for members.

The members of this team might include many of the same individuals who participated in the self-reflection process. However, this group should depend less on the involvement of individuals from beyond the congregation and should instead rely more on the contributions of lay people. Such teams also provide a way for people to contribute to these efforts when they are unable to have more direct involvement as a congregational guide, faith partner, or volunteer in the children's programs. Depending on the size of your congregation, around four to eight team members might make the most sense. Identify a leader who has both the passion and the time to devote to guiding congregational efforts in this area. This person does not have to have expertise in disability issues or a professional degree in disability services. Rather, he or she simply needs to be someone with a heart for transforming his or her congregation, as well as possessing strengths in leadership. In some larger congregations, this person might even be a paid staff member.

AVENUES FOR PARTICIPATION

A multitude of avenues exist for people to get involved within your congregation. Consider the following strategies for supporting the participation of people with disabilities in every aspect of your faith community.

Worship Services

People with and without developmental disabilities should worship alongside each other. A congregation is enriched by the presence and participation of people with disabilities. Making this happen involves several steps. First, be ready to welcome people with disabilities when they first arrive to your congregation for worship services. Ensure that greeters and ushers feel comfortable welcoming people with disabilities and are provided basic information on how best to extend a greeting, offer assistance, and make introductions to others in the congregation (see Box 3.1). In particular, make sure that greeters know about the programs, activities, and supports offered by the congregation so that this information can be shared with visitors and their caregivers. Greeters will be setting a very visible example of how to welcome people with disabilities for an often curious and sometimes reluctant congregation.

Second, worship leaders may need to consider how services could be designed to make them truly accessible to a larger proportion of the congregation. Different elements of a worship service speak to and hold meaning for people in different ways and there are many avenues through which people worship and learn. Dramatizing readings, incorporating visual imagery, conveying truths through music, and weaving movement or dance into worship are all possible avenues for reaching more members of the congregation. Consider the following excerpt from a statement commended for study, comment, and action by the World Council of Churches (2003) titled, *A Church of All and for All.*

> Sometimes people "hear" or comprehend God's Word, and know the mystery and majesty of God's presence in their lives through a sensory experience: perception of light or colour, a picture or sculpture, a whiff of incense, silence, music, dance, a procession, a hug, or clasped hands around a circle. This sensory experience in liturgy is important to all of us, but especially to children, elderly people and persons with disabilities. It should be considered in our planning of corporate worship and its setting. Many elements of worship are non-verbal, and we can be more intentional about how we incorporate them to enhance the service for everyone. There is the movement of dance, drama, hands clasped in

prayer or raised in blessing, making the sign of the cross, handshakes and hugs, lifting the eyes, bowing the head, offering gifts, and passing the bread and cup. There are tactile elements of anointing, baptism, laying on of hands, foot-washing, touching, and vesting. We can smell the incense, wine, flowers, and candles, and taste the bread and wine or juice. Besides words, we hear music, clapping, bells, sighs, and breathing. Centuries ago when many did not know how to read or have access to printed material, churches were filled with visual renditions of the Bible stories. There were murals, tapestries, sculpture, icons and stained glass windows. Today, some churches still have many of these visual elements and can also make use of banners, altar hangings, colourful vestments, scarves, flowers, balloons, liturgical dance and drama to portray the messages of our faith.

The point is simple: It might not be a developmental disability that is preventing services from being meaningful to a member of your congregation. Consider whether the worship experience really reflects the many different avenues through which people encounter God. *Are you really planning services with everyone in mind?*

Third, some children and adults with developmental disabilities may benefit from additional support to participate in the worship services. As suggested previously, the input of a congregational guide or the support of a faith partner offers two avenues for supporting participation. In addition, the following strategies might be used to include children and adults with autism or intellectual disabilities in worship services:

- Talk in advance about what to expect during the worship service. Use the bulletin to walk through each aspect of the service, explaining when and how the person might participate. Anyone who has ever visited an unfamiliar service can attest to being anxious about doing or saying the wrong thing. Offer a word of explanation of how things typically are done.

- Help a person acclimate to the many different sights and sounds within the sanctuary by visiting when a worship service is not in progress. Explore the pews, listen to the piano or organ, and rehearse rituals such as approaching the altar, handing an offering plate, passing the peace, and entering or exiting the sanctuary.

- Sermons can be the most difficult part of the worship experience for some children, especially when they are intellectually inaccessible. Consider bringing quiet objects or alternate activities that children can engage with during this time. For example, some parents create a folder containing activities that correspond with the ongoing sermon series.

- Create a visual schedule of the worship service using pictures (e.g., clip art, photographs, communication symbols) to represent each aspect of the service (e.g., prayer, hymns, fellowship, special music, sermon, Scripture readings, benediction). Such a schedule cues a person so he or she can anticipate what is coming up next and better handle changes in routine that might occur during special services and events.

- Allow for an early exit. It may take time for some children with developmental disabilities to sit through an entire worship service. Begin by staying for shorter periods of time, gradually increasing their presence as they become more comfortable.

- Remind congregation members to be supportive and extend grace to every child. Parents often feel "judged" when their children with disabilities are disruptive. Patience will go a long way toward making these families feel more comfortable.

> "It is not wise to assume that a person will 'get nothing' from attending services. Faith is not measured by how fast it develops, nor are we fully aware of the depth and breadth of what any one of us gains from worship. When we restrain someone with mental retardation from participating, we may be more worried about our own potential 'embarrassment' then we are concerned with his or her religious experience."
>
> —Ann Davie and Ginny Thornburgh (2000, p. 29–30)

Rituals, Sacraments, and Rites of Passage

Baptism, bar/bat mitzvah, confirmation, congregational membership, first communion—these and many other events hold incredible significance and serve as prominent markers in many people's faith journeys. Moreover, these ceremonies hold great importance for a gathering community, offering a time when the congregation together makes a commitment to support the spiritual growth of one of their members. As you observe these and other personal and spiritual milestones in your congregation, are children and adults with developmental disabilities among the participants and celebrants? For most people with developmental disabilities, inclusion in these important events simply requires a willingness to extend an invitation. Sometimes, however, congregations will need to find creative ways to adapt these rituals in ways that allow every member to participate. A baptism ceremony might be held at an accessible pool; communion might be served in multiple ways to allow an individual with a feeding tube to participate; a child might use a communication device to recite the Torah; or confirmation preparation may be taught using pictures, modeling, and adapted expectations.

> "A pastor, priest, or rabbi may simply have never done this before. Blend a recognition of their desire to protect the holy or what is most special with helping them to see why this may be so special for the person or family involved and how it could be a special moment for the whole congregation."
>
> —Bill Gaventa (2005, p. 115)

Fortunately, greater efforts are being made to prepare children and adults with developmental disabilities to participate in important congregational rituals and traditions. Vogel and Reiter (2004) described one such program aimed at preparing children with developmental disabilities for their bar/bat mitzvah ceremonies. After receiving instruction in small groups as part of a year-long program, the children participated in a ceremony that was adapted to include "both elements that are defined and prescribed and elements that are improvised as determined by the unique needs of the group" (p. 296). The ceremonies had a profound impact on the children, their families, and other members of the congregation.

> "Members of the congregation and other guests who were present were indeed moved by the experience. They found it one of the most meaningful and uplifting services they had ever attended, and they too felt a new sense of community. The feeling of inclusiveness resulting from the respect and the opportunity to share in the values, symbols, and rituals of the community offered to those with differing abilities created an energizing sense of interconnectedness for all who were present."
>
> —Gila Vogel and Shunit Reiter (2003, p. 319)

> "To my knowledge, this is the first time our 24-year-old congregation has received anyone with [developmental disabilities] into formal church membership. Over the years, we have had many people with disabilities attend our worship services, but this is the first time we have welcomed them fully as members. It's not that we deliberately excluded them—in fact, we weren't deliberate at all. That was the problem."
>
> —Pastor Scott, as cited in Vredeveld, R.C. (2005, p. 202)

A number of guides are available to help you support people with developmental disabilities to participate meaningfully in these important events, such as communion (Edwards, 1997b; Foley, 1994; Murdoch, 1995; O'Shannessy, 1995a), confirmation (Anderson and` Briarwood Task Force for Handicapped Ministries, 1999; Edwards, 1997a; Kruck, 2002; Meyer, 1995; O'Shannessy, 1995b), marriage (Vredeveld, 2001), bar/bat mitzvah (Leneman, 2003), congregational membership (Vredeveld, 2005), and funeral rites (Raji, Hollins, & Drinnan, 2003). See Appendix B for additional resources.

Service, Outreach, and Other Ministry Activities

Does your congregation nurture or leave untouched the gifts and passions of its members? Many congregations fail to recognize the deep reservoir of gifts, talents, and assets that reside among its members. When one's focus remains only on what a person cannot do—as is often the case with regard to people with developmental disabilities—it becomes easy to overlook all that a person might have to offer. It is not the presence of a disability that hinders a congregation from benefiting from the gifts of its members. Examples abound of the very concrete and visible ways that people with developmental disabilities can contribute within their faith community. These might include

- Greeting people as they arrive at a worship service or serving as a parking lot attendant

- Folding, stuffing, and passing out bulletins

- Assisting in the nursery, preschool, Vacation Bible School, or other children's activities

- Preparing or serving food at a Wednesday night dinner, potluck supper, or congregation picnic

- Reciting a prayer, sharing a short scripture passage, singing in the choir, or serving on the worship team

- Volunteering with the congregation's homeless shelter, food pantry, nursing home, or visitation team

- Serving as an acolyte, altar server, reader, usher, gift bearer, or catechist

- Assisting with holiday outreach efforts

- Collecting items left in the sanctuary after the service

- Helping in the congregation's library, resource center, or staff offices

- Preparing coffee, doughnuts, or other refreshments for fellowship times

- Passing out materials in classrooms or delivering snacks to children's classrooms

- Preparing communion or counting the offering

- Serving on a congregational committee, prayer ministry, or stewardship team

- Helping other youth put on a car wash, bake sale, or other fundraising activity

> "Although some friends with cognitive impairments will be able to serve independently, others may need the supervision of their mentor, church leader, or another member of the faith community to help them learn their tasks and to provide encouragement. Perhaps a group of people could take turns serving alongside a friend, thus enabling new relationships."
>
> —Ronald Vredeveld (2005, p. 24)

Everyone has something unique to offer and so it is important to avoid making assumptions that people with developmental disabilities should all serve in particular ways, whereas people without disabilities should serve in others. Opportunities to serve should be aligned with people's gifts and passions, not allocated according to one's disability label. It is quite often the case that acts of service that seem insignificant or inconsequential to one person hold profound meaning for another person.

> "I remember a man named Owen who had mental retardation who went to this church. I remember that greeting people was his gift. However, the Board of Deacons didn't want him to be a greeter because it was afraid that he would frighten visitors away. Owen was a big man and his size could be disarming to some. But, he was as harmless as anyone could be. He didn't know how to hate. He loved people and helping them. He would have been the perfect greeter in my estimation. By letting Owen become a greeter we would have shown him what discipleship and service to others meant."
>
> —William Rush (2003, p. 69–70)

> "It was with some excitement and anxiety that the congregation watched Keith, an individual with Down syndrome, serve communion and collect offerings his first Sunday as a deacon. Would he be able to follow the pattern of serving? Would he drop a serving plate? He served perfectly, with obvious care and pride. Some described his serving communion as the spiritual highpoint of the worship."
>
> —Jeannine Vogel, Edward Polloway, and David Smith (2006, p. 107)

If your congregation's starting point is recruiting people to meet specific programmatic and volunteer needs, someone with developmental disabilities often is not the first person to come to mind. In contrast, if your congregation begins by identifying the gifts and passions of each of its individual members—including those with developmental disabilities—and then proceeds to find opportunities and places in which to use those gifts, the task becomes much easier. Does a person have a gift for helping others, making people feel comfortable, offering encouragement, relating spiritual insights, creating things, sharing her faith, befriending people, praying for others, caring for children, or communicating creatively through the arts? To what and whom is she drawn? What things seem to energize and excite her? Once you have identified someone's gifts and passions, the next step is to think about how you will then connect the person with opportunities to share and build up those gifts. Sometimes these gifts will find a natural home within existing programs in your congregation. Other times, a newly discovered gift will challenge you to identify new avenues for supporting its expression.

PREVENTING AND RESPONDING TO BEHAVIORAL CHALLENGES

Sometimes, children and adults with developmental disabilities may act in unexpected ways that challenge congregations, leaving people unsure of exactly how to respond. Sometimes, congregations commit to problem-solving exactly why these behaviors are occurring and brainstorming pos-

sible solutions. Other times, congregations ask a person and their family or
caregiver to leave or clearly communicate that they are no longer welcome.

Challenging behavior should not be
ignored. In fact, many highly effective
strategies exist for addressing behavioral challenges of children and adults
with disabilities (see Chapter 4). Begin
by considering possible reasons for why

"Bob liked to sit next to women at church and touch them on the arm. It was his way of expressing sexual attraction—but needless to say, it made the women uncomfortable. The men in the congregation noticed what was going on and agreed to take turns sitting next to Bob to help keep his mind on the Lord and not on the ladies."

—Mary O'Connell (1988, p. 20)

a person is engaging in these behaviors. Is it because he is unfamiliar with
the expectations? Is she not feeling well? Is he trying to communicate
something? Is she anxious and unsure about what is going to happen next?
Is he encountering some sensory experience he finds intolerable, such as
loud noises, crowded rooms, or flickering lights? Is she trying to avoid
something? Is there something he wants, but cannot express it? Let your
first response be to seek out and address the possible causes of the behavior rather than simply to ask a person not to attend your congregation any-
more. Often, solutions become much clearer when these triggers are
identified. Consider the following situations and how they might best be
handled, and apply them to your own circumstances in your congregation.

- *Jacob is always making noises during the service.* Ask yourself: Is this his
  way of trying to communicate something to you? Does he know that
  people are expected to remain quiet during certain parts of the service?
  Are his noises really any louder than those that others his age in the
  congregation are making? Could the congregation learn to be more
  comfortable with certain distractions?

- *Rhonda just gets up and walks around whenever she wants.* Ask yourself:
  Does she need to stretch? Does she know that people are expected to
  remain seated during this particular part of the service? Is the pew
  uncomfortable? Is she bored? Are there other people who occasionally
  get up and walk to the back of the sanctuary during the service? Can
  we find times during the service when it might be okay for her to walk
  around?

- *Simon sometimes has a meltdown when the worship team begins playing.* Ask
  yourself: Is the music too loud? Did it startle him? Would he be more
  comfortable if we sat further away from the speakers or helped him
  anticipate what was coming up next in the service? Is he overly
  exhausted from staying up late last night or did he recently experience
  a medication change?

If you still struggle to understand these behaviors, ask for ideas and assistance from a support provider or family member. It is likely that others are encountering similar behaviors in other settings; perhaps they also have discovered appropriate responses. Numerous other resources also are available within your community, including school teachers, special educators, and other professionals from local agencies. For example, a congregation might ask the behavioral specialist working with a child with autism to observe during a service and offer recommendations for how best to support that child's positive behavior.

> "Rigid codes of 'acceptable' behaviour may need to be loosened. Just as some people cannot stand or kneel, others cannot sit still for a whole hour or more. They may need to stand or move about because of back pain or muscle spasms or some agitation related to their disability. Some may not be able to understand the 'rules' about silence and may mumble to themselves, speak out when others are quietly listening, or utter exuberant vocalisations at unexpected moments. In these situations, as with people who 'make a joyful noise unto the Lord' by singing off-key, we can acquire tolerance that acknowledges such behaviour as a mild distraction rather than a great annoyance."
>
> —World Council of Churches (2003)

Congregations should also consider whether their expectations for behavior are too narrow. There always will be people whose behaviors diverge from what is typical—a child who repeatedly flaps his hands, an adult who greets even strangers with a bear hug, a teenager who occasionally talks aloud to himself. Is there room within your congregation for such people? Are you willing to make room?

SUSTAINING INCLUSION EFFORTS OVER TIME

Over time, new people will join a congregation and old members may leave. In fact, only about one-third of worshipers report having attended services at their current congregation for more than 5 years (Woolever & Bruce, 2002). Therefore, one-shot or short-term efforts to create a welcoming environment are unlikely to produce lasting change. A congregation once known for their acceptance may find that their willingness to be supportive has faded over time as key people have moved away. The impassioned efforts of another congregation may have since stagnated, and the plans they formulated never really extended to every aspect of community life. To avoid these situations, it is important that congregations continually revisit and renew their commitment to welcome children, adults, and families with disabilities. Periodically check with parents, teachers, and other lay volunteers to make sure that they have needed information and resources and that they are comfortable and confident in their roles. Maintain communication with family members to determine the extent to which you are still addressing perceived needs. Keep the congregation and community members posted on the steps that the congregation is taking to remain a community whose invitation extends to everyone. As your response strengthens, return to those families who once did not feel welcome and re-extend an invitation. Let them know that they are valued and that you have made great strides toward making your congregation more accessible and welcoming.

PARTNERING WITH SERVICE PROVIDERS

Crafting a meaningful response to people with disabilities and their families can be enhanced when congregations seek out relationships with service and support organizations in their broader community. Service providers working in educational and community-based settings have much to offer in the area of training and support for inclusion and can be key allies as you seek to support people with disabilities within your congregation. In fact, many of these service providers are themselves members of a congregation—perhaps even yours—and would share your commitment to addressing the spiritual needs of people with disabilities and their families. Because much of what congregations do happens in the community, developing relationships with the people who are providing supports and services to people with disabilities in those settings is essential. Consider the following ideas for developing these relationships.

- Identify a person in your congregation who is willing to serve as a liaison with local agencies and organizations that provide services and supports to people with disabilities in your community.

- Visit local agencies and organizations to learn about the supports and resources they are providing to people with disabilities in your community. Talk with them about the needs they see in the community and discuss possible avenues for collaborations. Ask to be put on their mailing lists so that you can keep abreast of upcoming events and emerging needs.

- Produce and distribute a brochure or short video describing your congregation and the ways in which children and adults with disabilities can be and are currently involved in the life of your congregation. Include information about ways that you might partner with organizations to connect adults with disabilities with the faith community of their choice—perhaps yours, perhaps another.

- Offer to be involved on the advisory boards of these agencies and organizations. You will contribute an important perspective and can assist organizations in developing policies and procedures that ensure that people with disabilities are supported in participating in meaningful ways in communities of faith.

- Recruit the expertise of service providers when that same knowledge is not available within your congregation. Educators, job coaches, and residential staff all have much to contribute and some may have worked with other congregations around similar issues. For example, invite a special educator to serve as a consultant or resource for your children's ministry programs, ask a job coach to help you determine how best to support members of your congregation with disabilities who want to volunteer in your food pantry, or approach a social worker about meaningful strategies for supporting the parents and siblings of a child with a fragile medical condition.

- Ask service providers to tell you how to more effectively reach out to, serve, and be served by people with developmental disabilities in your community.

- Recognize that some support providers may have fewer staff on the weekends—the time when many activities take place within faith communities. Think creatively about how you might be willing to volunteer your support during this time of the week.

- Find out how you can support the work and recognize the contributions of caregivers and support staff who work daily to meet the needs of people with disabilities. Discover how you can support their call to this vocation and affirm the deep importance of their work.

- Encourage members of your congregation to individually volunteer their own time and resources to local organizations that serve people with disabilities. Such efforts will help facilitate the full participation of people with developmental disabilities in the wider community.

CONCLUSION

Is your congregation truly a *sanctuary* for people with developmental disabilities and their families? It could be. The opportunities awaiting your congregation are numerous. Prayerfully seek out how you might develop new relationships with people with disabilities in your congregation and the broader community. As you do, strive to continually improve your hospitality, making sure your welcome never wears thin.

Chapter 4

Designing Inclusive Religious Education Programs

Among the many important aspects of congregational life are the opportunities provided to help people mature in their faith, learn the teachings and practices of their tradition, and develop meaningful relationships with others on the same journey. More than 90% of all congregations offer some form of religious education opportunities to their members and attendees, whether Sunday or Sabbath school classes, children's and youth programs, men's and women's groups, confirmation classes, small group studies, or retreats (Woolever & Bruce, 2002). Yet, many congregations struggle with exactly how to include children and adults with developmental disabilities in these activities. This chapter affirms the importance of designing religious education programs that both welcome and engage every member of a congregation, including those with developmental disabilities. A commitment to respond, coupled with the resources and creativity that already reside within your congregation (perhaps still untapped), is all that you need to begin inviting children and adults with disabilities in the life of your congregation.

INCLUSIVE PROGRAMS FOR CHILDREN AND YOUTH

Children's programs are integral to the vision and the life of most congregations. Many adults can trace the beginnings of their faith journeys to key experiences within such programs, which lay important foundations for later spiritual growth. Parents want quality, dynamic programs for their children and many choose a congregation based largely on this factor. Although the desires of parents of children with developmental disabilities are no different, they often encounter great difficulty in finding a congregation willing to include their child. When activities and programs are not open to their children, it is unlikely that families will return to your congregation.

The call on congregations to serve children with disabilities often raises many questions. *How do we teach a child who may not read or speak, see or hear? How do we include a child whose behaviors may challenge our expectations or try our patience? How do we meet the needs of a diverse group of children within the same classroom or program?* Schools have long wrestled with these same questions and have discovered many effective strategies for including an increasingly diverse group of children. Does your congregation approach these questions with a sense of challenge and a willingness to explore new answers? Or, do these questions signal a stopping point in the conversation, in which efforts go no further?

> "When their son with autism was three, the parents explained, he attended children's worship for the first time. After class, a weary worker returned their son and said, 'Please don't take him back to this class. We can't handle him.' For the next four years, his parents took turns attending church. Too old to qualify for nursery but unable to sit though the service, their young son, they felt, had no place in their congregation."
>
> —Barbara Newman (2001, p. 7)

Casting a Vision for Every Child

Building an inclusive program begins with prayerful examination of your congregation's heart for children. Ask yourself: *Is there really a place for a child with autism in our kindergarten class? Do we truly believe that our youth group is less than it ought to be when a teenager with disabilities does not feel welcome to attend? Are our teachers willing to welcome only those children who learn most quickly, speak most eloquently, behave most predictably, or work together most easily? Is our congregation committed to nurturing the faith formation of most children or all children?* Revisit your mission to ensure that it really encompasses every child, regardless of disability label. Consider the following example:

> The vision of the children's ministry of Fellowship Congregation is to partner together with families in nurturing each child's spiritual development and lifelong relationship with God. We welcome every child, including those with special needs.

You may see only glimpses of this vision right now, but it should still describe where your congregation is headed. This purpose should fuel your work, compel your volunteers, and captivate your congregation. If your congregation has not always demonstrated a willingness to include children with disabilities, it may be necessary to clearly state to parents in your mission statement that your welcome really does extend to them.

To truly catch hold, a vision must be both articulated *and* shared with others. Make sure that it is communicated broadly to everyone in your congregation so that inclusion becomes the expectation. Place it on your brochures, hang it on your walls, and share it at volunteer trainings.

Parents should be confident that their child with autism is welcome in your programs for children and youth. Teachers, helpers, and other volunteers should anticipate that children with disabilities might be in their classes. This vision also should be shared widely beyond the walls of the congregation.

Concerns of Congregations

As you begin taking steps to develop program offerings that support children and youth with disabilities, expect to encounter some of the following challenges.

- *We tried inclusion once and it just didn't work!* It often takes time for new initiatives to find their place. Try again. Let any challenges you encountered push you to muster more creativity, ask better questions, seek more advice, and, perhaps, approach things differently. Remember that the potential impact of your efforts is too important to give up on.

- *I would like to help, but I just don't know how.* Even while affirming the importance of inclusion, lay volunteers may still feel unprepared to support a child with disabilities in their class. Religious education classes typically are taught by people who, unlike special educators and adult service providers, have not received formal training in disability-related issues. Reassure them that the gifts and passions that they bring to these efforts, when coupled with some basic strategies and good teaching, are more than sufficient. Dispel the myth that formal training or a specialized degree is required to welcome children with disabilities.

- *Children with disabilities will not be accepted by their peers.* As inclusion becomes the norm in elementary, middle, and high schools, most children already count their peers with disabilities among their classmates. So, do not be surprised when children express greater comfort with their classmates than do many adults. Moreover, adults can play an important role in creating classroom environments that promote acceptance and encourage positive relationships among all children.

Designing Inclusive Children's Programs

Most efforts to include children with disabilities begin just as they should continue: *one child at a time.* A need is recognized and a congregation responds. For example, a long-standing member has a son with fragile X syndrome who now is old enough to enroll in the preschool class, the congregation hires a new staff person who happens to have a teenager with severe cerebral palsy, or a new family with a sixth-grader with autism starts attending your congregation for the first time. As your congregation demonstrates its commitment to welcoming and supporting each of these children, trust that word will spread among other families in your community. As new families arrive, thoughtful and proactive planning will ensure that you are ready when they arrive at your door.

Establish a Planning Group   Many congregations find it helpful to gather a planning group to begin assessing needs and next steps for including children with disabilities into their programming. Identify a core group of interested people who are willing to meet together and brainstorm both where and how to begin. This team should include at least one person who is very familiar with program offerings and activities for children and youth in the congregation, such as the children's ministry director, youth pastor, curriculum coordinator, or a seasoned teacher. In addition, consider inviting members of the congregation who have experience working with children or adults with disabilities (e.g., special educators, therapists, health care workers), parents of children involved in the program, and a member of the congregation's leadership. The size of the group will, of course, depend on the scope of the efforts you intend to undertake.

Identify a Program Approach   Every person is unique. Thus, the specific strategies used to include one child in congregational activities might look quite different from those used to support another. Still, it is wise to decide from the outset on the general approach you will use to include children in congregational life. This book argues for the importance of an *inclusive* approach that supports children to participate fully and actively in existing programs, rather than creating separate programs specifically for children with disabilities (see Box 4.1). From this perspective, inclusion is much more than just being present in the same building. Rather, it is evidenced when children worship, learn, serve, and fellowship side-by-side. Commit to embracing a ministry model that affirms that every child belongs with his or her peers and that the only thing standing in the way of that happening is the resolve of your congregation.

> "We must be conscious that 'special' must not become a euphemism for segregated programmes."
>
> —Simon Bass (2003, p. 2)

Identify a Coordinator   Numerous congregations have demonstrated that hiring new staff is not a prerequisite for including children with developmental disabilities in their programs. As more children become involved in your congregation, however, it may be beneficial to identify someone whose role is to ensure that informational and support needs related to inclusion are being addressed. With all of the other things vying

Box 4.1
Choosing a Curriculum

As you outline your curriculum for the upcoming year, seek out ways to meaningfully include children and youth with developmental and other disabilities in every lesson and activity. By considering the needs of all children from the very outset, teachers and helpers will encounter less difficulty adapting lessons throughout the year. Select curricular materials that engage children in multiple ways and provide teachers numerous ideas for delivering lessons. Every time you design a lesson with children with disabilities in mind, it is likely to improve learning and engagement for every child. Unfortunately, religious education curricula offered by only a few publishing houses address how lessons and activities might be adapted for children with developmental disabilities or other special needs. Instead, most resources for people with disabilities often are designed to be used in separate classes. These resources, however, may still offer planning teams helpful ideas for how lessons and activities might be adapted in creative ways (see Appendix B). Remember, it is important to explore how the existing curricula for a given class can be modified to include a broader range of children, rather than introducing a special curriculum just for children with disabilities.

for the attention of children's program staff, designating someone to serve in a coordinating role can ensure that the needs of children with disabilities are not overlooked. This person might assume responsibilities for extending invitations to families within and beyond the congregation; coordinating or directly providing training to teachers, helpers, and other lay volunteers; maintaining communication with families; seeking out helpful resources for teachers; developing new avenues for meeting the needs of children and families; and keeping the leadership informed of emerging needs, inspiring successes, and future plans. In addition, this person would advocate on behalf of the needs of children and families with disabilities to the congregation's leadership. Some congregations identify an existing staff person to assume this role as part of his or her other responsibilities, such as an early childhood ministry leader, director of religious education, or youth director. As responsibilities increase in response to growing needs, some larger congregations eventually do choose to hire a staff person devoted specifically to disability issues.

Seek Out Supports and Resources As you pursue efforts to include children with disabilities, make certain to draw on the gifts, expertise, and passions of others already within your congregation. Perhaps your congregation counts special educators, job coaches, early childhood specialists, paraprofessionals, behavioral specialists, psychologists, or social services providers among its members. If they are not already involved in planning efforts, share with these individuals the steps you are undertaking and seek out their advice. Invite them to participate in brainstorming sessions or to assist in problem-solving any challenges that may arise. However, think more broadly than just traditional service providers. Perhaps there are artists, carpenters, engineers, hobbyists, and other creative or "tech savvy" individuals whose skills could be drawn on to make a particular classroom, activity, or lesson more accessible to children. Maybe there are people who just love trying new experiences, are full of energy, have a great sense of humor, like to "go with the flow," or are especially sensitive to the needs of others. Most people have never considered how their talents could readily be used to support the participation of children with disabilities.

Revisit Program Procedures   As with all programs for children, you should have already developed procedures for responding to accidents, injuries, or other unexpected incidents. For children with developmental disabilities, many of whom may have related special health care needs, clear procedures are especially critical. Similarly, procedures for screening volunteers and protecting the confidentiality of children should be firmly in place. When beginning any new endeavor involving children, contact your congregation's legal counsel or insurance provider about issues related to liability.

Identifying Children's Support Needs

Preparation to welcome children with disabilities into your programs should occur on at least two levels. First, you will want to be ready to welcome every child from the moment that he or she arrives at your classroom door. For example, a child with disabilities and her family may be visiting your congregation for the very first time or a regular member may be accompanied by a relative with disabilities visiting from out of town. It sends an incredible message to families when you were ready to receive their child whenever they arrive, instead of turning a child away because you feel unprepared (see Figure 4.1). Second, when families make the decision to call your congregation their permanent home, you will want to take steps to ensure that your teaching leaders or other volunteers are prepared to support the long-term participation of children as they grow up in your program. To do this effectively, consider taking the following steps.

Listen to Families   Scheduling time to meet with parents is one of the best ways to get to know their child and the supports that he or she might need. Share a conversation over a cup of coffee or offer to visit their home.

WE WELCOME KIDS WITH SPECIAL NEEDS!

We are committed to welcoming children with special needs into our programs and activities. We believe that every child is created and loved by God. We are excited to have the opportunity to meet and minister to your son or daughter. In order to best meet the needs of each child, we ask that families follow these steps:

1. Tell the welcome person at the registration desk about any special needs your child might have.
2. You will be introduced to your child's classroom teacher. Tell the teacher a little bit about your child. How best can we support your child? What are his or her gifts and needs?
3. If you feel your child needs one-to-one support, let us know. We will try to identify an additional person who can help your child in his or her class today.
4. If you decide to make this your congregational home, please contact _____. We will set up a time to meet with you to find out more about your child and the steps we can take to welcome and support him or her in our programs.

We are glad you have joined us!
If you have any questions, please do not hesitate to ask!

Figure 4.1. An example of a sign for welcoming first-time visitors. (From Spencer, S. [2005, May]). *Blackhawk Church procedures for kids with special needs.* Madison, WI: Blackhawk Church; adapted by permission.)

Reassure parents of your commitment to welcoming their child into congregational activities and explain that the purpose of your time together is to explore together how best to accomplish that goal. Ask parents to share what they have learned about how best to help their child adapt to a new setting; participate in various activities; and feel welcome, safe, and loved.

Invite parents to tell you about strategies that have worked particularly well (and not so well) in other places throughout the week, such as in school, at home, or during other community activities. Allow parents to share their concerns and apprehensions as well. Your conversation is aimed at gathering information that would be helpful for adults who will interact with the child as teachers and other lay volunteers. Thus, the meeting should be informal, encouraging, and focused on gathering ideas for supporting the child. Parents should feel confident that you are looking for ways to include, rather than exclude, their child.

> "Parents of children with special needs have experienced a great deal of rejection. It seems they have to fight for everything that their child needs—and they do not want to have to fight for their child in church. It is too easy to simply stay home and avoid the fight. So we must communicate to these families that we want their child in our programs and will do whatever it takes to make it work."
>
> —Cheryl Rosenberg (1999)

Table 4.1 offers sample questions that you might ask during your conversations with parents. In fact, many of these questions would be useful to pose to the parents of *any* child who has unique needs, whether or not those needs are related to a developmental disability. The information you

Table 4.1.   Sample questions for parents of children with disabilities

How long have you been attending our congregation? What first brought you here?

In what ways would you like to see your child involved in this congregation?

What has been your child's previous experience in other congregations?

Tell us about your child.

> What does she enjoy doing? Not enjoy doing?

> What are her gifts and talents? What does she do well? What does she love to "show off"?

> How does she communicate with others? How does she express excitement? Frustration?

Tell us about your family.

Tell us about your child's disability.

> How might her disability affect her involvement in congregational activities?

> Are there any treatments, interventions, or services that she is receiving that we should incorporate into our programs?

> Is there any special equipment or adaptive devices that we should consider acquiring to help your child participate more fully?

> Are there any environmental issues that might make your child uncomfortable and agitated?

> Does she have any allergies or food restrictions we should know about?

How can we best support the positive behavior of your child?

> Are there things we should definitely avoid doing or saying?

> Are there things we should absolutely do?

> What does she find most rewarding?

> What is the best way to respond when your child becomes upset?

How would you describe your child's faith? What are the best ways to communicate spiritual truths?

Are there important goals that you have for your child as she participates in our program this year? As you look into the future?

What could we do to make our children's program the most exciting time of the week for your child?

How would you like us to respond when other children or adults ask us about your child's disability?

What do you see as the biggest challenges to including your child in congregational activities?

How can our congregation help support your family as you raise your child? Can we _____ [offer specific examples]?

Is there anything else that you would like us to know about your child or family?

gather may be sufficient to get you started or it may be compiled into a more focused "religious education plan" or a brief "biography" to be shared with those adults who will interact with the child. Of course, parents may express various degrees of comfort with the information they are willing to have shared about their child. Therefore, it is essential that you ask parents about what they would and would not like relayed to volunteers and other children. An attitude of respectfulness and confidentiality are absolutely essential.

Developing Religious Education Plans

Individualized planning has long been a core principle of educational and adult services for people with disabilities. Recognizing that every person has unique aspirations and different needs, such plans offer personalized maps that sketch out a person's goals and detail the supports and resources needed to help him or her realize those goals. Religious educators and lay volunteers can draw on the best aspects of this planning process to ensure that every child with disabilities is meaningfully included and well supported in the life of the congregation. The outcome of this process—sometimes called a *religious education plan*, or *inclusion plan*—should be a plan tailored to address the specific needs of each child. In other words, these plans help you become an expert on how best to welcome a specific child, rather than on the specific disability condition. It is not important to know all of the details of a child's diagnosis, just how to support him or her best.

The starting point for developing a religious education plan is a meeting with the child's parents (described previously). It often is helpful to involve the adults who are (or will be) serving as the child's teacher or helper. Some congregations invite others who know the child well, such as a favorite teacher, neighbor, or family friend. As a group, consider the following questions when developing a child's support plan.

- *How does the child learn best?* It is a good question to ask of any child, but particularly children with disabilities who may appear to learn differently. Ask parents to explain the avenues and modalities (e.g., seeing, hearing, doing) through which their child seems to learn best. Discuss those instructional strategies that seem to work well at home, at school, and in other settings. You may discover new ideas that will benefit every child in the class.

- *Are there any health or medical issues that should be considered?* Some children with disabilities have special health care needs beyond those that teachers typically encounter. Find out if and how those needs can be addressed during the Sunday/Sabbath school hour or other children's activities. For example, a brief tip sheet might need to be given to adults working with a child who sometimes has seizures. Or, an emergency plan might need to be periodically revised as a child's health condition changes.

- *How does the child communicate with others?* Does he or she use any type of assistive technology to interact with others or his or her environment? For example, a child might use an augmentative communication device to talk to peers, an electronic switch to make basic choices, or modified sign language to express when he or she is hungry or needs to use the restroom. Ask parents to demonstrate for you any unfamiliar technology or communication strategies.

- *Are there behavioral issues that will need to be considered?* Ask about the extent to which the child engages in challenging or atypical behaviors. Such information should not be used as a reason to exclude the child, but rather to assist you in being proactive in identifying ways of reducing the likelihood that such behaviors will be displayed (see Box 4.2).

- *What goals and key spiritual concepts are most important?* Teachers often express hesitation about including a child with developmental disabilities who may struggle to learn the same curricular material in the

---

Box 4.2
Separate Programs for Children, Youth, and Adults with Developmental Disabilities

Even a cursory look at the history of people with developmental disabilities confirms society's propensity to segregate people who seem different. This same inclination is evident within many faith communities. Although national data are not available, the most common response in congregations appears to be to establish separate religious education classes, recreational activities, and worship services for children and adults with developmental disabilities. However, relegating children and adults with developmental disabilities to separate programs is neither welcoming nor necessary. Indeed, separate programs lack one very critical aspect of congregational life: *community*. As schools throughout the country are discovering, children with developmental disabilities can be served just as well—sometimes even more effectively— when they are included among their peers. When considering some of the arguments for inclusion described in Chapter 1, it is clear that the congregation misses out on something vital when they lose the opportunity to worship, learn, serve, and fellowship alongside their friends and neighbors with disabilities.

same ways as others in the class. But most parents are probably not expecting that their children will learn exactly the same things as other children. For many parents of children with more severe disabilities (and children without disabilities), it is most important that their children feel welcomed and valued in the classroom, as well as feel assured that they are loved deeply by God. For these parents, it might be most important that their children develop friendships with their peers, be accepted by others, and fulfill important roles in the class. Other parents may be working at home on learning important character traits—such as honesty, responsibility, or compassion—and would like to see those same traits reinforced in class.

- *What should the child's participation look like?* As you devise a support plan, think broadly about what it really means for a child to participate *fully* in your congregation and brainstorm strategies for supporting this type of participation. Although inclusion in Sunday/Sabbath school classes often receive the most attention, consider how you will help each child participate in the many other activities of your congregation, such as children's time during the worship service, choirs and musical groups, holiday pageants, summer programs, day trips, service projects, and other ceremonies and rites of passage (e.g., baptism, bar/bat mitzvah, confirmation, Shabbat services).

> "I talked with a father last week about his son, Brian. Brian just turned nine and is enjoying the new school year. The father was excited because this is the first year that Brian is in a class with other students who do not have a developmental disability.... The father expressed feelings of relief, excitement, and encouragement—finally his son had a place at the table. He then paused, thought for a moment, and said, 'I wish it was the same at our church.'"
> —Scott Landes (2001/2002, p. 28)

Also recognize that even though some children may only be able to participate partially in certain activities, their involvement still should be supported.

- *What can you learn from others?* Most children with developmental disabilities will be receiving specialized services in other settings throughout the week in places such as early childhood centers, schools, or community recreational programs. Ask if there are support strategies and adaptations used in those settings that might also be helpful for the child as he or she participates in your congregation. For example, parents might be willing to share a copy of their child's behavior support plan from school if it is relevant. Ask parents about whether there are other individuals who work with their child (e.g., a respite worker, former teacher, or paraprofessional) with whom it might be helpful for teachers or helpers to talk.

Religious Education Support Plan for Children and Youth

I. Overview

We are excited that your child will be involved in our programs! We would like to ask you to provide the following information so that we can ensure that our programs meet the needs of your child.

Date: _____

Child's name: _____ Date of birth: _____

Parent's/caregiver's name: _____

Address: _____

Telephone: _____ E-mail: _____

If absolutely necessary, where can we find you while we are with your child?

❑ Main sanctuary _____   ❑ Classroom: _____   ❑ Other: _____

What are some things that your child really enjoys doing?

_____

_____

_____

_____

In what ways does your child learn best? Are there teaching strategies that work particularly well?

_____

_____

_____

_____

How does your child communicate with others?

_____

_____

_____

_____

What types of assistance (if any) will your child need with eating, getting around, or using the restroom?

_____

_____

_____

_____

What behavioral challenges might we encounter when interacting with your child (if any)?	For each challenge, what are some strategies for responding that seem to work well?
•	•
•	•
•	•
•	•

Figure 4.2. Sample religious education support plan.

How would you describe where your child is right now in his or her faith journey?

_____

_____

_____

_____

What are the most important goals and concepts that we should be focusing on?

1. _____

_____

_____

2. _____

_____

_____

3. _____

_____

_____

4. _____

_____

_____

Other information:

Describe any allergies that we should know about.

_____

_____

_____

Is your child on medications that may impact his or her behavior? If so, describe.

_____

_____

_____

Is your child at increased risk for getting sick from other children? How can we reduce this risk?

_____

_____

_____

Are there other medical issues of which we should be aware? If so, how should we be prepared to respond to these issues?

_____

_____

_____

Do you have any other specific concerns that we can try to address?

_____

_____

_____

_____

(continued)

Figure 4.2. *(continued)*

II. Participation Plan

Describe the strategies and supports that will be used to involve the child in the following aspects of congregational life:

Activities	What will the child's involvement look like?	What supports will the child need to participate?
Small group activities		
Large group activities		
Summer programs and camps		
Other programs for children and youth (children's choir, recreational activities, etc.)		
Worship services		
Rites of passage, preparation classes, and other activities		
Service and outreach opportunities		

Figure 4.2 displays one possible format that a religious education plan might take. The first section is an overview used to gather information. The second section of the form will help to organize the plan. Of course, it can (and should) be adapted to reflect the unique aspects of your congregation. Other formats have been presented elsewhere (e.g., Carter, 1999; Mose, 2001; Newman, 2001; Pierson, 2002; Tada & Miller, 2002). A religious education plan does not have to be so comprehensive as to cover every conceivable situation that might arise. It simply offers a starting point for including a child; one that can be built on as others get to know him or her better. An overly extensive plan that is "time intensive" is likely to either discourage people or go unused. Plans also should be revisited as often as needed, such as when the child transitions to a different class or teacher, becomes involved in a new activity, encounters unexpected challenges, or experiences a dramatic change related to his or her disability. However, an annual review and update of the plan is probably sufficient.

Creating Biographies

Simply passing on information about the causes and characteristics of a particular diagnosis is generally much less helpful than sharing information about the interests and needs of a specific child. Although children sharing the label of autism or Down syndrome may have many things in common, there still remains incredible diversity in strengths and needs from one child to the next. It is far more important that teachers understand exactly what Tamisha, Sophie, or Madeleine need than to know what children with a particular disability generally need. Although it is usually hoped that a disability label will communicate helpful information, it can also have the opposite effect. Being introduced to a child through his or her label (e.g., Stefan has autism) often evokes only images of what he or she cannot do, leading people to feel overwhelmed and ill-equipped before they ever have the chance to get to know the child.

A biography offers a more informal approach to introducing a child with disabilities that can be used in conjunction with or in lieu of a religious education plan. A biography offers a brief, but informative, description of a child, accompanied by examples of ways that he or she can be supported to participate in children's activities. An example biography is included in Figure 4.3. Biographies can take many forms and might contain general information about the child, including his or her interests and strengths; ideas for how a child can participate, even partially, in typical activities; and tips for making the child feel welcome and safe. The biographies should also include information about who to contact when more information is needed.

Who is Sam?
- Sam is 12 years old and in sixth grade; he has been attending our program for 3 years.
- Sam has three siblings: Meredith is 7, Wesley is 9, and Eric (his twin) also is 12.
- Sam's parents are Tim and Sandy.
- Sam has a genetic condition called Williams syndrome.

What does he like to do?
- He loves country music, race cars, and any kind of crafts.
- He enjoys drawing and is very good at doing portraits.
- Sam sometimes likes to rock back and forth. It keeps him calm.

How does Sam communicate with others?
- Sam is incredibly social and loves to talk with anyone he meets; he tends to interact more with adults, but he really wants to make new friends among his peers.
- When he is frustrated, he sometimes raises his voice or paces around the room.

What are some ways that you include him in activities?
- Sam has great difficulty reading, so ask him questions orally or pair him with a peer whenever reading is necessary.
- Find alternative ways to help him to participate, such as having him pass out worksheets and supplies, turn pages in the readings, or call on classmates during discussions.

What are some of the goals you can be helping Sam work toward?
- His parents are working with him on the importance of telling the truth and taking responsibility.
- Sam is noticing differences related to his disability. His parents would like us to find opportunities to reaffirm for Sam that God loves him very much.

How might you encourage Sam when he is doing something well?
- He loves adult attention and that is usually sufficient. An occasional "high-five" goes a long way.
- Sam loves going out for sub sandwiches after church; this can be used to encourage good behavior when he seems to be a bit agitated.

What should you keep an eye out for?
- Recently, Sam has had some behavioral challenges. They tend to occur when he feels rushed to finish something. Providing him cues that the class is almost over often helps.
- If he starts to pace, it is a sign he is about to lose his temper. Offer him a break to regroup.

Is it okay to talk about his disability?
- Sam's parents definitely want to increase understanding and acceptance among his peers, so it is okay to explain to other children about Williams syndrome to dispel any myths they may hold. Attached is a brief information sheet about his disability. Sam also is comfortable with answering questions from peers.

If you need any addition information, do not hesitate to ask Sharon Paulin (Room 108) or Sam's parents (555–2453).

Figure 4.3. Sample biography of Sam. (From Spencer, S. [2005, May]. *Blackhawk Church procedures for kids with special needs.* Madison, WI: Blackhawk Church; adapted by permission.)

One advantage of biographies is that a substitute teacher, new helper, or occasional volunteer can easily pick one up and quickly review it to provide a starting point for supporting a child. It is not uncommon for a volunteer to be absent some mornings. Having basic information ready and available for a temporary substitute can ensure that the child does not have to miss activities that week or have his or her parents leave worship services or classes to stay with him or her. As you get to know the child better, periodically update his or her biography to reflect the new information and strategies that you have learned. As children grow up in your congregation, their goals will certainly change, new needs will often surface, and new avenues for participation will emerge.

Conducting Ongoing Communication

It is essential that the lines of communication between program leaders, families, teachers, and volunteers always remain open. After a child has been involved in activities for several weeks, follow up with his or her parents, teachers, helpers, and other volunteers to find out how everything is going. Discuss additional questions and challenges that have arisen as everyone has accumulated experience working with and getting to know the child. Often, it is during these follow-up discussions that teachers raise more specific questions about the disability and its impact on the child.

EQUIPPING LAY VOLUNTEERS TO SERVE ALL CHILDREN

Most activities within programs for children and youth are carried out by lay people who volunteer their time and who likely have had little, if any, formal training in issues related to children with disabilities. Some may feel unequipped to include a child with disabilities in their program. Others may respond initially with hesitation or reluctance to your request to include a child with disabilities in their class. Equipping children's workers to meet the spiritual needs of every child, including those with developmental disabilities, is an incredibly important task.

Roles of Lay Volunteers

There are many different avenues through which members of a congregation might contribute their time and gifts toward including children and youth with developmental disabilities. Teaching comes quickly to mind because teachers assume responsibility for leading activities for a class or group of children—one or more of whom might have a developmental disability or other special needs—on a regular basis. In addition, it may be necessary to identify people who are willing to provide any additional assistance that may be needed. Finally, there is an important role for other lay volunteers whose involvement will be more occasional and short-term. The following section describes roles people may assume in supporting the inclusion of children with disabilities. Because the titles attached to these roles vary from one congregation to another, consider how these responsibilities might be met in your faith community.

Lead Teachers Lay people working as teachers and leaders in religious education programs feel called to nurture the spiritual development of children in their congregation. Some teachers may have less confidence in their ability to carry out this call with children who happen to have disabilities. Your efforts can go a long way toward assuring teachers that they really do know more than they think they do and that they and their class have much to gain from welcoming a child with disabilities. Help teachers learn to communicate lessons in multiple ways to capture the attention and promote the learning of a wider range of students. Teachers often rely too heavily on reading and writing activities. Equip teachers to vary their teaching methods by incorporating storytelling, drama, music, skits, role playing, games, activities, crafts, and other interactive approaches. Adapting activities to meet the needs of every child is a key quality of good teaching, but it is absolutely essential when working with children with developmental disabilities. Using such a "universal design" approach, in which curricula and activities are designed with all children in mind right from the beginning, serves to increase the participation of children with disabilities and keep teachers from having to adapt activities at the last minute or not at all.

To support teachers to meet the needs of the children and youth in their care, let them know that you will invite additional people, such as helpers or "buddies," to assist them in their efforts. This extra assistance is especially important in larger groups, where it would be difficult for the teacher to provide extra attention to a single child or when a child has more substantial support needs.

Helpers Many children with developmental disabilities will benefit from having additional support to participate fully in activities. Identifying a helper who will accompany the child is one avenue for providing this support. Often called an *assistant, companion, mentor, shadow,* or *support,* helpers accompany the child during programs and provide one-to-one assistance, as needed. Helpers seek out creative ways of including a child in ongoing activities and facilitating interactions with classmates. Although their primary focus is to ensure that children with disabilities are well supported and meaningfully included, helpers should view their role much more broadly by helping the lead teacher to address the needs and participation of every child in the group. During times when a child with disabilities does not require one-to-one assistance, helpers should also be interacting with other children in the class. This "only as much support as is needed" approach will help children fit in better and enjoy increased independence.

Buddies   Other children can play a vital role in welcoming children with disabilities into religious education classes and activities. For example, older children might serve as buddies (e.g., *friendship partners, mentors, or peer supports*) to younger children with disabilities, providing the help they might need to be involved in various activities. Moreover, as children get older—particularly during middle and high school—they often desire less dependence on adults. Adolescents with disabilities may prefer not to have an adult accompanying them all of the time, especially because the constant presence of an adult can make other youth reluctant to interact with them. With just a little instruction and guidance, teenagers often prove to be quite capable of providing support to their peers with disabilities (Carter, Cushing, Clark, & Kennedy, 2005). In fact, they often turn out to be even more creative than adults at discovering effective ways to include their peers with disabilities.

Substitutes   As more children with disabilities become involved in your congregation's programs, it may be wise to devise a backup plan for when helpers or buddies must be absent. Identify others in your congregation who are willing to serve as an occasional substitute when the usual helper is unavailable or an unexpected child visits for the first time. Having someone you can call on at the last minute can keep a child with disabilities from being turned away because necessary support is not available. For example, you might compile the names of several members of the congregation who would be willing to provide additional assistance in a classroom on very short notice. Often, there are people within a congregation who would like an opportunity to work with children in your program, but are only available occasionally. Perhaps they are involved in their own class or they frequently travel out of town. Participating as a substitute allows them a way to contribute to your congregation's vision. Of course, a parent of the child also may be willing to occasionally fill in, but generally you should rely on family members only as a last resort. Remember that your ministry is not just to children, but also to their families.

Identifying Lay Volunteers

Prior to identifying individuals to serve as teachers, helpers, buddies, or substitutes, it is important to outline your expectations for volunteers. In what capacities will you be asking them to serve? Some congregations develop written descriptions of these ministry roles. If you are unsure of what to include, consider describing the nature of the commitment you are asking people to make (e.g., one month, one summer, one year), the types of interactions they will have with children with disabilities, and the ways in which you will equip them to serve effectively in their new roles. As you gain experience, you can tailor these descriptions to reflect the ongoing lessons you are learning.

As with any position, your goal is not simply to find *any* volunteer, but rather to find dedicated individuals who recognize this role as an opportunity to use their gifts to meet the needs of children in their congregation. Prayerfully seek out people who have gifts and passions that would advance your congregation's vision for welcoming and nurturing every child. Explain that past experience with people with disabilities is not the most essential quality; anyone can learn how to offer support. When a person brings both past experience and related gifts, it is a wonderful combination. However, many people have either never considered or not yet found an opportunity to share their gifts in this way and their contributions should still be encouraged. Distinguish between skills a person can learn with help and qualities they should already possess. Seek out people who express a willingness to learn, who love children, who are willing to be flexible, who enjoy thinking creatively, and who recognize this as an avenue for connecting their gifts with needs.

Finding helpers who are consistent and reliable sources of support is essential, particularly when first welcoming a child into your program. In addition to adults in your congregation, consider college-age young adults and mature high school students as potential helpers. Some congregations try to identify more than one person willing to provide support to a given child. This ensures that someone is always available to provide support and it reduces the commitment required by any single person. Some children, however, have difficulty adjusting to frequent changes in routines, so it is important to consider the needs of the particular child.

Several approaches can be used to identify people to serve in the roles of lead teachers, assistants, buddies, and substitutes.

- If your congregation distributes a survey as part of its awareness efforts (see Chapters 2 and 3), make sure that the survey includes a place for members to indicate their interest in volunteering with children.

- Some congregations have developed other approaches for connecting gifts and opportunities within and beyond their congregation, such as time and talent surveys, resource mapping, or spiritual gift questionnaires. As gifts are identified, make sure that supporting children with disabilities is included among the many avenues offered for engaging those gifts.

- Ask parents if they can suggest people who have shown a special interest in their child with disabilities.

- Keep an eye out for members of your congregation who seem to make extra effort to seek out and interact with people with disabilities.

- Buddies can be identified from among peers within a child's class or by approaching older children in other classes. For example, some congregations invite high school students to serve as buddies to elementary students with disabilities.

- Post opportunity announcements throughout your building, on your web site, and in bulletins and newsletters. Consider interviewing a teacher, helper, or buddy who currently is working with a child with disabilities. Write up a summary of his or her thoughts and distribute it for others to read.

Educating Religious Educators

The approach you take to train and equip children's ministry workers to welcome and support children with disabilities will be influenced by many factors, including the number of children with disabilities, the nature of those disabilities, and the specific activities in which the children will participate. As you seek to tailor training opportunities to meet the specific needs of your congregation, several issues should be considered.

Who Will Lead the Training Sessions? For just one or two volunteers, it may be sufficient to meet with parents and the child's lead teacher to brainstorm inclusion strategies. Parents often are the best source of information about their children, so it is wise to turn to them for ideas and strategies. Invite past helpers or buddies to meet with the new volunteers to share strategies they have learned over time.

As additional children with disabilities become involved in your programs and your inclusion efforts broaden, consider offering more focused learning opportunities for lay volunteers. Look within your congregation to find current members who can contribute to training efforts. For example, an elementary school teacher from your congregation could share ideas for adapting activities and curricula; a doctor, nurse, or other health care professional may be willing to talk about how to address basic medical issues or strategies for responding to specific concerns (e.g., toileting, choking, seizures); a counselor could talk about strategies for promoting positive peer relationships among classmates; and a clergy member could talk about creative ways to communicate important spiritual truths.

It also can be helpful to bring in people with specific expertise from another congregation, organization, or agency. Extend an invitation to one or more of the following individuals: disability consultants from within your denomination or faith group; members of other congregations involved in disability ministry; special educators, paraprofessionals, and related service providers (e.g., occupational, physical, or speech therapists) from your local school system; professors from local colleges and universities working in departments that address disability-related issues (e.g., communication disorders, counseling, elementary/secondary education, rehabilitation psychology, social work, special education); or staff from organizations that serve people with disabilities. Many of these people would be excited to partner with you in your training efforts. Have them come to your yearly kick-off for volunteers to set the tone and introduce themselves as an available resource.

Who Should Be Involved in Your Training Efforts?   Training needs will vary depending on the role that each person will play in supporting children with disabilities. Lead teachers will benefit from broader training on quality and creative teaching strategies that are likely to capture the hearts, minds, and attention of the diverse group of children in their class. Good teaching will be good for every child. Helpers will need information that is focused more directly on the specific child or children whom they will be supporting. Buddies usually only need basic information about their classmates, as well as general strategies for interacting with and assisting them to participate in ongoing activities. Often, other information is provided on an "as needed" basis.

What Information Should Be Shared?   Some of the topics you will want to cover can be woven into the general training activities provided to all children's volunteers (see Table 4.2). Begin by explaining the focus and importance of your children's program, drawing on the vision you have articulated (e.g., to assure children that they belong and are loved by God; to nurture their spiritual formation; and to help them discover their needs, gifts, and place in the world). Teachers, helpers, and others should understand the ways that their efforts can contribute to and be fueled by this vision. To help others catch hold of this vision, share God's perspective on disabilities, drawing on scriptural passages and other theological and doctrinal teachings of your faith tradition (see Appendices A and B). Remind volunteers that their efforts will not only affect children with disabilities but also the family members and classmates of those children. In fact,

Table 4.2. Topics to address when training teachers, helpers, and other volunteers

- Describe the mission of your program and how each person contributes to that mission
- Share insights into God's perspective on disabilities (see Appendices A and B)
- Talk about the impact of inclusive programs on children with disabilities, peers, family members, and lay volunteers
- Answer questions about how to interact with people with disabilities and offer tips for using affirming language
- Present basic strategies for adapting lessons and activities
- Offer ideas for facilitating relationships among children with and without disabilities
- Share relevant information about the specific children who will be participating (e.g., interests, strengths, communication strategies, unique needs)
- Discuss any emergency procedures or expectations about confidentiality
- Offer basic strategies for managing children's behavior
- Communicate your expectations for volunteers and address any other information specific to their roles

they should expect their own lives to be affected by the relationships they develop.

Share general strategies for adapting activities and programs for children with disabilities (see Table 4.3). In fact, these general strategies are useful for any teacher to know when working with any group of children. Remind teachers that there are many different ways to communicate a lesson and children may grasp the message different ways. However, the most important lessons often are not even contained in the written curriculum, but are communicated through the relationships that develop among children and teachers. Demonstrate some of the different ways that activities might be adapted for children who learn somewhat differently.

Because every child with disabilities is unique, some of the information and strategies that you share will need to be child specific. Additional training might be provided individually to the teachers and helpers who will be working with a particular child. Draw on the information that you have learned from conversations with parents and your previous experiences including other children. The goal is not to make teachers and helpers experts in every aspect of a particular disability, but rather to provide them with the information and strategies they will need to begin supporting a specific child. *Is there special equipment that she uses? Does she communicate in alternative or different ways? What adaptations might be helpful to use during certain activities? With what activities might she need extra help?* Behavioral issues are likely to be a primary concern of many volunteers, so make certain that strategies for preventing and de-escalating challenging behaviors are addressed (see Box 4.3). If disability-specific information is

Table 4.3. General strategies for adapting activities and programs for children with disabilities

Adaptations	Comments	Examples
Curricular	Begin with the existing curriculum, identify the main concepts, find out how the child learns best, and adapt the materials and activities accordingly. Lessons and materials may need to be simplified or supplemented, but they should always remain age-appropriate.	Augment the lesson with pictures, videos, or other concrete examples. Reduce the amount of reading required. Supplement the lesson with additional activities.
Participation level	Allow children to participate in multiple ways and at various levels. Some children may only be able to participate partially in some activities, but their involvement should still be valued and supported.	Add motions to songs to include children who are nonverbal. Have a child cut out pictures and symbols to describe a concept or story. Allow a child who cannot read to turn the pages and/or act out part of the story.
Instructional level	Vary your teaching methods, rather than relying exclusively on reading and writing activities. Connect lessons with students' life experiences. Communicate concepts clearly and in multiple ways, using repetition to reinforce important concepts.	Use a variety of approaches to communicate lesson truths, including drama, stories, puppets, music, and role-playing. Rephrase a story so that it is more understandable at the child's level of understanding.
Expectations	Be clear about your expectations for appropriate and inappropriate behavior in the classroom, remembering that expectations may have to be adjusted for students with specific needs. Encourage good behavior by reinforcing it often.	Allow a child who has difficulty sitting still for extended periods to move around the classroom. Use a picture calendar to help a child anticipate the next activity. Use a token system to support positive behavior.
Environmental	For a child to participate fully, it may be necessary to change the classroom setting in some way. Providing physical accommodations, removing distractions, and providing special equipment all may enhance the learning environment.	Rearrange a classroom to accommodate a wheelchair. Purchase adapted writing/drawing tools, scissors, or tables to enable a child to complete crafts and other activities.
Supports	Providing the child with additional assistance from an adult or pairing the child with one or more peers who can support participation in class activities.	Have children work together in groups to present a Bible story as a skit. Ask a classmate to help a peer with disabilities paint a mural about loving others. Recruit a college student to help a youth with disabilities serve coffee during fellowship time.

Box 4.3
Addressing Behavioral Challenges

The issue of challenging behavior often emerges as one of the primary concerns voiced by teachers, helpers, and other volunteers. Every program should establish clear procedures for how adults are to address disruptive behaviors exhibited by any child. For most children with developmental disabilities, these procedures will be sufficient. However, some children may engage in behaviors that are especially challenging, and additional considerations may need to be addressed. Consider the following general strategies for supporting positive behavior among children and youth.

- Model the behaviors that you expect children to display.

- Convey your expectations using clear and simple language; set understandable limits.

- Break down complex directions and tasks into smaller, more manageable, parts.

- Offer frequent opportunities for children to experience success; catch students being good and let them know it.

- Remember that inappropriate behavior may stem from many different causes, including not understanding classroom expectations, difficulty communicating preferences and needs, unexpected changes in routines, or the effects of medications. Try to determine the root cause of the behavior when deciding how you will respond.

- Find out what people, activities, or settings seem to anticipate behavioral challenges. Then, brainstorm ways of addressing those triggers. For example, a child may struggle when the room gets crowded, noises get loud, or routines are disrupted unexpectedly.

- Visiting a congregation (or any new place) for the first several times can be stressful and unpredictable for children with disabilities. Recognize that it may take some time for some children to settle in to a new place, different routines, and unfamiliar people.

- Talk with parents about their recommendations for handling specific behavioral concerns that you are encountering. They can be key allies.

When challenging behavior persists, consider drawing on the expertise of a behavioral consultant, special educator, or other professional who works with the child in other settings. These individuals may be able to offer keen insight into approaches for reducing the occurrence of challenging behaviors. What seems unpredictable at first glance may be readily understandable by someone with more experience. Several published books may also be helpful (see Janney & Snell, 2000; Koegel, Koegel, & Dunlap, 1996; Luiselli, 2006). Your goal should be to develop a plan so that parents are called out of worship services only as an absolute last resort.

important, helpful information sheets and resource guides can be downloaded for free from the National Dissemination Center for Children with Disabilities (www.nichcy.org).

The support needs of some children with more severe disabilities can be quite substantial. The more a helper can learn about a child, the better equipped and more confident he or she will be to provide support. With a parent's permission, consider arranging a time for a teacher or helper to spend time with the child during school or at home. For example, a helper might observe the child during several class periods at school, talking with a special educator or paraprofessional about the support strategies he or she has found to be effective. Parents may even be willing to have a helper spend some time interacting with the child at their home or watching the child participate in a therapy session. These approaches not only serve to acquaint the helper with strategies others are using to include a child but they also serve to increase the child's familiarity and comfort with the person who will be providing support. It is not unusual for some children to need extra time to warm up to a new person. Other approaches might include inviting a staff from the child's school to visit your congregation to offer hands-on guidance or having the child's teacher or helper observe at another congregation where people serve in similar support roles. Sometimes, the best way to learn something new is by watching other people doing it.

Supporting the Contributions of Lay Volunteers

Any new undertaking can be accompanied by challenges, and inclusive children's ministries are certainly no exception. Some children will exhaust you and some days will leave you feeling unsuccessful. Yet, this work is deeply rewarding. Most volunteers express great satisfaction with their contributions and recognize that they are making an eternal difference in the lives of children and their families. It is essential that everyone working in your program be well supported and encouraged as they use their gifts and engage their passions to welcome children and youth with disabilities. The following strategies can be taken to support the ongoing work of volunteers.

Encourage Open Communication   Lines of communication between program leaders, volunteers, and parents should be kept wide open. Encourage teachers, helpers, buddies, and other volunteers to ask frequent questions, share their apprehensions, and offer suggestions. It is critical that teachers know to whom they can go for support. Everyone has much to learn from each other about how to include children in meaningful ways. In addition, make sure that families and volunteers both know whom to contact when they will not be in attendance on a given week. It also may be helpful for teachers and parents to share a periodic e-mail or conversation after class to keep communication lines open.

Extend Learning Opportunities   Nurture the gifts of volunteers by offering occasional learning opportunities. Consider holding monthly or quarterly workshops that explore different aspects of serving and meeting the needs of children with and without disabilities. Partner with other congregations in your community to attract a larger audience and divide planning responsibilities. In addition, let volunteers know about regional, state, and national conferences that include sessions or strands on inclusive ministry. Because conferences can be expensive, set aside funds to help to defray the expenses associated with attending these learning events. Finally, compile print and video resources into a lending library for teachers, helpers, and others who want to seek out more information on their own (see Appendix B for a list of books and other resources that might comprise this library).

Recognize Efforts   Celebrate the contributions that each person is making to the lives of children and their families. Reassure everyone that the efforts that they are making really matter, even when success seems hard to recognize. Write notes of appreciation to staff, volunteers, and others who contribute their time, energy, passions, and creativity to these endeavors. Hold an annual dinner to reflect on the successes of the past year and cast a vision for the upcoming year.

Share Stories   As you hear stories from parents, children, and other members of your congregation, share them with your volunteers so that everyone recognizes the impact that their efforts are having. For example, a child with autism who rarely spoke now excitedly sings along during music time, a member of the congregation who always felt like she had little to offer found an opportunity to use her gifts through serving as a helper to a first grader with autism, a middle school student who serves as a buddy to a peer with disabilities in his youth group begins advocating for including that peer in his school, or a parent shares of how her daughter with Down syndrome received her very first invitation to a birthday party from a peer in her confirmation class.

HELPING CHILDREN AND YOUTH WELCOME THEIR PEERS

When first including a child with disabilities in activities within your congregation, other children naturally will be curious. Adults can prepare children and youth by addressing their questions and concerns as well as by helping them consider ideas for interacting with their peers with disabilities. As schools increasingly adopt inclusive practices, children are enjoying more opportunities to develop relationships with their peers with disabilities. You might be surprised at just how welcoming most children can be, especially when provided with just a little guidance.

The following strategies can be used to guide children in welcoming peers with disabilities into their class or program:

- The most important step you can take is to model the behaviors that you expect children to display. Children will be watching how you interact and, for better or worse, they will follow your lead. This includes how you speak to (and about) children with disabilities. Make sure your language is age-appropriate and affirming.

- Some children initially might be uncertain of how to interact with their peers with disabilities. Offer children some specific ideas, such as helping someone to complete a craft, follow along in a workbook or songbook, play a musical instrument, participate in a game, pass out snacks, relate a lesson to his or her own life, or get around the building in a wheelchair.

- Involve children in brainstorming ideas for helping their peers with disabilities "fit in" socially and become more involved in the class. Ask them: *How can we help Thomas talk with us more? What can we do to make Sharon feel more welcome? When Zora gets anxious and upset, what do you think we could each do to make her feel okay?* Children often are among the most creative problem solvers.

Children are likely to have many questions and usually are not shy about asking them. Answer honestly and respond directly to their reactions to disabilities. Such situations present great learning opportunities for everyone in the class. Think carefully about whether these conversations should happen with or without the child with disabilities being present. Talk to the parents of the child with disabilities to find out what information they are comfortable having shared with the class.

- Explain to children that there are certain roles they should not assume. Your goal should be to foster friendships among classmates, not to promote relationships that resemble those of a tutor and tutee.

Even if a child with disabilities is not yet participating in your congregation's programs, you can take certain steps to increase children's awareness of disabilities (Miller & Sammons, 1999; Newman, 2001).

- Talk with children about their experiences with people with disabilities in their families, schools, and neighborhoods.

- Invite people with disabilities to come to your class and talk about their life experiences and faith journeys. Parents or siblings of children with disabilities also may have much to share.

> "I have found that *accurate information* is one of the most powerful tools in creating a successful program for including children with special needs in classrooms at school or in church. I believe that educators, children, and parents of peers need to be given the right glasses in order to practice greater acceptance and understanding."
> —Barbara Newman (2001, p. 9)

- Have conversations about the gifts and needs that each person has. Stress the idea of interdependence and illustrate how everyone has times when they give and receive support.

- Incorporate stories about children with disabilities into your lessons to jumpstart conversations. Draw on scriptural passages and existing children's literature (see Dyches & Prater, 2000; Kupper, 2001) to find such stories.

- Involve children in an accessibilities project within the congregation or in the wider community. For example, a youth group might build a ramp to the fellowship hall, volunteer to help out at a community respite program, or offer to do yard work for members of the congregation with disabilities.

- Disability simulations may inadvertently reinforce wrong stereotypes about people with disabilities (Brew-Parrish, 2004). Think carefully about the messages that your awareness efforts will send.

INCLUDING ADULTS WITH DEVELOPMENTAL DISABILITIES

As children grow up, the need for adult programs that are responsive to the needs of people with developmental disabilities will only increase. Anticipate these needs and begin planning ahead of time by keeping adult education leaders in your congregation abreast of your efforts and involved in future planning. Although many of the strategies and considerations presented in this chapter remain relevant when supporting the participation of adults, several additional issues should be addressed.

> "My church is very welcoming. It has a warm setting where you feel you have friends and family in the congregation that you can turn to. The people in my congregation don't treat me any differently than they would treat anyone else. They listen to me. They come up to me, hug me and talk to me. I also have a best friend I met through church. She emails me and I email her back."
> —Kelly Barnes (2005, p. 4)

First, the process of getting to know the support needs of adults might differ somewhat. The involvement of family members in the lives of adults with developmental disabilities may not be as prominent as it is for children. If asked, many adults will be able to tell you about the types of supports they will need to be involved in your programs. For others, it may be helpful to have conversations with service providers or adult siblings to discern how best to support a person's participation. Second, parents are less likely to be involved in advocating for the inclusion of their adult children. Therefore, congregations will have to be especially intentional about connecting with and extending invitations to adults with disabilities in their community. Several strategies for communicating these invitations were described in Chapter 3. Third, many activities designed for adults take place at various times throughout the week, including small groups, social events, and outreach projects. Leaders will need to make sure that information about these events is communicated to adults with disabilities and those who support them, as well as helping to ensure that transportation is made available. Fourth, the faith partner approach described in Chapter 3 seems to offer a more appropriate strategy for supporting the participation of some adults with developmental disabilities. Consider identifying one or two people who would be willing to serve in this capacity. Finally, many people with severe disabilities continue to live in restrictive living situations, such as long-term care facilities, nursing homes, and institutions. When people experience great difficulty coming to your congregation, think creatively about how you might bring the community to them.

CONCLUSION

A wonderful opportunity awaits your congregation when it commits to opening its doors and hearts to every child. Communicate boldly that people with disabilities are integral to the life of your community. However, your commitment must be much more than a symbolic one. Strive to be known by what you do and how you do it; rather than by a well-worded mission statement that has found no place in members' hearts.

Chapter 5

Supporting Individuals with Developmental Disabilities and Their Families

The Other Six Days

The life outcomes experienced by people with developmental disabilities offer a challenge to faith communities to respond in new, inspired, and meaningful ways, as well as an opportunity for faith communities to improve life outcomes for these individuals. Too many children and adults remain disconnected from others in their communities; experience lives of poverty; or lack the resources, opportunities, and supports to pursue and attain personally important goals (e.g., Gardner & Carran, 2005; Park, Turnbull, & Turnbull, 2002). Yet, many congregation members are simply not aware of the needs of people with disabilities and their families, as well as the many ways that they—both individually and collectively as a faith community—might offer support. The potential for congregations to dispense grace, extend relationships, and affect the lives of people with developmental disabilities and their families is enormous, but these rich and deep reservoirs of support remain largely untapped.

How can you be responsive to the needs of people with developmental disabilities and their families in your congregation, neighborhood, and city? What can you do to help people with disabilities participate more fully within your congregation *and* in the wider community? Congregations are still discovering all that is possible. This chapter describes both ordinary and creative ways that congregations might reach out to meet the needs of children and adults with developmental disabilities and their families. Congregations usually want to be responsive, but often lack direction; service providers desire to engage people in their communities, but frequently lack natural partnerships with members of those communities;

119

and families may hold great hopes for their congregation, but remain unsure of how to invite their involvement and ask for their support. The purpose of this chapter is to 1) challenge congregations to grasp hold of a vision for how they might participate in meeting the needs of their neighbors with developmental disabilities; 2) help service providers recognize new avenues for partnering with congregations to promote community inclusion throughout the week; 3) and stimulate people with disabilities and their families to consider the source of support their congregation could be in their lives and to communicate their needs. Consider the many ways in which you might affect the lives of people with disabilities—not just on the days when they enter your building—but throughout the rest of the week.

THE CASE FOR CONGREGATIONAL RESPONSES

With more than 300,000 churches, parishes, synagogues, mosques, temples, and other places of worship in the United States (Chaves, 2004), the potential availability of support is astonishing. Imagine how the landscape would change if 300,000 congregations each made a commitment to support a person with developmental disabilities with some aspect of his or her life. Suppose that just one person attending each of these 300,000 congregations decided to hire a person with a disability in his or her business or organization. Imagine what would happen if 300,000 congregations made a commitment to advocate for the inclusion of people with developmental disabilities in their wider communities. If even a fraction of these congregations took steps to reach out to and engage their neighbors with disabilities, the impact would be enormous.

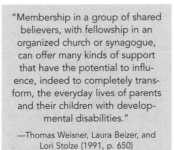

"Membership in a group of shared believers, with fellowship in an organized church or synagogue, can offer many kinds of support that have the potential to influence, indeed to completely transform, the everyday lives of parents and their children with developmental disabilities."

—Thomas Weisner, Laura Beizer, and Lori Stolze (1991, p. 650)

Inviting faith communities to play a role in providing supports and opportunities to people with developmental disabilities and their families makes sense for several reasons.

Natural Supports

Too many people with developmental disabilities live their lives within a system of services, rather than within a network of supportive personal relationships. Advocates, service providers, and other professionals are calling for greater reliance on more natural sources of support—the informal people and resources that most people typically draw on—when promoting community inclusion. Many people count faith communities as among the most natural forms of support. Indeed, some families feel more comfortable drawing on informal supports, such as their congregation, rather than turning to community and state agencies. For these families, there is something qualitatively different about support from these sources. Providing respite service is viewed simply as "lending a hand to Sarah and her family"; supported employment is nothing more than "helping Tyrell find a good job"; and supported living services are really just about "making sure Sujata has the help she needs to live on her own in an apartment." Congregations can support people with disabilities and their families, just as they meet the needs of others within their congregation and broader community. To a great extent, this is what congregations feel they are called to do. That they do not always serve this role in the lives of people with disabilities may be a result of not recognizing potential opportunities or not knowing how to proceed.

> "Society must recognize that a significant number of individuals and families attend houses of faith. For these individuals, the local church is a significant resource providing life sustaining and enriching support."
>
> —Jeff McNair (2000, p. 52)

Community Assets

Transforming the dreams and aspirations of people with severe disabilities into realities sometimes requires an interconnected web of support emerging from a constellation of sources within a community. Involving congregations as partners in these support efforts ensures that the full range of assets and capabilities available in a community are being drawn on (Kretzmann & McKnight, 1993). Efforts to improve quality of life for people with disabilities are enhanced when congregations join in those efforts and mobilize their own members and resources to respond in concert.

> "These are some forms of support that have successfully pulled together the energies and talents of community people to break down the barriers keeping people with disabilities out of the ordinary life of communities. People who belong to them are modern-day Joshuas: They help make the walls come tumbling down."
>
> —Mary O'Connell (1990, p. 24)

Many Purposes

Congregations are all about nurturing the spiritual growth of their members. However, they also play an important role in addressing other needs. Consider the tremendous number of educational, recreational, vocational, and outreach programs undertaken by congregations to meet the physical, social, emotional, *and* spiritual needs of members of their community. Congregations have long sponsored a multitude of groups, programs, and activities within and beyond their walls, including counseling and support groups, housing projects, hobby clubs, immigrant and refugee support programs, literacy programs, scouting groups, senior citizen assistance programs, sporting activities, substance abuse/recovery programs, and many others. People with developmental disabilities would benefit from invitations to participate in the numerous outreach and community services *already offered* by congregations.

Enduring Support

Reductions in available public funding, long waiting lists for services, increasingly scarce external resources, and an aging population—each of these factors argues for the importance of identifying new and innovative approaches to ensure that people with disabilities can live rich and varied lives (Nerney, 2003). Congregations have the potential to offer a stable and long-standing source of support for people living within a service system that usually is fragmented and fractured. Unlike public educational services, which end before age 22, and community residential and vocational services, which often fail to emerge until adulthood, the support provided through congregations has the potential to last indefinitely. Congregations need not be constrained by eligibility requirements, waiting lists, or time-limited services. Amidst times of transition, they can offer a consistent and trusted source of support, shared resources, and social capital.

> "Joel knows that Temple Chai is a second home, a 'safe place' where his participation is valued, and he never questions the appropriateness of his being there. During the period of transition from school to adulthood, when all that is familiar and comforting is taken away from a young adult, being able to return to the security and regimen of weekly prayer and participation in synagogue activities becomes the reassuring anchor during this tumultuous period. Attending services and being greeted by fellow congregants reminds this young adult that he is still respected and valued in his community."
>
> —Rebecca Hornstein (1997, p. 487)

Existing Relationships

It makes good sense to draw on the relationships and supports that people already hold and value. Many children and adults with developmental disabilities and their families are known by and have a long-standing history with their congregations. These families may place a special trust in these relationships and supports. Congregations can work toward transforming these relationships into a strong and integrated network of support for people. Service providers can then build on, rather than trying to replicate, these forms of support.

SUPPORTING PEOPLE WITH DISABILITIES: MEANINGFUL OPPORTUNITIES

Congregations are comprised of an extensive network of connections—often complex and usually unexpected. This chapter presents several avenues by which faith communities might choose to take intentional efforts toward supporting people with disabilities to live, work, learn, play, and contribute in their communities. The opportunities are numerous (e.g., Fewell, 1986; McNair, 2000; Stiemke, 1994), limited only by the imagination and creativity of a congregation. These ideas are intended to be neither proscriptive nor exhaustive, but simply suggest a range of potential ways in which your congregation might respond. As you read these ideas, notice how few require special training or past experience. Rather, the gifts and resources already present in your congregation simply need to be awakened to and connected with these needs.

> "It is not enough merely to affirm the rights of persons with disabilities. We must actively work to realize these rights in the fabric of modern society.... All of us can visit the homebound, offer transportation to those who cannot drive, read to those who cannot read, speak out for those who have difficulty pleading their own case."
>
> —United States Conference of Catholic Bishops (2001, pp. 8–9)

A Few Caveats

First, this discussion of congregation-provided supports should not imply that the involvement of more formal support providers no longer is necessary or desired. Support provided through congregations can indeed be instrumental in a person's life, but it rarely is sufficient to meet all of a person's support needs—whether or not that person has a disability. At the same time, it should be noted that the support of paid service providers also is insufficient to meet all of a person's needs. Think creatively about avenues for combining these varied sources of informal and formal support, lacing them together in ways that make the most sense for a given person. Second, individual congregations will differ in the supports that they are able and willing to provide. The contributions of each congregation will be unique and so this chapter is written to explore *possible* responses, not proscribe specific actions.

Third, congregations should carefully examine the roles they wish to assume when partnering with community service providers to promote the inclusion of people with disabilities. Although both groups may share many goals in common, congregations should consider closely their role in light of their unique and particular mission as a community of faith. Accomplishing shared goals in partnership with outside agencies without relinquishing this mission may require deliberate thought on the part of congregations. Fourth, drawing on supports offered by congregations will feel more natural to some people than to others. Although many people with developmental disabilities and their families would welcome a connection and relationship with a congregation in their community, others would not. The choices and preferences of each individual should always guide every decision.

Friendships and Social Relationships: Connecting One with Another

Relationships matter. Most people's lives involve a network of casual acquaintances, neighbors, co-workers, fellow members of organizations, friends, relatives, and romantic partners. Yet, too many people with developmental disabilities remain disconnected from the important relationships that others often take for granted. The social networks of many children and adults with disabilities often are fragile, small, and dominated by family members and paid service providers. Consider research by Orsmond, Krauss, and Seltzer (2004) that found that almost half (46%) of adolescents and adults with autism were reported to have no friendships with similar age peers. This absence of relationships should serve as a loud call to congregations.

Consider how this isolation might affect the hearts and lives of people with developmental disabilities. Like everyone else, people with disabilities desire close friendships and need supportive relationships. Although this common need is shared by everyone, similar opportunities for developing relationships often are not. Segregated classrooms, schools, workplaces, day programs, and group homes cause people with and without developmental disabilities to live in parallel worlds that too infrequently intersect. It is not surprising, then, that promoting friendships remains a central goal identified by parents, educators, service providers, and others.

Faith communities can play a role in restoring disconnected lives by intentionally fostering enduring and mutual relationships among all of their members. Supporting a person's involvement in congregational life multiplies his or her opportunities to meet new people. But simply bringing people together into the same location 1 or 2 days a week may not be enough to ensure social connectedness or a sense of belonging. Building meaningful relationships takes time and effort and members of a congregation should seek out ways of getting together with their neighbors with disabilities and extending relationships throughout the week. For example, consider these ideas drawn from congregational efforts to weave people with disabilities into the social fabric of their community:

- Encourage members to make efforts to get to know people with disabilities outside the walls of your congregation. A gesture can be as simple as inviting someone to go for a walk, share a meal, watch a movie, grab a cup of coffee, visit a museum, go to the mall, or shoot a game of basketball.

- During the week, stop by to see people at their homes to check how they are doing, ask about their family, see how their job is going, and pray with them. People with developmental disabilities encounter the same ordinary and unexpected life experiences as everyone else—the death of a family member, the loss of a job, the breakup of a romantic relationship, a personal illness. It is essential that everyone know someone who cares deeply about him or her and is available to talk, listen, and offer comfort. Most visitation programs, however, focus on people who are elderly or sick. Expand these hospitality efforts to include homebound or hospitalized children and adults with developmental disabilities.

- Members of a congregation can initiate a "support circle" for someone with disabilities or become involved in his or her existing network of support (see Box 5.1).

- Invite people with disabilities to be part of small groups, attend potluck meals, serve on congregational teams, contribute to ministry activities, and to attend prayer meetings. As your congregation plans events throughout the year, be certain that invitations are extended to people with disabilities throughout your community.

- More than half of all congregations organize groups designed for young adults and singles (Dudley & Roozen, 2001). The social activities hosted by these groups offer excellent opportunities for getting to know others in their congregation. Invite and support people with disabilities to participate in these groups. Other congregations sponsor social groups in which people with disabilities get together, enjoy their community, maintain existing relationships, and meet new people.

- Many congregations offer companionship ministries, in which deliberate efforts are made to befriend and engage those who seem to live on the margins of community life. If you have such a program, con-

Box 5.1
Creating Circles of Support
for People with Developmental Disabilities

Congregations know that relationships matter! In genuine communities, people walk alongside each other, rely on one another for support, and receive
assurance that they belong, are accepted, and are loved. As people journey
together, strength is found in community. In the same way, people with
developmental disabilities have need of supportive relationships characterized by love, mutuality, and grace. Unfortunately, such relationships often fail
to emerge for many people with developmental disabilities. Creating a circle
of support can provide one avenue for helping a person enter into relationships with others, discover their gifts and passions, recover a sense of
belonging, and become more deeply woven into their communities (Galvin,
2001; Preheim-Bartel & Neufeldt, 1986). Consider the following steps for
getting started:

1. Determine the interest of the person with disabilities (i.e., the focus per-
    son) in having a circle of support. For individuals with communication
    difficulties, it may be helpful to also talk with a caregiver or support
    provider. In addition, advertise the availability of these circles so that
    interested persons know who to approach.

2. Have one person assume primary responsibility for serving as a facilitator.
    Roles might include getting the circle started; coordinating gathering
    times; communicating with members of the circle; serving as a liaison
    between the circle and other supports; problem-solving challenges; and
    making sure the circle maintains, even as members have to come and go.

3. Together with the focus person, identify several other individuals who
    are willing to make an ongoing commitment to participate in the circle
    of support. These people can be drawn from among members of the
    congregation and from the broader community, such as a neighbor, a
    co-worker, or a support staff. At least one of the members should know
    the person well. Others might simply have an interest in getting to know
    the focus person better. In general, family members should not be part
    of the circle unless desired by the focus person.

4. With the focus person, decide on the primary purpose of the circle.
    Begin by listening to the person's hopes and aspirations for his or her
    life. Spend time getting to know him, seeking out the gifts he possesses,
    the supports he needs, and the kind of involvement he would like to
    have in his congregation and community. Ask what obstacles prevent
    this vision from becoming a reality.

5. Assist the focus person in identifying several goals and brainstorm ways
    that circle members can use the connections and resources they have to
    support him in accomplishing those goals. For example, the circle might
    identify creative approaches for including her on the church softball
    team, finding a new job in the community, volunteering at a food pantry,

attending Wednesday night services, or meeting new friends. Prioritize those goals as immediate or long-term and determine what should be accomplished first.

6. Assign primary responsibility for each of the goals to at least one member of the circle.

7. The circle of support can be the vehicle for accessing and drawing on other resources in the congregation. Help connect the person with others who are not members of the circle, but who can offer various forms of support or assistance.

> "The key word in this model is support, which does not mean taking over. In building relationships within this model of support, the concept of mutuality must be emphasized. People involved in caring for and supporting a married couple or individual need to realize early on in the relationship that they are not just giving, but they are also receiving."
>
> —Ronald Vredeveld (2001, p. 33)

8. Meet periodically to revisit goals and reassign tasks. Once every month or two is probably realistic.

9. Reflect on how involvement in the circle is affecting each member. People often share how they have been profoundly affected by the new relationships they have developed.

sider expanding your efforts to include people with developmental disabilities.

- Faith-based programs are among the largest sources of mentoring in the United States, yet children and youth with developmental disabilities rarely take part in these programs. Invite and support the participation of people with disabilities in mentoring programs, fostering relationships with adults that reinforce spiritual values, offer guidance, and present strong role models.

- Encourage your congregation to establish relationships with local group homes and other community residential providers. Discuss ways in which members of your congregation might get to know and support the community inclusion of adults with disabilities living in these settings.

- Many adults with developmental disabilities who have recently left state institutions or who live outside of their home community have little regular contact with their family members or relatives. In addition to personal visits, regularly send cards, letters, and e-mails to remind people with disabilities that you are thinking about them, especially during holidays, birthdays, and other important life events.

Relationships may take time to develop, but this is true for everyone. The key is to keep providing and nurturing opportunities for people to develop new relationships. How will you know when a person is socially connected? Ask yourself some of the following questions: *Are there people he can call late in the evening if he has a problem he needs to discuss? Are there people who will invite her to spend a holiday dinner with them? Are there people who are willing to pray with him and for him? Are there people who know when her birthday is and will make sure it is celebrated? Are there people who are seeking him out each week before and after services, noticing when he is not there and following up to find out why?* Members of your congregation can play a part in making sure the answer to each of these questions is a resounding *"Yes!"* (Gaventa, 1993).

Recreation and Leisure Activities: Having Fun with Friends

Involvement in recreation and leisure activities contributes greatly to a person's quality of life and provides the context for social interactions, friendship development, and learning of new skills. Yet, many people with developmental disabilities have few opportunities for inclusive recreation or the resources to access those opportunities. Instead, most of these individuals are involved only in activities that can best be described as solitary, sedentary, stereotypical, and/or segregated. Finding meaningful ways to include people with disabilities in enjoyable recreational and leisure activities is cited as a perennial concern of parents, support providers, and people with disabilities themselves.

In addition to activities focused on worship and spiritual nurture (e.g., prayer groups, scriptural and doctrinal studies, spiritual retreats), numerous congregational activities are designed around sports (e.g., bowling, basketball, softball, soccer leagues), leisure (e.g., scrapbooking groups, cappuccino clubs, walking groups), arts (e.g., music, drama, and painting groups), fitness (e.g., exercise, aerobics, and weight loss programs), and personal enrichment (e.g., self-help/personal growth groups, budgeting workshops, book clubs) (Dudley & Roozen, 2001). Such activities are even more prevalent in larger congregations with broader resources. These activities offer a natural place for people with disabilities to participate actively in their community and engage in recreation and leisure activities with their peers.

In addition to supporting involvement in these existing activities, consider the following ideas.

- Sponsor a Unified Sports team through your local Special Olympics program. These inclusive teams involve people with and without developmental disabilities competing as partners in events such as basketball, softball, golf, and bowling.

- Host inclusive recreational activities at your own congregation, using the facilities you already have. To include individuals with more severe disabilities, consider how you might creatively adapt recreation and sports activities (see Block, 2007; Getchell & Gagen, 2006).

- Summer camps, weekend retreats, and day trips all offer opportunities to enjoy the company and fellowship of others. Plan well in advance how you might support the inclusion of people with disabilities and select destinations that will be accessible to all participants.

- If your congregation is planning to construct a playground area or gymnasium on its property, make sure it is fully accessible for all children. The United States Access Board (www.accessboard.gov) publishes guidelines for accessible design on their website.

- Remember that most people with developmental disabilities have limited financial resources, which may hinder their participation in many recreational activities. Consider suspending or reducing registration and other related fees for people who lack the income to otherwise participate.

Congregations will want to address several common barriers that often limit the involvement of people with developmental disabilities in community recreational activities. In addition to ensuring that activities are offered in accessible locations, consider providing or arranging for transportation, offering basic information to activity sponsors, sharing strategies for supporting various levels of participation, and identifying creative avenues for extending invitations. Moreover, it may sometimes be helpful to informally

"Faith communities are also often overlooked as places to recreate and meet new people. Religious organizations often have singles groups, social action committees, environmental groups as well as many other opportunities for members to get together outside of services."

—Brian Abery and Matt Ziegler (2003, p. 13)

partner participants with and without disabilities to facilitate and support their participation in various congregational activities. For example, when David expressed an interest in joining the church basketball league, a couple of other players made sure he had a ride to practices, learned the fundamentals of his position, and joined the team out for pizza after the games.

Employment Connections and Opportunities: Finding One's Vocation

A meaningful career offers opportunities to develop new relationships, learn valuable skills, generate needed income, contribute to an organization, and build personal assets. Moreover, employment is a gateway to many other important outcomes, affecting one's residential lifestyle, educational opportunities, community involvement, self-sufficiency, and quality of life. Yet, for many youth and adults with developmental disabilities, the job outlook remains quite bleak. As many as 90% of adults with intellectual disabilities are unemployed or underemployed (President's Committee for People with Intellectual Disabilities, 2004). Moreover, only about one-quarter of young adults with autism, intellectual disabilities, and multiple disabilities were reported to be working just 2 years after leaving high school (Wagner, Newman, Cameto, & Levine, 2005). These statistics in no way reflect an inability or lack of desire to work. In fact, community businesses and organizations are finding that people with disabilities, when simply given the opportunity, are making valuable contributions in the workplace. However, several barriers hinder their introduction to and participation in the workforce, offering congregations an opportunity to respond to this pressing need. How might congregations assist in improving the employment outcomes of people with developmental disabilities?

First, consider the tremendous number of faith-based and congregation-sponsored organizations and businesses located in every community across the country, including hospitals, nursing homes, child care centers, schools, community programs, and nonprofit groups. Add to this the number of congregations and denominational offices that employ paid staff. Faith communities might simply commit to hiring a person with disabilities in their workplace. The most prominent barrier to employment for people with disabilities is not limited skills, but rather, limited willingness on the part of employers to hire them. *Are there jobs within your congregation or related programs that a person with disabilities might assume, even if only part-time? Are you willing to think creatively about how you might carve out such a job?* Remember that most employees with developmental disabilities usually have access to job-related supports, such as a job coach or personal assistant, funded by community vocational programs. Moreover, most service providers would eagerly assist you in finding ways to support the employment of the person with disabilities.

Second, congregations are rich sources of job connections because they are comprised of networks of people who work in a wide variety of different employment sectors and places of businesses. Even small congregations are likely to represent dozens of potential employment opportunities in a community. Think about all of the people who attend your congregation who own businesses and/or make hiring recommendations. Moreover, congregation members have their own personal connections in the community and may know of receptive workplaces. Each of these contacts offers an informal avenue for connecting the strengths, talents, and interests of people with disabilities with meaningful employment opportunities—most people simply need to be asked. Indeed, it is through personal connections and existing relationships that most people find their jobs. Employers may be more likely to take a chance on hiring someone who attends their same congregation. A casual conversation with a men's group leader, an announcement from the pulpit, or a brief note in the bulletin may be just enough to find a teenager with autism the job she wants assisting in a doctor's office, working with animals, or learning to be a cook.

Third, some faith communities actually provide employment assistance or services directly to members of their congregation and the wider community. Approximately one-quarter of all congregations provide— either on their own or in partnership with other congregations and faith-based agencies—employment-related outreach programs (Dudley & Roozen, 2001). People with developmental disabilities should be invited to benefit from these program efforts. In fact, research suggests that congregations may be quite willing to assist people with disabilities in finding employment (McNair & Schwartz, 1997).

Fourth, the numerous activities and programs that take place in most congregations offer an excellent context through which adolescents and young adults with disabilities might obtain initial job training experiences. Opportunities for gaining work-related experience might include working in a nursery or child care program, preparing food in the kitchen or food pantry, working with the maintenance staff, assisting in a church office, or helping teachers in children's programs. Such settings are likely to represent supportive environments within which youth and young adults can learn valuable work skills.

Finally, congregations recognize that there is a difference between finding a job and finding one's vocation. A paid job is certainly important and remains elusive for many adults with developmental disabilities. But it is a sense of calling that sustains and drives a person throughout a lifetime, imbuing meaning into their work. Congregations should offer guidance to youth and adults with and without disabilities on discerning their vocation, something that is deeper than just one's strengths and interests. Such an understanding, coupled with the connections and supports to fulfill that calling, can be the difference between a job that is eminently fulfilling and one that feels more like a prison sentence. Too often, traditional vocational placement programs focus narrowly on simply getting a person a job—sometimes any job—and fail to recognize and harness one's sense of calling.

Transportation: Navigating One's Community

Transportation remains one of the most prominent barriers to community inclusion for people with disabilities (Abeson, Bosk, Timmons, & Lazarus, 2005). Put simply, it is impossible to participate in congregational and other community activities if you cannot get there. Most people with developmental disabilities lack a driver's license, depend on support staff to drive them from one place to another (staff that often has limited availability), lack the freedom to set their own schedule, or require accessible forms of transportation. Transportation that is both reliable and accessible is essential to enabling people with disabilities to participate fully in the life of their community by going shopping, attending appointments, seeing movies, enjoying hobbies, meeting with friends, and participating in congregational activities. Recognizing this need, consider the following ways you might address the transportation needs of people with disabilities in your community.

- Establish a ride share program by compiling a list of congregation members who are willing to provide transportation to and from worship services, social events, and other activities. Determine who has vehicles that are accessible to a person using a wheelchair. In addition, find out which of these members would be willing to occasionally take a person shopping, to a movie, out to eat, or to other community events.

- Some group homes and supported living programs may have fewer staff available on weekends, making it difficult for residents to attend the congregation of their choice. Offer to pick up interested adults with disabilities each week to enable them to participate in congregational activities.

- Utilize the congregation's lift-equipped vehicles to provide transportation to people with disabilities throughout the week. Often, these vehicles sit unused during the weekdays.

- For people who travel using city paratransit services or contracted transportation, identify another person attending the event who is willing to arrive a little early or stay a little late. Sometimes, these transportation services can only provide pick-up and drop-off windows, making it important that someone is available to meet or wait with the person.

- Coordinate and communicate with family members or residential staff about transportation issues far ahead of an event. Transportation arrangements often require advance notice and can be difficult to make at the last minute.

- If you do not already have one, consider raising funds to purchase an accessible van. Having such a vehicle would not only benefit people with developmental disabilities, but also would increase the accessibility of your congregation to senior citizens or others in your community who might have physical disabilities. Several congregations—especially those that meet at different times during the week—could combine resources to purchase a lift-equipped van.

- When planning activities in the community, try to identify locations that are accessible via city bus lines.

Service Opportunities: Using Gifts for Others

Look across almost any congregation and you will find members involved in a multitude of volunteer activities within their communities. Whether an interfaith-sponsored homeless program, neighborhood food pantry, community health clinic, new parent ministry, nursing home and assisted living visitation ministry, Meals on Wheels program, community fundraiser, or Habitat for Humanity project, opportunities for serving others abound. Such contributions may engage a sense of calling, increase self-confidence and self-determination, develop social and personal skills, and expand social networks. Youth and adults who contribute to service

> "Every single person has capacities, abilities, and gifts. Living a good life depends on whether those capacities can be used, abilities expressed, and gifts given. If they are, the person will be valued, feel powerful and well-connected to the people around them. And the community around the person will be more powerful because of the contribution the person is making."
>
> —Jody Kretzmann and John McKnight (1993, p. 13)

activities also may encounter a new sense of value and respect by the community, as others come to recognize the meaningful contributions that they are making. Most importantly, such acts of service offer concrete ways for people to put their faith into action. Yet, people with developmental disabilities enjoy few opportunities to serve others; in part, because of attitudinal barriers; limited transportation; or, most likely, they are simply never asked (Miller et al., 2002; Roker, Player, & Coleman, 1998).

Congregations can help overcome these barriers by making sure that invitations to service and outreach projects are regularly extended. Often, involvement can be supported by pairing people with developmental disabilities with other volunteers who are willing to acquaint them with the service project, guide their involvement, and offer assistance as needed. In programs sponsored by your congregation, make sure volunteer coordinators are aware of the importance of involving people with disabilities, know how and where to invite new participants, and are familiar with congregational and community resources on which they can draw, if needed. For example, your congregational inclusion team (see Chapter 3) or local advocacy organizations, therapeutic recreation specialists, and parents are all potential resources who can help to brainstorm strategies for opening the doors to everyone. In addition, congregations can assist in connecting people's gifts and talents with other service opportunities within the larger community.

A Home of One's Own: Living in the Community

Recent legislation and advocacy efforts are expanding community living possibilities for adults with developmental disabilities. Public policy is shifting away from institutional and congregate living and moving toward living situations that are typical of how others in a community live. Whereas people with developmental disabilities once resided primarily in institutions, the recent trend has been toward residing in smaller group homes or purchasing a place of their own. Despite this progress, more than 125,000 people with developmental disabilities are still waiting to receive residential supports in their community (Coucouvanis, Prouty, & Lakin, 2005). Faith communities can help make community living a reality by offering support to people as they return to their neighborhoods.

- Many congregations, denominations, and faith-based organizations already operate residential programs that include group homes or supported living programs (i.e., a person with disabilities shares a place with one or two roommates without disabilities). Others may financially sponsor or otherwise support these religiously affiliated living options. Such programs can ensure that people with developmental disabilities have the option of choosing a place to live where staff will support—and may even share—their values, faith commitments, and religious traditions.

- Congregations can play an instrumental role in supporting people with disabilities who are transitioning out of state institutions and other large-scale congregate facilities and back into life in the community. For example, a congregation might commit to "adopting" people moving out of an institution, ensuring that they are welcomed as they enter a new community and connected with needed resources and relationships (see Carlson, 2004).

> "Faith communities are now called to embrace a new resettlement model. Citizens with disabilities who were, many years ago, removed from their communities and admitted to state-run institutions, are now being given the opportunity to return to their home communities and build new and more hopeful lives."
>
> —Mary Carlson (2004, p.5)

- Some congregations offer housing assistance to individuals who demonstrate financial need. Because the financial resources of many adults with developmental disabilities are extremely limited and cost is a major barrier to home ownership, congregations might decide to offer down payment or closing cost assistance.

- Ask adults with developmental disabilities and/or their support providers about their material needs. With their permission, compile a list and share it with a group within your congregation, asking them to facilitate meeting these identified needs. For example, a Sunday school class or youth group could purchase or gather donations of furniture, appliances, household supplies, and other material resources for people with disabilities moving into a home of their own. Many congregations undertake similar initiatives for single parents, refugees or new immigrants, and former prisoners.

- Identify individuals within your congregation who are skilled in different aspects of home maintenance and are willing to share their talents. For example, some congregations have developed home repair or auto mechanic ministries, serving single parents, the elderly, and others in financial distress. The occasional contributions of this group might be influential in enabling people with disabilities to live more independently in their community.

- Careful budgeting and financial planning are important aspects of maintaining one's own home. Many congregations offer budgeting and financial workshops to assist members to be better stewards of their money. Consider how you might involve youth and adults with disabilities in these valuable learning opportunities. As you invite people to participate, recognize that the materials that are typically part of such programs will likely need to be adapted. In addition, conversations may need to take place with family members or support staff who are familiar with the specific government benefits, incentives, and programs the person receives.

> "It is almost as easy to ignore someone across a big suburban lawn and behind some well-placed shrubbery as it is behind the wrought-iron fence of a developmental center."
>
> —Paul Leichty (2003, p. 10)

- Congregations should advocate for accessible, affordable, and inclusive housing options in their local community. Partner with area housing coalitions to identify existing needs and potential avenues for serving as a voice for change.

Congregations must work to ensure that *living in the community* speaks not only of people's physical location but also describes their relationships with others. Many people live in a community but remain detached from all of the personal relationships and meaningful activities that give that community life. Efforts to support a person to live in a neighborhood should be coupled with

> "Being *in* a community is not the same as being *part of* a community."
>
> —Robert Bogdan and Steven Taylor (2001, p. 192)

efforts to make sure he or she feels welcomed, socially connected, and valued.

Religious Education: Growing in Faith

Each year, almost four and a half million children and youth attend more than 22,000 religiously affiliated private schools in the United States (Broughmann & Pugh, 2004). Many parents choose these schools because they desire an education for their children consistent with their values and faith commitments. Although many faith-based schools are making considerable strides to address the educational and spiritual needs of children and youth with disabilities within their classrooms, these efforts often only include students with learning disabilities. As a result, parents find that they are left with few options for religious education for their children with developmental disabilities. When private schools do choose to serve students with developmental disabilities, they generally offer only separate programs where students are educated apart from their classmates without disabilities.

Does your congregation operate or support a private school for children and youth? What is the mission of the school? Does this mission include children and youth with developmental disabilities? Religious schools should carefully examine the extent to which they are meeting the educational needs of families of children with disabilities within their faith communities. As you explore ways in which you might serve students with disabilities, realize that numerous resources are available to guide you. For example, religious schools might draw on the resources, professional development opportunities, and expertise of public schools when serving children with special education needs (see Eigenbrood, 2004, 2005). In addition, articles and resources addressing topics related to inclusion are appearing with increasing frequency in religious educational journals, books, and curricula, suggesting growing recognition of the importance of providing inclusive religious education. Moreover, numerous professional organizations offer resources on inclusive education upon which you can draw (e.g., Council for Exceptional Children, National Association of Christians in Special Education, TASH; see Appendix B).

SUPPORTING FAMILIES: AREAS AND OPPORTUNITIES

Almost 30% of all families in the United States—approximately 20.9 million families—have at least one relative who experiences some type of disability (Wong, 2005). A child with a disability can impact a family in substantial ways. The presence of a "disability, like a rock thrown into a pond, has repercussions that reverberate through the elements and routines of the family's life" (Hanson & Lynch, 2004, pp. 92–93). Families should not have to meet the challenges of raising a child with disabilities without the love, care, and support of their congregation. Congregations must commit to standing alongside parents in raising their children with disabilities, just as they do for all other parents.

How might your congregation support families of children with disabilities? What actions can be taken to ensure that families feel welcome and supported in your congregation? What supports would allow families to become more deeply involved in congregational life? In other aspects of community life? The remainder of this chapter offers avenues through which your congregation might address the needs of families with disabilities. Of course, every family is different and parents should be asked about the supports they need and would like to receive. By truly investing in the lives of families with disabilities, you should be able to learn the needs of a family without having to guess.

> "Martha Bess came to the hospital and she said the very best thing that somebody can say to somebody in our situation which was, she just picked up Rob and held him and said, 'We will love this child.' There were no conditions attached. There...was no specialness about him, other than he is special because he is a child."
>
> —Glenn Funk, as cited in Haythorn, T. (2003, p. 195)

Respite Care

Raising any child has its difficult times, but the unique demands associated with caring for a child with developmental or other disabilities can pose additional challenges to parents. Respite care is designed to provide a much-needed break to parents, allowing them to attend to the needs of other family members, be present at medical and educational appointments, run errands, re-energize themselves while pursuing personal interests, maintain involvement in community activities, or enjoy a night out alone with a spouse. Moreover, respite care can allow parents to be involved in congregational activities and ministries in which they might not otherwise have been able to participate, such as a potluck dinner, prayer meeting, planning committee, outreach event, choir practice, or parent support groups. For the exhausted parent who frequently shuttles a child from one doctor to another, struggles to balance the needs of one child with those of siblings, or avoids going out altogether because it is too difficult to find a babysitter, respite care can offer a brief sabbatical from the challenges of raising a child with disabilities. More than three-quarters of parents affirm that respite care would improve their family's well-being (Abelson, 1999). Unfortunately, such care is usually available inconsistently or not at all. More than half of respite care programs report having waiting lists, and many have to turn families away altogether (ARCH National Respite Network, 2001). Furthermore, respite services are expensive and typically are provided by professionals who may not be well-known by families.

Congregations are using a variety of creative approaches to offer respite opportunities to families. First, respite can be provided informally and on an individual basis to families. This might involve having a person come to the family's home to watch their child. For example, members of a high school youth group or adults from a Sunday school class may commit to being available to families on a periodic basis. Or, congregations may choose to identify a core group of "host families" who are willing to welcome children with disabilities into their home for short periods of time. Still others compile an "emergency list" that includes individuals within the congregation who are willing to provide respite care on a short notice.

> "Her recent divorce forced Miriam back into the workplace to support her family. But the only available day care for Angela—her youngest daughter who had cerebral palsy—was a half day. When the Baptist women's group at Miriam's church learned of her problem, five mothers who did not work outside their homes each volunteered to babysit Angela one afternoon a week. The women's kindness was a blessing and needed support for Miriam. It gave five families a chance to know and love her daughter."
>
> —North American Mission Board (2000, p. 1)

Second, congregations can infuse respite opportunities into existing programs and activities. By expanding preschool programs, child care services, Vacation Bible School, summer camps, and weekend retreat activities to include and accommodate all children, parents will gain access to many of the existing respite opportunities *already* available to other families with children in the congregation. For example, congregations offering "morning out" programs for parents or child care for congregational events should be more intentional about stating that children with disabilities are encouraged to attend. Basic information and training can be provided to volunteers to ensure that they feel prepared to welcome these children. Another small, but meaningful, gesture of respite is to identify someone who periodically will watch a child with disabilities for a few minutes before or after worship services so that parents have a chance to catch up with friends.

Third, respite care can be offered more formally as a stand-alone activity open to additional families of children with disabilities in the broader community. For example, a congregation may offer evening respite activities weekly, biweekly, or monthly, providing several hours of time that parents can use to take care of errands, enjoy a date, reconnect with friends, or reenergize themselves in other ways. Respite care activities are usually provided in the congregation's gymnasium or children's area and volunteers often are drawn from among students involved in high school youth groups, local college students, and/or adults from the congregation. Participating children are provided snacks and recreational activities, which might include a movie night, games, crafts, and other fun activities. This serves as a powerful outreach to families in your neighborhood and city.

Fourth, volunteers from several congregations might join together to provide various respite offerings, either rotating activities across congregations or holding them consistently at the most accessible location. Or, they may host a respite co-op for families (Hoecke & Mayfield-Smith, 2000). Moreover, instead of hosting their own respite activities, congregations might choose to encourage their members to volunteer with local organizations that already are providing occasional respite care, such

> "Initially, the thought of asking for help filled us with apprehension. When Pastor Bill spoke to our congregation and asked for volunteers, I was sure the sign-up sheet would stay empty. Then we found out that 12 families had volunteered! We were relieved and filled with joy; we were being heard and understood instead of being judged. Just knowing that other people were willing to help did a lot to make us feel better about ourselves as a family...."
>
> —Teri Mika (1995, p. 43)

> "The people from a congregation who provide respite care while parents with [a child with autism] have a rest are just as much ministers as the chaplain who sits and prays with a family while a baby with hydrocephalis has an operation to have shunts put in. Each level of the institutional church and each person within it may have a contribution to make and each level is in a unique position to enable ministry and service."
>
> —Ellen Cook (1998, pp. 18–19)

as the Arc, Easter Seals, or United Cerebral Palsy (see Appendix B). These programs often struggle to find consistent volunteers and would welcome contributions from your congregation.

When designing respite care activities, use the steps outlined in Table 5.1 to guide your efforts. In addition, the following strategies should be considered.

- When initially planning respite activities, engage in conversations with parents to ensure that your efforts will be provided in ways that address real needs in your congregation and wider community.

- Draw on the resources of local agencies and service providers for help with designing your program or providing any needed training for volunteers (see *Potential Community Partners* in Chapter 3). What type of training will volunteers require? Most will simply need general information about the participating children, ideas for activities they can engage in together, and tips for interacting with children who may communicate and participate in different ways.

- Think proactively about how to ensure the safety of all participating children. Develop an initial set of safety and emergency procedures and continually refine them. Conversations with other community

Table 5.1.   Steps for creating respite opportunities for families of children with disabilities through your congregation

1. Identify a core group of people committed to prayerfully designing and organizing respite opportunities through your congregation.
2. Identify a dedicated, passionate, and organized person willing to coordinate respite activities.
3. Determine potential interest among families within and beyond your congregation and identify which avenues for respite care families prefer.
4. Seek out advice and recommendations from existing community respite providers, including other congregations offering similar outreach ministries.
5. Address logistical issues, such as where respite care will be provided, what activities will take place for children, how volunteers will be recruited and trained, potential costs, emergency plans, and procedural and liability issues.
6. Recruit volunteers from within your congregation and/or other partner congregations. Consider youth groups and college programs as a source of volunteers.
7. Train volunteers by drawing upon the expertise and guidance of professionals within your congregation and from local service providers who already serve people with developmental disabilities.
8. Implement the respite care activities; start small and grow strategically.
9. Spread the word about your efforts and celebrate the impact they are having on families, children, and volunteers.
10. Periodically evaluate and, if necessary, realign your efforts to meet changing needs among families in your community.

Sources: Gaventa (1990); Hoecke & Mayfield-Smith (2000); Pierson (2002); Van Dyken (1995).

respite providers will assist you in determining what form these procedures should initially take. For example, you will need to consider
issues such as volunteer screening and supervision. In addition, contact your congregation's legal counsel and/or insurance provider to
better understand safety and liability considerations.

- To feel comfortable leaving their children with you, parents will want
  assurance that someone is trained to respond to unique situations that
  may arise. For children who are medically fragile or who have special
  health care needs, it may be essential that someone be present who has
  received training in first aid, CPR, feeding procedures, and/or changing routines. In such cases, perhaps a health care professional attending your congregation will volunteer to help.

- Congregational respite care programs often begin with great enthusiasm, but can gradually diminish over time as volunteers find themselves exhausted or "burned out." Listen to your volunteers; ask for
  their feedback and respond to their concerns. Most importantly, publicly recognize and celebrate the efforts of these volunteers before the
  rest of the congregation.

Spiritual and Emotional Support

A mother hearing a new diagnosis wrestles with decisions concerning
services and placement; a brother struggles to understand why his sibling
with Down syndrome occupies so much of his parents' time; a sister feels
exhausted from the new responsibilities
of taking care of her older brother with
autism after her parents have died; a
father is frustrated with the roadblocks
he encounters trying to navigate the
service system; a family nervously
launches their adolescent with disabilities into adulthood. These struggles cry
out for a response from communities of
faith. Congregations should be a place

> "We trust in our church communi-
> ties to bear us up during the diffi-
> cult portions of our journeys,
> providing practical support, prayer
> support, listening ears, shoulders
> to cry on, or perhaps just an affirm-
> ing word. We also trust in our com-
> munities to share and celebrate the
> joys of our lives."
>
> —Kathleen Bolduc (2001, p. 24)

on which families should be able to lean for support—both from individual members and corporately. In fact, research has shown that religious
beliefs and the informal and formal supports provided within congregations can have a powerful influence on families' quality of life (e.g., Marshall et al., 2003; Miltiades & Pruchno, 2002; Poston & Turnbull, 2004).
Many parents find their faith to be a critical source of support and view

their congregations as an important context through which that support is dispensed.

Much more than cliché responses, families need genuine support that meets real needs. There can be enormous variation in the ways that families are affected by the presence of disabilities. Some families may feel overwhelmed by the multiple and often competing demands made on their time and energy, whereas others may encounter a strong network of support. Some families may feel isolated from relatives, friends, and neighbors, whereas others feel tightly embraced and supported by these individuals. Some families may articulate feelings of loss, fear, guilt, anger, or sadness, whereas others express a sense of acceptance and appreciation. To minister effectively to families, you have to invest time seeking to understand their needs. Then, commit to generously dispensing presence, prayer, encouragement, friendship, and support.

Congregations also should understand that a family's need for encouragement and support might be especially salient during certain periods of transition, including when 1) first discovering the presence of a disability; 2) their child initially enters the school system and the family has to learn to navigate a new system of services; 3) their adolescent begins preparing for life after high school; and 4) aging parents come to recognize that they are no longer able to provide direct care to their child (Pierson, 2002; Turnbull, Turnbull, Erwin, & Soodak, 2006). Remember that disability is only one challenge that families might be experiencing. Other issues also affect families—regardless of disability—including poverty, marital discord, job loss, substance abuse, and loss of a family member. A congregation should be a place to which a family can turn with *all* of their support needs, not just those related to a disability.

> "Local congregations have the human resources to say 'yes' to families directly. 'Yes—someone will care enough to share the journey, to struggle with questions that have no immediate answers, to find a way for a person [with intellectual disabilities] to be an equal and functioning part of the believing community.'"
>
> —Ellen Cook (1998, p. 19)

Supportive Groups

Many congregations host or facilitate support groups that provide companionship to and connections among people traveling similar life paths or wrestling with common concerns, such as grief, divorce, adoption, disease, substance abuse, or career transitions. These groups offer a safe and supportive environment for people to exchange encouragement, companionship, and information with others sharing a similar faith commitment. For parents of children with developmental disabilities, a support group can be an invaluable resource by reducing parents' sense of isolation, providing a place for mutual support to be exchanged, and connecting people with empathetic ears, understanding, practical advice, information about local services and supports, and prayer support (e.g., Solomon, Pistrang, & Barker, 2001). Congregations can offer meeting space for these events to take place, provide child care, and even offer a facilitator. Unfortunately, relatively few congregations appear to offer such groups. Table 5.2 describes strategies for beginning such a group in your congregation.

Amidst the attention devoted to providing for the needs of children with developmental disabilities and their families, the needs of siblings sometimes get overlooked. Brothers and sisters may experience a range of bewildering emotions—struggling to find focused time with their parents; wondering whether they will have to take care of their siblings when they are older; or wanting support, information, and advice from their peers in similar situations (Gallagher, Powell, & Rhodes, 2006; McHugh, 2002;

Table 5.2.   Steps for starting a support group for families of children with disabilities

1. Identify someone who has the time and gifts required to organize, schedule, and maintain the group.
2. Talk with leaders of other support groups within your congregation and community to seek their advice on starting and sustaining a group. Numerous support groups already exist, so there is no need to reinvent the wheel (see Klein, 2000).
3. Identify several members of your congregation willing to commit to attending until the group gets off the ground. Continuity is often important in helping people to open up.
4. Establish an initial format for your group, considering how often you will meet, how long sessions will last, and how many people will be invited. For example, several congregations might decide to work together to establish a single group of five to seven parents that meets monthly.
5. With other group members, establish some initial ground rules for discussions, especially around issues of confidentiality. Revisit these guidelines periodically as concerns arise.
6. A strong facilitator is a critical element of a successful group. Identify a person who is sensitive, has a gift for drawing people out, can keep the conversation positive, and is comfortable enforcing the group's ground rules.
7. Your time together could involve inviting guest speakers to talk about various topics (e.g., parenting, community services, futures planning) discussing concerns of members, exchanging ideas, or sharing stories, successes, and challenges.
8. Create a comfortable environment—physically and socially—where members can share freely without interruption or reluctance. Snacks and coffee are always well-received.
9. Provide child care for group members by drawing upon the efforts of youth or college-age groups.
10. Promote your group through announcements in your congregation's bulletin and notify other congregations, community organizations, parent groups, and schools.

Meyer, 2004). Creating opportunities for children to meet and spend time with others who have siblings with disabilities may offer another avenue through which congregations can offer support. For example, congregations may serve as host to a Sibshop (www.thearc.org/siblingsupport), sponsor a panel discussion of siblings, or make other efforts to connect siblings with mentors or other relationships.

Providing Resources and Informational Support

Information can be powerful. Congregations can compile and share informational resources (e.g., books, magazines, newsletters) and offer educational opportunities addressing raising children and building strong families. Make sure that your congregation's library includes resources and information about people with disabilities (see Appendix B). Consider subscribing to periodicals such as *Exceptional Parent* or denominational magazines and newsletters (e.g., *Breaking Barriers*, Christian Reformed Church; *Breakthrough*, Bethesda Lutheran Homes; *Special Education Newsletter*, Jewish Education Service of North America; *Special Education Today*, Southern Baptist Convention). Partner with other congregations to create your own lending library or donate faith-based materials to local parent resource centers. Finally, consider collaborating with other congregations to develop directories or lists of local, statewide, and national faith-based service providers affiliated with your denomination or similar faith traditions. Compiling such information can help parents navigate more easily an often disconnected and confusing service system.

Financial Support

The medical and service needs associated with raising some children with disabilities and special health care needs can be financially overwhelming. Congregations can respond by raising money for special equipment, supplies, therapies, or services not covered by insurance or other funding sources. Identify the needs that exist in your congregation and solicit donations of items from families, schools, and local organizations. For example, a resource exchange board would benefit everyone in your congregation, providing a forum for connecting needs with available resources. Gestures of support need not be expensive. Recognizing the stresses experienced by some families, a congregation might surprise parents by offering a night of respite for parents at a nice hotel, periodic cleaning or cooking services, or financial support and respite care to attend a weekend retreat (Pierson, 2002).

Relationships

Many parents or family members of individuals with disabilities share that they feel isolated and disconnected. Others in the congregation may be unsure of what to say or uncertain of how to interact with their child or sibling. Often, this reluctance translates into silence. One of the most important responses your congregation can make is simply to take initiative to establish new and maintain existing social relationships.

Pastoral Counseling

Many people turn to their clergy and congregational staff when they are struggling and need support and counseling. Yet, parents of children with disabilities often find the response from their clergy to be wanting. In a survey of 233 parents of children with developmental disabilities, almost half reported that the social support of religious leaders was not available to them (Herman & Thompson, 1995). Most of the other parents felt this source of support was only sometimes helpful. Take steps to ensure that those who provide counseling in your congregation feel equipped to minister to families with disabilities. For example, some congregations offer specific training for lay care providers, such as Stephen Ministries or parish nurses. Direct these people to resources, workshops, and organizations that offer support and training in this aspect of ministry. Once clergy feel equipped, make sure that parents know that it is okay to approach their leadership about issues related to raising a child or supporting a sibling with disabilities.

CONCLUSION

Numerous opportunities await congregations desiring to make a real difference in the lives of people with disabilities and their families. As you explore new avenues of hospitality and ministry, be assured that the benefits will be mutual; as people share their gifts with people with disabilities they rarely emerge unchanged. Through the avenues described in this chapter, you will benefit from having the opportunity—perhaps your first—to get to know and come to love children and adults with developmental and other disabilities. When you do encounter needs that you cannot address on your own, partner with other congregations to craft a meaningful response. If other congregations are already offering supports that you are unable to provide, make sure you are directing people with disabilities and their families to those communities. However, be careful that your only ministry is not solely one of referral; your congregation is also called to respond personally.

Chapter 6

The Contributions
of Service Providers

Supporting Spiritual Expression

It has been more than 3 years since Mark moved out of a large state institution and into a comfortable home that he shares with a housemate. Because Mark has significant cognitive disabilities and is unable to speak, he receives ongoing assistance from direct support staff funded through a local residential program. Since moving back into the community, Mark has received support from four different weekend staff people. The first was a fairly pious woman who brought Mark to the local Presbyterian church twice on Sunday—once in the morning and again in the evening. She knew the congregation to be very welcoming and she just assumed that Mark held similar beliefs and traditions. The second was somewhat antagonistic to religion and immediately stopped taking Mark to church. After all, she thought, it really isn't appropriate for her to be involved in anything religious, anyway. The third was very involved in her own faith community, but it never really crossed her mind that Mark might want similar involvement for himself, and so Mark remained at home on the weekends. Since November, however, Mark has been faithfully attending a local synagogue. This came about because his new support staff person took the time to contact a distant relative and discovered that Mark had always enjoyed attending synagogue services as a youth. She even arranged for several members of the synagogue to take him to services each week.

The services and supports provided to people with developmental disabilities should increase their presence in the community, help them assume valued roles, cultivate their gifts and strengths, champion their preferences, and enhance their full participation and sense of belonging (O'Brien & Mount, 2005). As described in Chapter 1, values surrounding supporting the personal aspirations, community inclusion, natural relationships, self-determination, and quality of life of people must be at the core of what service providers do. Recognizing and honoring the spiritual needs and strengths of people with developmental disabilities is entirely consistent with each of these values. Indeed, overlooking this dimension of people's lives runs counter to these principles. Put simply, the spiritual support needs of people with developmental disabilities should be considered right alongside educational, vocational, residential, recreational, social, behavioral, and other support needs (AAMR/The Arc, 2002; TASH, 2003).

Yet, service providers often struggle to navigate this important dimension of people's lives. *How do I discover what brings meaning, joy, and inspiration to a person's life, especially someone who has difficulty communicating in the usual ways? What does it even look like to support someone in exploring and expressing his or her spirituality? How do I figure out what help a person will need to participate meaningfully in congregational life? Is this even my role? After all, isn't faith a private matter? Shouldn't someone else take responsibility for making sure these needs are being addressed?* Supporting the spiritual expression and faith commitments of people with developmental disabilities raises important questions that require thoughtful consideration. For Mark, these questions were ignored for too long. Most of his support staff never invested the time to find out what was most important to Mark.

> "Everyone has the right to freedom of thought, conscience and religion; this right includes freedom to change his religion or belief, and freedom, either alone or in community with others and in public or private, to manifest his religion or belief in teaching, practice, worship, and observance."
>
> —United Nations General Assembly (1948)

If truly committed to promoting full community participation, self-determination, and quality of life, the spiritual and religious needs and strengths of people with developmental disabilities and their families must be on the agenda of service and support providers. This chapter highlights the importance of supporting all of the preferences and aspirations of people with disabilities, including those related to faith and spirituality. Several strategies exist for discerning the preferences people have in these areas, as well as the supports needed to enable this expression. Connecting people with the faith communities of their choice requires serious reflection and thoughtful planning. To do this well, organizations and agencies must develop meaningful policies and establish rela-

> "Although the field of mental retardation and developmental disabilities embraces a commitment to full societal inclusion, the supports available to achieve such inclusion may be inconsistent when it comes to participation in religious life."
>
> —Jeannine Vogel, Edward Polloway, and David Smith (2006, p.105)

tionships that support the religious expression of those individuals whom they serve.

CONTRIBUTIONS OF SERVICE AND SUPPORT PROVIDERS

Most Americans decide on their own whether and how they wish to explore and express their spirituality. So, why might service providers become involved in this very personal aspect of the lives of people with developmental disabilities? In part, the answer lies in the very prominent role that they play in the lives of many individuals with developmental disabilities and their families. People with developmental disabilities have received this particular label because of their need for individualized and coordinated services and supports to participate fully in the life of their communities. For some people, the involvement of service providers will be occasional and slight. For many others, their involvement will be lasting and quite extensive. When people's lives are dominated by paid service providers to the virtual exclusion of other relationships, the silence of staff in this area often leads to this important dimension of life remaining unaddressed.

Service providers might include residential staff, case managers, respite providers, social workers, rehabilitation counselors, job coaches, educators, counselors, therapists, health care professionals, or other specialists. Of course, the roles each assumes in the lives of people with developmental disabilities and their families varies widely. And so, their interactions around issues of faith and spirituality also will each look different. In some cases, understanding the spiritual needs, strengths, and resources held by people and their families may enhance the design of service plans, making them more relevant, valued, and effective. For example, a counselor might explore relationships and sources of strength that can assist someone in coping with a new diagnosis, a health care practitioner might seek to understand how the spiritual beliefs of parents influence their care decisions, or a special education team might draw on the informal supports and connections within a youth's congregation when designing a comprehensive transition plan (e.g., Nangle, 2001; Poston & Turnbull, 2004; Speraw, 2006). Indeed, professionals across many different disciplines are acknowledging the benefits of considering the spirituality, religious beliefs, and informal supports of the people whom they serve, whether or not they have a disability. In other cases, service providers may be more directly involved in supporting people to explore or express their spirituality. For example, residential staff may accompany someone to weekly worship services, a physical therapist might provide services to a student attending a church-sponsored elementary school, or a job coach might work with a faith-based organization to develop jobs for people with disabilities (e.g., Butterworth, Hagner, Helm, & Whelley, 2000; Eigenbrood, 2005). Sometimes service providers directly deliver these supports themselves; other times, they make introductions and referrals to someone who is better equipped to provide the supports a person needs.

The involvement of service providers in providing spiritual supports also will look different across the age span. For children and youth with disabilities, families and caregivers usually take primary responsibility for ensuring that their children have the opportunities and supports they need to discover and grow in their faith. As children enter adulthood, however, they should assume a more central role in decision making and planning. Thus, service providers should expect to work more directly with adults with disabilities to ensure that their preferences are

> "When a community service provider says, 'We cannot address faith or religion because we are funded by the state,' they are simply wrong. The question is how you do so, not whether."
> —Bill Gaventa (2005, p. 51)

sought out and well-supported. Finally, the roles that service providers assume also will be influenced by their program's unique mission. For example, staff at private, religiously affiliated organizations may provide spiritual supports somewhat differently than would publicly funded agencies.

AVENUES OF EXPRESSION

What does it mean to address someone's spiritual needs or to support them in their faith journey? Spirituality can be expressed in a wide variety of ways—expect to hear a different answer from everyone you ask. For some, spirituality is nurtured through involvement in a local congregation—attending worship services, going to Sunday school, serving on committees, or contributing to ministry activities. It might involve studying the scriptures, praying with friends, visiting those who are sick, or attending religious celebrations. For others, it is expressed primarily in times of private devotions, prayer, or reflection. Even within the same religious tradition, denomination, or congregation, two people may understand and express their faith in very different ways. Sometimes, spirituality is articulated apart from involvement in organized religion. People may find purpose and hope through relationships with friends, service to their community, encounters with nature, quiet contemplation, and creative expressions. Moreover, the things that bring meaning to people's lives can deepen or change over time; the importance people attach to these expressions is rarely static. You should expect to see the same spiritual diversity among people with developmental disabilities as is evident in the rest of society.

RELUCTANCE OF SERVICE PROVIDERS

Faith and spirituality clearly are important in the lives of many people with developmental disabilities (see Gaventa & Coulter, 2002; National Organization on Disability/Harris Interactive, 2004; Schulz, 2005; Swinton & Powrie, 2004; Webb-Mitchell, 1993; Zhang & Rusch, 2005). However, the extent to which they find meaningful expression can be influenced greatly by the opportunities and supports provided to people with disabilities. Many service providers express uncertainly about their role in supporting this dimension of people's lives, and so the spiritual and religious support needs of people with developmental disabilities are often left unaddressed. The explanations offered for this omission can vary:

- I never really thought about it.

- It is not relevant to this population of people.

- It is not my responsibility to address it.

- I do not have time to address it.

- I feel uncomfortable addressing it.

- I do not know how to address it.

- I am not permitted to address it.

- Someone else is addressing it.

Certainly, tensions arise when it comes to supporting another person's personal choices. How do you find out what a person really wants for himself or herself? How do you support someone in making choices about an issue with which you have very little familiarity? How do you support decisions that you personally disagree with or would not make for yourself? How do you offer meaningful guidance without imposing your own values? How do you proceed when someone's preferences are not entirely clear? These are very real concerns that staff may hold; but they are not unique to issues of spirituality. After all, service providers are charged with providing supports around many issues of deep importance, including social relationships, sexuality, politics, personal care, and even decisions about how to spend leisure time (Ban-

> "It is as legitimate to find out whether someone would like to go to church and to take them there as it is to inquire about an interest in going swimming and to take them to the pool."
>
> —Tom Hoeksema (1995, p. 292)

nerman, Sheldon, Sherman, & Harchik, 1990; Hingsburger & Tough, 2002). Society has a long history of failing to recognize the preferences and empower the choices of people with developmental disabilities. *We can and must do better.* In some cases, questions just need to be asked, perhaps for the first time. In other cases, determining people's true preferences will be hard work. Still, we must learn to seek out, listen to, and support the preferences of the people with disabilities.

IDENTIFYING SPIRITUAL PREFERENCES, STRENGTHS, AND SUPPORT NEEDS

A meaningful life is determined individually by each person. For some people, religious faith and congregational participation are absolutely integral to their lives. For others, purpose is found elsewhere, apart from involvement in a specific faith community. And so, supporting a meaningful life begins with identifying each person's aspirations and the supports and opportunities he or she will need to pursue these goals. Informal conversations about people's preferences can take place at any time. Listening carefully to people's stories, learning about their lives, and finding out what they want for themselves is just good practice. Conversations about spiritual issues often happen naturally when people spend lots of time together. These interactions are perfectly fitting for exploring such issues. At the same time, there also are good reasons to be more intentional about considering this aspect of people's lives.

First, the spiritual and religious needs of people with developmental disabilities, especially those individuals who require more extensive supports, often are overlooked. To illustrate, a study by Minnes, Buell, Feldman, McColl, and McCreary (2002) revealed that almost two-thirds of service providers indicated that spiritual activity was not applicable to the adults with developmental disabilities whom they supported. Less than one-quarter of these caregivers indicated that the spiritual needs of adults with disabilities had been identified and supported through involvement in the community. Moreover, a glance at tools designed to assess community integration, support needs, or to determine how satisfied people with disabilities are with services reveals that they rarely address the area of spirituality. Of those that do, items typically only ask about attendance at congregational activities, rather than exploring a broader range of potential spiritual expressions. Unless thoughtful consideration of spiritual needs already is well integrated into your existing planning processes and routine service practices, it may be necessary to be a bit more deliberate about this issue.

Second, for various reasons, people may not initiate conversations about this issue on their own. Many people with developmental disabilities have speech and language impairments or communicate using alternative methods. They may experience difficulties expressing their preferences in ways that are clearly understandable to staff. Others have been given few opportunities to explore spiritual practices and, absent such past experiences, they may not know what support to ask for. Some people may even be unsure that their support providers are willing to talk with them about this aspect of their lives. Thus, silence on this topic should not automatically be interpreted as disinterest. Asking thoughtful questions can sometimes start new conversations; or, it can help you determine when a person is just not interested in these issues.

Third, knowing a person well is essential to providing quality services and supports that enhance his or her quality of life. When you understand the beliefs and relationships people draw on for strength, their sense of calling or purpose in the world, the gifts they possess and wish to share, and the ways in which they view and relate to others, you can do a much better job of designing supports and creating opportunities that incorporate these values. What is most important to the people whom you support? What contributions do they want to make to their community? How do they understand their place in the world? In what ways do they wish to express their beliefs and commitments? Do not assume that these questions are irrelevant or unimportant to someone just because someone has a label of developmental disabilities.

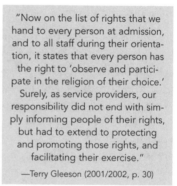

"Now on the list of rights that we hand to every person at admission, and to all staff during their orientation, it states that every person has the right to 'observe and participate in the religion of their choice.' Surely, as service providers, our responsibility did not end with simply informing people of their rights, but had to extend to protecting and promoting those rights, and facilitating their exercise."

—Terry Gleeson (2001/2002, p. 30)

General Guidelines

There are many ways to identify the spiritual needs and strengths of people with developmental disabilities, as well as the avenues through which they would like to contribute to congregational life and the supports they will need to do so fully. Before discussing these approaches, it may be helpful to consider some general guidelines.

Personalize Supports   Every person is different. A common disability label does not mean that people with developmental disabilities all desire the same expressions of spirituality. Individualization must always guide assessment and planning. What is important to Juan? What does his faith mean to him? How does he wish to express it? The challenge for service providers is to suspend their own assumptions about what forms spirituality should take and instead seek to discover the desires of the people whom they support (see Box 6.1).

Be Respectful   Strive to create an atmosphere in which people feel comfortable talking about issues that are important to them. The topic of spirituality is one that should always be approached respectfully and with permission; it requires the same sensitivity given to other personal issues. If someone prefers not to talk about this aspect of his or her life with you, respect that choice. Perhaps they feel more comfortable talking with someone else. Spiritual issues also will be more important to some people than others. On the other hand, do not automatically assume that these issues are unimportant without asking.

Consider Your Own Commitments   When given the opportunity to support people with developmental disabilities in pursuing things that are important to them, it is essential that you reflect carefully on your own beliefs, values, and biases. What brings meaning to your own life? What preconceived ideas do you have about what role spirituality should play in the lives of people with disabilities? Why do you react to this issue in the ways that you do? Such reflection can help ensure that you are supporting people's preferences, rather than projecting your own expectations.

Move Beyond When and Where   Your goal should be to do more than just find out which congregation a person would like to attend and how often. What does Sarah want her church involvement to look like? In which other activities might she like to participate? What spiritual practices and traditions does she want to engage in at home or elsewhere? What supports and relationships will she need to make these things happen? Questions such as these should lead to a clear plan for how each person will be supported in this, as well as every other, area of his or her life.

Understand that Expressions of Faith Can Change   It is not uncommon for people at different times in their life to decide to attend a new congregation, deepen (or lessen) their involvement, discover new callings and spiritual connections, or even radically change their faith commitments. Faith can grow, stagnate, or disappear altogether. Therefore, the support needs of people with developmental disabilities should be revisited peri-

Box 6.1
Offering Real Choices

Agencies and organizations increasingly are learning how to design services and supports that enable people with developmental disabilities to live self-determined lives. Essential to this movement is a commitment to provide people with opportunities to make meaningful choices about what they want for their lives. But, not all choices are the same. Many situations that are given the label of choice more closely reflect the decisions of staff, rather than the preferences of people with disabilities. Table 6.1 offers just a few examples of when a "choice" really is not a choice. Make sure that the services and supports you provide truly reflect the aspirations of people with developmental disabilities.

Table 6.1.   Examples of when a "choice" is not really a choice

Reason	Example
Never asked	At the time she first moved to her apartment, Audrey was not attending worship services. In the 5 years since, Audrey's support staff have never asked her if she would like to visit a local congregation.
Limited choices	Having grown up attending a Lutheran Church, Jeremy is frustrated that, due to staffing patterns, his only two options are to attend the same church as his housemate or to stay at home on Sunday mornings.
Choices without support	Kimberly has expressed a desire to continue attending her local synagogue, but the weekend group home staff person has stated that he is unwilling to accompany Kimberly to morning services.
Choices without information	When planning activities for the week, Fong's support staff asked him if he wants to go to a potluck sponsored by a local nondenominational church. Unsure of exactly what a *potluck* was, Fong said no.
Static choices	Over the past couple of years, most of Cheryl's friends have stopped attending First Congregational Church. Because she has multiple disabilities, she is unable to clearly express her desire to find a new congregation. Unfortunately, she is never asked by staff whether she would like to visit a different church.
Artificial choices	On mornings when her support staff is particularly exhausted, Ruth is asked, "Wouldn't you rather stay home and watch the service on television this week?" It is abundantly clear what the staff person wants and so Ruth timidly defers to her.

odically. At a minimum, this might occur during meetings in which formal planning takes places, such as when designing an individualized service plan. In addition, service providers should always be cognizant of potential indicators that someone no longer is satisfied with his or her existing supports or current degree of congregational involvement. Moreover, spiritual issues sometimes become more prominent in people's lives when they have experienced a personal tragedy or loss.

Areas to Explore

Capturing the expressions of faith that are most important to the individuals whom you support, as well as the opportunities and supports they would like to receive in this aspect of their lives, will require planning teams to ask thoughtful questions and engage in careful listening. Many physicians, nurses, social workers, counselors, psychiatrists, and other professionals draw on informal or formal spiritual assessments to improve the quality of care and support they deliver to people (see Box 6.2). Sometimes, this simply involves listening to people as they share their stories and circumstances, noticing expressions of spiritual interest, and following up with related questions. Other times, a more structured approach is taken, which may involve asking more focused questions about people's spiritual beliefs and support systems. Of course, the approach you take will depend on many factors, including your particular role as a service provider, the quality of your relationship with the person, the interests they may have expressed in the past, and the type of planning you are doing together.

What areas of need, strength, and support might you explore? Although numerous spiritual assessment tools exist (see Fitchett, 2002;

Box 6.2
Tools for Exploring Spirituality and Congregational History

Increasingly, human services professionals are recognizing that conversations about people's personal beliefs, values, and sources of support can be invaluable in designing services that are relevant and effective. Yet, many service providers feel uncertain about how to broach the subject. Several approaches have been developed for gathering information about people's spiritual needs and resources in ways that are thoughtful and respectful. The acronyms HOPE (Anandarajah & Hight, 2001), FICA (Puchalski & Romer, 2000), or SPIRIT (Maugans, 1996) offer mnemonic devices that can be used to facilitate such discussions. Table 6.2 explains each of these acronyms and offers brief explanations of the kinds of information they can be used to elicit. You might draw on these frameworks to craft your own questions.

Table 6.2. HOPE, FICA, and SPIRIT approaches to discovering a person's spiritual needs and supports

HOPE Approach		
H	Sources of Hope, Meaning, Comfort, Strength, Peace, Love, and Connection	What are your basic spiritual resources? What gives you support? What sustains you in difficult times?
O	Organized Religion	What role does organized religion play in your life? What aspects are most and least important to you?
P	Personal Spirituality and Practices	What spiritual practices are important to you? How would you describe your relationship with God?
E	Effects on Care	How should your spiritual needs, strengths, and resources impact the supports and opportunities we provide?
FICA Approach		
F	Faith and Belief	What brings you meaning? Do you consider yourself to be spiritual or religious?
I	Importance and Influence	How important are those beliefs in your life? What influence do they have on the decisions you make?
C	Community	Do you belong to a congregation or other spiritual community? How important is this community to you?
A	Address or Application	How (if at all) would you like us to address these issues through our supports and services?
SPIRIT Approach		
S	Spiritual belief system	How do you describe your formal religious affiliation?
P	Personal spirituality	Are there particular beliefs and practices that are more or less important to you?
I	Integration with a spiritual community	Are you a member of a particular congregation or community group? What supports do they provide?
R	Ritualized practices and restrictions	What activities and behaviors are encouraged or forbidden within your personal belief system?
I	Implications for care	What should we keep in mind as we provide services and supports to you?
T	Terminal events planning	What should we know about how you wish to be supported and cared for? (For people nearing the end of their lives)

Sources: Anandarajah & Hight (2001); Maugans (1996); Puchalski & Romer (2000)

Hodge, 2003; Plante & Sherman, 2001), few have been designed specifically with people with developmental disabilities in mind. When your goal is to find out the types of congregational involvement and opportunities for spiritual growth a person desires, the following issues might be explored.

- *Congregational history.* Have they attended services and other activities in a church, mosque, synagogue, temple, or other faith community in the past? Was participation in these activities an important part of family life when they were growing up? Have they since felt welcomed into or excluded from congregational life?

- *Current involvement.* How are they involved in a local congregation at the present time (if at all)? What do they find to be most important about these experiences?

- *Desired involvement.* What kind of involvement would they like to have in a congregation? Are there spiritual practices in which they would like to take part? Why are these choices important to them?

- *Support needs.* What supports will they need to have the experiences they desire? Who should provide those supports? What skills might make their involvement more meaningful?

Table 6.3 includes a list of sample questions that might be asked as you explore each of these areas. This list should not be used as a script; neither is it exhaustive. Feel free to add, rearrange, and rewrite questions so that you can truly discover the preferences and support needs of the individuals with whom you work. Of course, the questions will have to be individualized and adapted so that they are clearly understandable to the individuals whom you support.

Approaches for Identifying Preferences and Support Needs

Determining people's spiritual and religious preferences and support needs does not need to take place apart from consideration of other dimensions of their life. Indeed, this is just one of many areas that are important to address during the planning process. When seeking to improve quality of life for people with developmental disabilities, support needs related to social relationships, health, employment, community participation, self-determination, spirituality, and other areas of life should usually be considered together. After all, think about the transportation and social supports someone might need to participate fully in the faith community of his or her choice. Or, consider the opportunities that exist within a congregation for recreation, volunteering, lifelong learning, new relationships, and community inclusion. Approaches for determining the supports,

Table 6.3. Sample questions to explore preferences and support needs

Congregational involvement

- Do you currently attend a congregation?
- Tell me about it.
- Who do you go with?
- What do you do there? How do you participate in services and activities?
- How often do you go?
- What do you like most about your congregation? What do you wish was different?
- How is being part of this congregation important in your life?
- In what ways would you like to be more involved? Less involved?
- If you could try out any new class, program, or activity, what would it be?
- Is your congregation supportive for you? How so?
- Are there particular people who are especially friendly or helpful?
- What keeps you from being involved in the ways that you would like?
- Were you involved in a congregation when you were younger? Was this an important part of family life?

Religious and spiritual expression

- What are some things that give you joy or happiness? What brings meaning to your life?
- Do you have religious or spiritual beliefs that are important to you? What are those beliefs?
- What are some of the ways that you express your faith or spirituality?
- What traditions, rituals, or practices are especially important to you?
- Are there holy days, festivals, or other special events that you observe?
- What gives you strength?
- How do you cope when going through difficult times? To whom do you turn?
- What would you say are your gifts? What are you good at? What do people compliment you on?
- Have you experienced a sense of calling in your life?
- What else is important for us know about your religious and spiritual beliefs?

Support needs

- What supports will you need to be involved in your congregation in the ways you would like?
- Which of these supports can we provide? Which would you prefer come from someone else?
- Would you like help finding a congregational home?
- Do you have the spiritual supports, relationships, and connections that you would like?
- Are there religious practices or restrictions that we should keep in mind as we support you?
- Would you like us to help you address your spiritual needs? If so, how?
- Would you like help finding out more about your faith?
- How well are we doing at helping you meet your spiritual needs?
- Do you have any needs that are not being addressed?

skills, and opportunities people need to live a full life are discussed in greater detail elsewhere (see Holburn & Vietze, 2002; O'Brien & O'Brien, 2002; Thompson et al., 2004). The following section briefly highlights three of these approaches and raises some considerations related to addressing spirituality and congregational participation.

Individual Conversations   One of the best ways to find out what people value and want for themselves is simply to ask them. For some people with developmental disabilities, a meaningful conversation about their hopes and plans and desired involvement will be fairly straightforward. However, many people experience difficulties with comprehension or expression—sometimes slight, sometimes very extensive—which may require you to be more deliberate with how you go about determining what people really want for themselves. The following tips may be helpful when planning this conversation:

- Create a comfortable atmosphere where everyone feels open about sharing. If possible, someone should facilitate the conversations who knows the individual with disabilities well.

- It may be helpful to invite someone else to join the conversation who is known and trusted by the individual, such as a family member or friend. This person may be able to clarify or supplement any information that is shared. However, questions should always be directed first to the individual with disabilities; it should be his or her voice that is ultimately heard.

- Explain the purpose of your conversation—to find out what experiences and relationships are most important to the individual and to explore how best to support him or her in enjoying these things.

- It may take time and some creativity to find out what someone really wants for him- or herself, especially if he or she has had limited experiences with faith communities in the past. You may need to revisit this conversation several times to make sure that you have it right.

- To ensure that you cover everything, sketch out an initial list of questions to ask or areas to explore. If you are unsure of where to begin, consider drawing from the questions listed in Table 6.3.

- When necessary, confirm an individual's preferences by talking with others who know him or her well. When someone has difficulty recalling past experiences, ask others to fill in gaps.

Sometimes, it can be challenging to discern the preferences of people with severe cognitive impairments (see Box 6.3). The following tips may be

Box 6.3
Identifying Preferences

Some people with developmental disabilities may not be able to verbalize their preferences, but that does not mean that they have none. Seek out other avenues through which people can indicate what is truly important to them, as well as the opportunities and supports that would enhance their lives. Pay close attention to people's body language, gestures, facial expressions, and affect when exploring new experiences. Learn to listen to the subtle ways in which people sometimes communicate their preferences. Help them to become proficient in some alternative form of communication, such as using modified sign language, picture boards, or computer technology. It also may be necessary to invest time in teaching choice- and decision-making skills. Whenever preferences are still difficult to discern, turn to family members, friends, and others who are known and trusted by the person.

helpful when having such a conversation (Perry, 2004; Tassé, Schalock, Thompson, & Wehmeyer, 2005).

- Adapt your questions to match the individual's level of understanding or preferred mode of expression. For example, you might ask open-ended questions (e.g., "Tell me about your church."), offer several options from which to choose (e.g., "Would you like to join the choir, serve as a greeter, or help out in the nursery?"), or phrase questions so that they require only a yes or no response (e.g., "Do you want me to go with you to the potluck supper?").

- Keep your questions simple and concrete, but not patronizing; remember that you are speaking with an adult. If possible, provide examples that you know will be familiar to the individual. Avoid abstract concepts and jargon.

- Encourage questions. This should feel more like a conversation than an interview.

- It may take time for the individual to think about your question and formulate an answer. Provide plenty of time to respond, especially when he or she uses assistive technology to communicate.

- If you have difficulty understanding a comment, ask for clarification. If you are still unsure, restate what you think you heard and ask whether you have it correct.

- If the individual has trouble understanding you, rephrase the question or ask it in a completely different way.

- Sometimes, the individual may answer in ways that he or she thinks will please you, rather than expressing his or her true preferences. Be careful not to influence responses. When someone always answers yes, ask your questions another way to make sure this really reflects his or her preference.

- Respect decisions not to talk about certain topics or to stop the conversation altogether. Notice any reactions or body language that suggests the individual is uncomfortable.

Person-Centered Planning   Person-centered planning often is recommended for exploring the preferences, strengths, and aspirations of people with developmental disabilities. This approach focuses on helping people articulate a vision for their lives (i.e., their ideal future), identifying the steps needed to take them there, and gathering an alliance of supportive people who will commit to making this vision a reality. Its emphasis on strengths (rather than deficits), its recognition that people should have primary control of their own lives (rather than service providers), and its focus on creating supportive relationships (rather than fitting people into programs) are just a few of the things that distinguish this approach from traditional planning processes.

Anyone can be part of the planning process. Obviously, the individual for whom the planning is being conducted (i.e., the focus person) must be present. Identify people who have an existing relationship with the focus person or a vested interest in improving his or her quality of life. For example, you might invite family members, friends, neighbors, co-workers, or support staff. If the focus person already is involved in a congregation, invite members of that community to take part in planning. They might be able to share a unique perspective on the gifts and talents a person holds, as well as describe opportunities for using those gifts in their congregation. A skilled facilitator who can guide the process, as well as someone who can creatively (usually graphically) and accurately record and summarize the contributions of the group, are especially critical to successful planning.

Person-centered planning can be implemented using a variety of approaches, including Essential Lifestyle Planning (Smull, 1997), Personal Futures Planning (Mount & Zwernik, 1994), McGill Action Planning System (MAPS; Vandercook, York, & Forest, 1989), Plan-

> "Think of the difference it might make, to many, if there was a voice and presence at those meetings who said, 'We care what you all do here, and we want to learn as well, so that we can support them back in our congregation and community. We too have heard their concerns about the services they receive and are here to support their voice.'"
>
> —Bill Gaventa (2005, p. 53)

ning Alternative Tomorrows with Hope (PATH; Pearpoint, O'Brien, & Forest, 1993), and Whole Life Planning (Butterworth et al., 1993). These approaches vary, but common steps include identifying the dreams people have for their life, the immediate goals and priorities they hold, the gifts and strengths they possess, the relationships and experiences they already enjoy, the informal and formal supports they will need to move forward, and the next steps that everyone will take. As you can see, people's spiritual needs, preferences, and aspirations should emerge as part of the process. To ensure that this dimension is not overlooked or ignored, everyone who is part of the planning process should make sure these spiritual needs are addressed and well-supported.

The outcome of the planning process should be a clear roadmap for moving the focus person closer toward the life he or she envisions for him- or herself. Sometimes, the group will have to brainstorm creative strategies for supporting people to explore their spirituality, participate more fully in congregational life, practice their faith in meaningful ways, or assume valued roles in their communities. New connections and relationships may have to be sought out or nurtured further. For other people, everything may be going very well in this aspect of their lives. Still, it may be helpful to discuss what needs to continue happening to make sure this situation is maintained. To ensure that progress toward this vision remains steady, the group should periodically reassemble to problem-solve challenges and celebrate successes.

Exploring Preferences   Some people have had limited involvement in their communities or few opportunities to explore their spirituality. In such cases, difficulty articulating their preferences does not necessarily mean that spirituality is unimportant to them. It may just suggest that people need more information or an opportunity to try out new experiences for themselves. Provide the opportunities and support that people need to visit local congregations and other activities that take place in their communities. Allow people to decide for themselves whether a particular faith community feels like the right fit for them.

> "I would encourage them to do the same thing I did when it came to choosing the right church. I would tell them to go first and check it out.... So they need to know that they are all welcome. It's all about a partnership, an attitude or a feeling whether you have a disability or not. You have to be comfortable. If you feel comfortable in the church you pick, then that's where you should be."
>
> —Kelly Barnes (2005, p. 5)

To help people feel comfortable when they first visit a worship service or other congregational activity, Sieck and Hartvigsen (2001) suggest the following strategies.

- Talk with the person about what to expect beforehand. Walk through each aspect of the service or activity, explaining its purpose and describing the different ways in which people can participate. If the particular congregation or faith tradition is unfamiliar to you, talk to another staff person or invite someone from the congregation to meet with you both.

- Arrange to visit the congregation at a time when services are not taking place. Look around the building and introduce the person to members of the congregation's staff.

- Find out more about the culture of the congregation, including expectations for appropriate dress and behavior. Some congregations are very casual, while others are more formal; some are highly energetic, while others are more subdued.

- Contact the congregation and ask if someone would be willing to accompany the person to worship services, showing him the ropes and introducing him to others before and after the service (see Chapter 3).

- Explain to the person that, as a visitor, others in the congregation might be curious about who he is. Some people may eagerly extend their welcome, whereas others may be shy or uncertain about how to introduce themselves.

- Belonging takes time. It may take several—sometimes many—visits to become familiar and feel comfortable with all of the activities that comprise congregational life.

MORE THAN LIP SERVICE: IMPROVING POLICY AND PRACTICE

Organizations and agencies must be thoughtful and deliberate about recognizing and honoring the preferences, strengths, and aspirations of people with developmental disabilities in meaningful ways. What steps might you take to ensure that spiritual supports are addressed through your programs?

Reflect on Current Practices

Invest time reflecting on your existing policies and current practices as they relate to the spiritual and religious needs of the people whom you serve. Forest and Pearpoint (1997) suggest posing four simple questions:

What are we doing well right now? What could we be doing better? What could we be doing differently? What can we begin doing right now to get us started moving toward these goals? Engage everyone who is employed or served by your organization in contributing answers to these questions. Ask members of your management team or advisory board to look closely at the organization's priorities and service offerings. Table 6.4 displays several reflection questions that might help get this conversation started. Interview or survey your direct service staff about the ways they currently are supporting the spiritual expression of people with developmental disabil-

Table 6.4. Reflection questions for organizations and agencies supporting people with developmental disabilities

- What evidence can we point to that indicates that we view spirituality as being important to the people with developmental disabilities whom we serve?
- What values do we espouse as an organization? Does our mission statement reflect a commitment to support the choices of consumers, including those related to spiritual exploration and expression?
- Do our written policies explain the importance of supporting people's religious preferences, as well as point to practical strategies for doing this well? Are our staff and the people we serve familiar with these policies?
- Do we have an advocate or board member who is responsible for ensuring that spiritual supports are being addressed? Is someone ensuring that our policies are evidenced in practice and woven throughout our programs?
- Do we understand the different ways that we should be addressing the spiritual and religious needs of the people whom we serve?
- Do we discuss with new staff the importance of listening for, seeking out, and supporting people's choices and preferences, including their religious preferences? Do we provide the training staff need to do this effectively?
- Do we ask about the spiritual needs, strengths, and connections of people with disabilities when they first begin receiving our services? Are these conversations periodically revisited?
- Do we orient people with disabilities and their families to the types of supports we make available for individuals interested in being involved in a faith community?
- Do we provide the opportunities, space, and support people need to explore and express their spirituality at home, within a congregation, or elsewhere, if they so choose?
- Do we periodically assess and seek to remove potential barriers that hinder us from addressing the spiritual and religious needs of consumers?
- Are the people whom we serve involved in the faith community *of their choice*? Does everyone attend the *same* congregation? Do few attend any congregation?
- Is participation in community activities, including attending congregational activities, used to reinforce good behavior or punish inappropriate behavior?
- To what extent have we established relationships with local congregations and faith-based organizations?
- Do we recognize and affirm the sense of calling and vocation held by our staff providing direct support to people with developmental disabilities?

ities, as well as their need for additional information and training on how
to do this well. Meet with people with disabilities, as well as their family
members and friends, to obtain feedback on the quality of the supports
they are receiving and their satisfaction
with existing services. To find out what
people truly think, you might consider
holding separate focus group meetings
with consumers, parents, and staff mem-
bers, each facilitated by someone not directly affiliated with your organization or agency. Finally, talk with local congregations to gauge their
familiarity with your services and their willingness to partner together to
support the inclusion of people with disabilities in your community.

> "If faith and worship could enhance
> quality of life, shouldn't it be part
> of our delivery of quality services?"
>
> —Terry Gleeson (2001/2002, p. 30)

Refine Your Policies

Many organizations and agencies have crafted thoughtful policies addressing issues such as community inclusion, consumer choice, and self-
determination. Unfortunately, these principles have not always been articulated in relation to supporting the spiritual needs of people with disabilities (Hatton, Turner, Shah, Rahim, & Stansfield, 2004a). Sometimes even
good policies go overlooked or unheeded. Do your staff know whether,
when, and how to find out about the spiritual needs and strengths of the
people whom they serve as well as the supports these individuals need?
Do they know when to provide direct support and when to serve as a connector or bridge builder? Do they know who they can turn to when they
have questions? Staff will approach their work with greater confidence
when their roles are defined clearly. If you do not already have written
policies addressing these issues, draft them. The language contained in the
policy statements of the American Association on Intellectual and Developmental Disabilities, The Arc, and TASH may be helpful to consider. In
addition, collaborate with other organizations and agencies in your community to learn about each other's work in this area. Continuously refine
your policies as you learn more about what it look like to provide meaningful, effective supports in this area of people's lives.

Revisit Your Practices

Strong policies must be accompanied by quality supports. Supporting the
spiritual and religious needs of people with disabilities may require some
organizations to change how they deliver services. Approaches to planning, staffing patterns, transportation arrangements, and staff development opportunities may need to be revisited to ensure that people have

supports they need to pursue the experiences and relationships that are important to them. For example, inquiries about religious preferences may need to be incorporated into your intake or referral process. Additional staff may be needed on weekends or certain evenings to ensure that people wishing to attend worship services or other congregational activities can do so. Or, time may have to be dedicated to developing relationships with local congregations and faith-based organizations.

Equip Your Staff

Staff should be equipped with the skills and sensitivities they need to support effectively a diverse population of people, including one that is diverse religiously. Help staff become fluent in the core values articulated in Chapter 1 and to deliver supports in a culturally competent manner. In addition, explain the important role that staff can play in supporting the religious expression of people with developmental disabilities in their care. For example, a workshop might be offered during which staff 1) discuss the meanings of spirituality and religion, 2) describe the different avenues through which each is apparent in their own lives, 3) reflect on the importance of

> "It is far more important for staff to know how to listen to a person to find out how they understand their faith and what it means to them, than to apply a textbook knowledge of *religion* [emphasis added] that might not fit the person at all. Staff will then learn about the person's faith in a way that is relevant to the person and that will help staff support the person in their religious interests."
>
> —Chris Hatton and colleagues (2004, p. 12)

each in the lives of people with disabilities with whom they spend time, and 4) brainstorm practical strategies for discovering and supporting the spiritual and religious expressions throughout the week (Arnold, 2005; Hatton, Turner, Shah, Rahim, & Stansfield, 2004b). If you spend time reflecting on your current practices, you likely will identify common concerns raised by staff, consumers, and family members. Make sure that these issues are addressed thoroughly during staff development sessions.

Develop Support Plans

It benefits people little when you seek out their preferences, but fail to deliver the supports and experiences they desire. Make sure that people's preferences are clearly communicated to everyone who works with them. A meaningful and individualized support plan is necessary to ensure communication and coordination when people draw on a variety of formal and informal supports and services. It is not unusual for one staff member to do a wonderful job of learning about and supporting someone's preferences, only to have those same preferences overlooked by other staff.

Clearly detail what staff need to know about a person's preferences and desired supports. What relationships and experiences are important to her? Does he celebrate certain holy days? Does she follow particular dietary practices? Are there worship services or other activities that he likes to attend? Is it important to give her space and privacy for prayer or meditation? Does he like to listen to religious music or watch certain programming on television?

Gather Resources and Establish Relationships

Staff sometimes express uncertainty with how to provide meaningful support to people who adhere to a faith tradition that differs from their own. Gather informational resources about different faith groups that are represented in your community. If your staff reflects the diversity apparent within your community, it is likely that you can draw on the personal experiences of other staff who are working in programs. Furthermore, most congregations would be pleased to meet with staff to talk about the traditions, practices, and beliefs of their faith.

Support Self-Advocacy

If you are really serious about providing quality services that truly reflect the preferences of people with developmental disabilities and their families, equip recipients of your services to voice their feedback and advocate for their needs. Create opportunities for people with disabilities to explore their spirituality and discover what is important to them. Teach them how to voice their preferences, request the supports they need, and make it known when they are not satisfied with your services. Give people with disabilities real control over their own resources and let them choose for themselves how they receive support and from whom. Finally, invite people with disabilities and their families to have a prominent voice in shaping your policies around this issue.

PARTNERING WITH CONGREGATIONS

As you strive to support the personal aspirations, community inclusion, natural relationships, self-determination, and quality of life of people with developmental disabilities, local congregations can be important allies in your efforts. Such relationships can be mutually beneficial—helping congregations to realize their calling and enabling service providers to fulfill their charge to promote full community participation. Certainly, some congregations will be more willing than others to collaborate with you around these goals. For many, however, the possibility simply has never crossed their minds. Consider the following avenues for partnering with local congregations.

- Provide the supports that people with developmental disabilities need to participate meaningfully in the faith community of their choice. This might involve you serving as a bridge between people and local congregations, making initial introductions, working with congregations to arrange transportation to services and other congregational activities, and helping them brainstorm ways for providing support. To make these connections, you will have to know what opportunities are available in your community. Invite congregations to tell you about their programs. Compile a list of congregations that desire to welcome people with disabilities.

- One important role that agencies and organizations assume is to prepare communities to include people with developmental disabilities. Help interested congregations improve their capacity to welcome and support people with disabilities in the life of their faith community. Let them know of your willingness to share information and resources about how to create a welcoming atmosphere, remove common barriers, provide meaningful support, and discover the many gifts their newest members have to offer. Host occasional workshops on topics related to developmental disabilities or offer consultation on issues such as accessibility. Assure congregations that you are willing to come alongside and support them as they seek to become more inclusive.

- Invite congregations to join you in supporting people with developmental disabilities in *all* aspects of community life. Let congregations know about the services and supports you provide, as well as the specific ways that they might contribute to these efforts. Perhaps you could share your desire to see more people making efforts to befriend, spend time with, offer rides to, or otherwise get to know the individuals with disabilities whom you serve. If congregations are not aware of the presence and needs of people with disabilities in their community, they can hardly be expected to reach out in these ways. Of course, many congregations will choose not to take you up on your invitation. Do not let lack of awareness be the reason for their decision.

- Faith community representatives can play a valuable role in improving the quality of services your agency or organization offers to people with disabilities and their families. Invite them to contribute their perspectives as part of your advisory board or evaluation team. Ask them for feedback on your program policies and service offerings.

- Many direct service staff are actively involved in their own faith communities. If this describes you, let others in your congregation know of your willingness to share your experiences and gifts to help the community become a more inviting place for people with disabilities and their families. Most children's program coordinators and ministry leaders would be thrilled to discover that someone might be available to help them in this area.

- Demonstrate a willingness to explore novel and creative partnerships with local congregations. Be patient. This will be new work for many people.

CONCLUSION

The service and supports provided by agencies and organizations play a prominent role in the lives of many people with developmental disabilities and their families. Identifying the experiences and relationships that people want for their lives and the supports they will need to attain these goals can be challenging work, but it is fundamentally important. Quality services are characterized by a commitment to seek out and support the personal aspirations of people with disabilities. An understanding of people's spiritual needs and strengths is essential to providing these services well. Strive to develop policies and implement practices that reflect the importance of this dimension of people's lives.

Chapter 7

Launching Communitywide Efforts

![decorative banner]

Partnering Together for Inclusion

A small church is learning how to receive the gifts of adults with intellectual disabilities living in a congregation-sponsored group home.

A local synagogue is discovering exciting ways of weaving two high school students with severe disabilities into their youth and summer programs.

A core group of parents are meeting together each month in a church fellowship hall to exchange emotional and spiritual support.

A residential program is offering workshops to staff on how to honor the faith commitments of consumers.

An advocacy organization is reaching out to congregations as they explore new partners for increasing community participation.

S tories abound of individual congregations, families, organizations, and agencies striving to be responsive. Yet, in other corners of these same communities, Sunday school teachers are struggling to include children with extensive needs, adults with disabilities still feel unwelcome in their congregations, parents feel isolated and alone, residents of a group home have no one to take them to congregational activities, and organizations lament that they have few natural partners in the community. To truly transform the religious landscape for people with disabilities, the often scattered and disconnected efforts of individuals will need to be brought together.

This chapter offers strategies for gathering together families, congregations, service providers, and other community members to articulate and pursue a bold vision for inclusion throughout their faith community, neighborhood, city, or state. Communitywide efforts are essential for ensuring that the religious and spiritual preferences of *every* person with developmental disabilities is honored and supported. Establishing a community network, engaging in community mapping, and hosting a gathering on congregational inclusion represent three avenues for initiating and sustaining efforts throughout your community.

BUILDING A COMMUNITY NETWORK

One avenue for broadening your impact and multiplying partnerships is to establish a community network. Community networks can be coalitions of congregations, organizations, agencies, or other interested people who work together to ensure that the spiritual, emotional, material, and other support needs of people with disabilities in their community are being addressed. These groups might meet monthly or quarterly to share information, engage in advocacy, and serve as a common voice for inclusion throughout their community. There are several reasons to consider establishing a community network.

First, community networks provide a forum for identifying efforts that are already underway in your community, as well as discovering needs that have yet to be tackled. Who is already making strides to support the congregational participation of people with disabilities? What supports and relationships already are in place? What unmet needs remain to be addressed? A single congregation, agency, or organization would feel overwhelmed at the prospect of trying to meet every need within its community. Perhaps someone else already is offering respite care services, initiating a parent support group, training children's ministry leaders about inclusion, starting a ministry to people who are deaf, educating service providers about honoring spiritual preferences, or spearheading citywide inclusion awareness efforts. Sometimes, awareness of existing efforts can serve to reduce redundancy. In other cases, it can spur collaborative relationships around common goals.

> "Individuals and organizations interested in the inclusion of people with disabilities can be found in every community. The challenge is to build bridges, make connections and ultimately nourish a healthier, more integrated community, where people of all faiths and ethnic backgrounds work together."
>
> —Janet Rife and Ginny Thornburgh (2001, p. 13)

Second, sharing information, experiences, strategies, connections, and expertise increases the capacity of every congregation, agency, and organization to be more responsive and more supportive. Put simply, community networks multiply the resources available to everyone, enabling each to accomplish more than they would have otherwise been able to do on their own. So much can be learned through conversations with other congregations, even when they are associated with a different denomination or faith tradition. These interactions can keep you from having to reinvent the wheel.

Third, it is not uncommon for individuals doing this kind of work within congregations and organizations to feel isolated and somewhat disconnected from others. Gathering with people who share your passion and commitment to inclusion can be encouraging and energizing. It is exciting to hear about inspired and innovative efforts taking place in other corners of your community, motivating to hear stories of meaningful participation and

> "The group turned out to be a welcome haven of support, networking, and resource sharing among people who often felt isolated and alone in their local settings. Simply gathering together to share successes and frustrations was empowering. New friendships and working relationships emerged across denominational lines."
>
> —Betsy Sowers (2001/2002, p. 15)

progress, and empowering to hear from others who are further along in their journey than you are. These networks can also provide a forum for sharing with others the work you are doing.

Fourth, community networks can serve as an influential voice for inclusion in a community. They might call on congregations to be more inclusive of people with disabilities and their families, appeal to agencies to incorporate spiritual supports into their services, and challenge communities to rethink what it really means to be a place of welcome. Moreover, they can serve as a catalyst for mobilizing members of the community to fulfill unmet needs. In doing so, expect that new partners will emerge and be drawn to the work that you are doing.

Possible Partners

Community networks can be organized in many different ways. For example, participating partners might be drawn from congregations throughout a particular city, region, or state. Sometimes, networks are comprised of congregations associated with a single denomination; other times, they adopt a more ecumenical or interfaith approach. The focus of a network's efforts can also vary, with some groups deciding to address specific disability groups (e.g., people with mental illness, people who are deaf, people with autism) and others assuming a cross-disability approach. For example, representatives from all of the Lutheran churches in a large metropolitan area might be invited to meet monthly to exchange ideas, resources, and encouragement. Or, invitations to meet quarterly could be extended to *every* congregation in a small city in an effort to raise awareness of the needs of people with disabilities in the community.

It is wise to develop a network that includes more than just congregational partners. As emphasized in Chapter 1, barriers to congregational participation often exist throughout communities. A constellation of people can affect whether people with developmental disabilities are able to participate fully in congregational life. Invite representatives of relevant local service and support agencies, organizations, advocacy groups, school systems, or civic organizations to join you. People with developmental disabilities and family members also should be among the voices contributing to the network. Table 7.1 lists some examples of various networks throughout the country, demonstrating just a few of the different forms that these groups might take.

Developing Plans

Transforming the religious terrain for people with developmental disabilities in your community will take time and sustained effort. A strong community network, however, can serve as a guiding force in realizing this

Table 7.1.   Examples of community networks addressing congregational inclusion

Organization	Web site
All God's Children	http://www.all-gods-children.org
Anabaptist Disabilities Network	http://www.adnetonline.org
Atlanta Alliance on Developmental Disabilities/Interfaith Disabilities Network	http://aadd.org/newsite/programs/idn.html
Bridge Ministries	http://www.bridgemin.org
Bridges to Faith	http://www.bridgestofaith.org
Christian Council for People with Disabilities	http://www.ccpd.org
Disability Outreach Partnership Ministry	http://www.dopm.org
Ecumenical Disability Advocates Network	http://www.oikoumene.org
Faith Inclusion Network	http://www.faithinclusionnetwork.com
Inclusion Network	http://www.inclusion.org
Lutheran Services in America-Disability Network	http://www.lsa-dn.org
Massachusetts Council of Churches-Disability Network	http://www.masscouncilofchurches.org
New Jersey Coalition for Inclusive Ministries	http://www.rwjms.umdnj.edu/boggscenter/projects
Special Needs Parallel Professional Advisory Committee	http://www.pjll.org

vision. Begin by developing a mission statement that explains your purpose, articulates your core values, and orients your efforts. This mission should guide you in determining the avenues through which you will endeavor to impact your community. Consider the following ideas for equipping your community to do a better job of including people with disabilities.

- Develop a directory of local congregations and organizations that are making efforts to welcome people with disabilities and their families. Briefly describe how they are including people with disabilities in congregational and community life, as well as the supports and resources they are willing to offer. Provide contact information and update the directory periodically. This directory can then be shared—either in print or on-line—with families seeking a congregational home within their particular faith tradition or local neighborhood.

- Compile a list of people who are willing to share their expertise, perspectives, talents, and time to equip congregations to include people with disabilities. For example, you might gather names of people willing to assist with issues such as architectural accessibility, inclusive children's programs, family support, pastoral counseling, congregational advocacy programs, or respite care. Advertise the availability of this resource to congregations through newsletters, listservs, and on your web site.

- Design a web site through which families, people with disabilities, congregations, service providers, and others in your community can obtain information about the work of your network, the activities of local faith communities, upcoming events and learning opportunities, and local resources (see Table 7.1 for examples). In addition, provide a way for visitors to your site to provide feedback, ask for assistance, or request more information.

- Offer workshops and other training opportunities to local congregations, agencies, and organizations interested in improving how they support people with disabilities. If the necessary expertise is not already available from within your network, invite people beyond your community to address issues with which you are less familiar.

- Community networks are ideal for making new connections. Offer to serve as a primary liaison between local congregations and community organizations that serve people with developmental disabilities. Host a networking reception or dinner aimed at bringing together people throughout the community whose interests and involvement in disability and ministry intersect in obvious and unique ways. Identify congregations who are willing to serve as a resource, guide, and encourager to the congregations just beginning their journey toward inclusion.

- Arrange for several partners from your network to visit local congregations that have developed a reputation for their hospitality to people with disabilities and families. Talk with congregational leaders and members to hear about their journey so far, including the challenges they encountered and the steps they have taken to become more inclusive. Compile these strategies into a brief guidebook or brochure as a source of inspiration and direction for other faith communities.

- Develop a team of people who are willing to assist interested congregations in reflecting on their own strengths, needs, policies, and practices in the area of inclusive ministry (see Chapter 2). This team might offer to hold listening sessions with lay leaders and congregation members, provide an "outsider's" view on the congregation's accessibility, give suggestions for next steps, and answer questions that arise as congregations strive to improve their welcome.

- Numerous organizations—such as the American Association on Intellectual and Developmental Disabilities, The Arc, Autism Society of America, Council for Exceptional Children, National Organization on Disability, and TASH—hold annual state, regional, or national conferences that address topics such as inclusion, community building, self-determination, and congregational participation. Enable one or more network partners to attend some of these different conferences, each bringing information and strategies back to be shared with the network and broader community.

- Most individual congregations, organizations, and families have limited access to the growing number of materials addressing people with disabilities and religious participation. Local libraries and parent resource centers rarely have more than a few resources addressing this issue. Develop a lending library of practical resources that can be shared with any interested members of your community. Gather articles, books, curricula, and videos that address this important dimension of people's lives (see Appendix B for resource ideas).

- Speak up as a voice for congregational participation within larger conversations about community inclusion. Sponsor a booth or resource display at local and state gatherings addressing issues such as education, employment, community living, family support, health, and community services. Consider presenting a session or leading a panel discussion at these conferences.

- Seek out avenues for recognizing, supporting, and stimulating the efforts of individual congregations, organizations, and agencies to remove barriers to participation in faith communities. You might raise funds to support small initiatives, such as a synagogue's efforts to start a sibling support group, a religiously affiliated camp's plans to make their cabins more accessible, or an agency's efforts to train staff to incorporate spiritual supports into their services. Hold an awards banquet or media event to publicly acknowledge the innovative awareness, advocacy, and support efforts being made by local congregations.

- Compile and retell stories that illustrate how people with developmental disabilities are participating in and contributing to local congregational and community life. Develop booklets, bulletin inserts, videos, or other materials that could be shared with interested congregations (see Swedeen, 2002).

When developing an overall plan for your community network, make certain that you are gathering input from an array of stakeholders, including people with disabilities, parents, professionals, and congregational leaders. Prioritize your goals, recognizing that there is probably much yet to do and that everything cannot be tackled at once. As you work toward your vision, make sure to let others in your community know about the steps you are taking by contacting local parent resource centers, congregational associations, disability-related organizations, and agency clearinghouses.

Resources and Funding

Funding is not necessary to this work, but it certainly expands what a network can accomplish. Some networks are able to find support for a part- or full-time staff member; others rely on the energies and efforts of volunteers. If funding would facilitate your work, contact local public and private foundations that support community development projects. Apply for grants from organizations and agencies that serve people with developmental disabilities, including your Council on Developmental Disabilities, United Way, or state or county department of health, family, or children's services. Invite congregations to support your work through yearly donations, special gifts, or fundraisers.

DEVELOPING CAPACITY THROUGH COMMUNITY MAPPING

The task of transforming communities into places of continuous welcome and abundant support for people with disabilities and their families should begin with recognition that communities already have much to offer to this end. Communities are rich reservoirs of relationships, resources, and opportunities, much of which has simply gone unrecognized, remained untapped, or has never been connected with this particular vision. The challenge lies in identifying those strengths and capacities—often called assets—that already reside within your community. The efforts of individual congregations, organizations, groups, and individuals often are made in relative isolation and with little publicity, leaving most people unaware of the full spectrum of resources and supports that are potentially available.

Community mapping offers one approach for revealing and unlocking these numerous assets and engaging them to realize a particular vision. It is a process through which stakeholders are brought together to inventory the resources available within their community collaboratively and direct those assets toward achieving a shared goal. Often considered a key component of effective community building, community mapping has been used to facilitate goals related to economic development, civic engagement, environmental issues, educational outcomes, health promotion, and youth transitions. The approach also has great potential for promoting the inclusion of people with developmental disabilities, both in the broader community and in the faith community of their choice (e.g., Crane & Skinner, 2003; O'Connell, 1990; Rans & Green, 2005).

The outcome of the mapping process is a comprehensive portrait of all the resources and relationships a community might have to contribute to a particular goal. What skills, talents, people, services, institutions, and organizations exist in your community? What are congregations, organizations, families, self-advocates, and other groups already doing to advance full participation? What religious, cultural, financial, and other resources might be available? What formal and informal relationships already are in place? Community mapping provides information about all that is already available, often uncovering resources that you never knew existed. For example,

- A Jewish social services agency already offers support to families experiencing stress.

- Three congregations have recently begun respite care activities.

- Special educators from an area elementary school are willing to share inclusion strategies with Sunday school teachers.

- A Center for Independent Living offers resources and guidance on architectural accessibility.

- A local priest is willing to mentor other clergy on counseling families with disabilities.

- A self-advocacy group is volunteering to help congregations assess their welcome.

- A local university offers training to the public on behavioral support strategies.

You also might discover assets that have never been considered in relation to supporting community inclusion. For example, a temple may be willing to use their van to support the transportation needs of people with disabilities in their neighborhood, a Christian businessmen's group may be willing to offer their numerous connections to help job developers locate receptive employers for people with disabilities, or a parish may be glad to host a parent resource day in their gymnasium.

By now, it should be apparent that community mapping is *strength-based*. Rather than pointing fingers at where a community (or segments of the community) has fallen short in the past, it is designed to identify the good work that is already happening, the opportunities that are just emerging, and the capacities that still await untapped. Engaging in this process can be especially helpful when you are unsure of what assets exist in your community, when current supports and services are especially fragmented and disconnected, when community members' gifts and connections are underutilized, or when existing relationships need to be further developed or strengthened.

Community Mapping Process

A number of approaches and strategies can be used to identify the assets and resources within your community. Readers interested in undertaking the community mapping process are encouraged to read guides written by Kretzmann and McKnight (1993), Rans and Altman (2002), or Snow (2004). One version of this approach is described briefly here.

Focus Your Efforts Begin by articulating a vision for your work and crafting goals that will take you there. What is it that you hope to accomplish? What is the context for this work? Perhaps your focus will be broad—promoting the inclusion of children and adults with disabilities in schools, business, and neighborhoods throughout your city. Or, maybe you are more narrowly focused on increasing the capacity of faith communities to include people with disabilities and their families. A very large church might even decide to apply this mapping process just within their own congregation, seeking to discover and deploy the myriad gifts and talents their members possess in order to more fully welcome people with disabilities—or anyone, for that matter—into the life of their church. Your goals will help you to determine who should be invited to partner in this process, as well as the approach you will take to inventory your assets.

Gather Participants   Achieving a vision of community inclusion for people with developmental disabilities will require a commitment to work across the traditional boundaries of sacred versus secular, informal versus formal, and disability versus generic programs. Assemble a diverse group of partners to undertake the mapping process. Faith communities have much to share with service providers; service providers have much to offer to congregations; people with disabilities, as well as their families and friends, have much to give to both; and numerous other community members just need to be asked what they have to share. A group composed of a wide range of partners is less likely to overlook important community assets. It also expands the number of stakeholders who will benefit from what you discover.

> "By uniting the resources of local religious institutions with those that already exist in other aspects of the community, churches, synagogues, and other religious institutions can become actively connected to the most vital issues of their community and can be empowered to build a series of strong relationships though whose combined perspective these issues can be confronted and most effectively resolved."
>
> —Jody Kretzmann and John McKnight (1993, p. 143)

Determine Your Approach   How will you go about learning what your community already has to offer? You might visit local organizations, meet with congregation leaders, mail out surveys, telephone community leaders, contact parent groups, interview a sample of community members, drive through your neighborhood, or look through the yellow pages or existing community directories. Tasks should be divided up among different members and can be carried out over a period of weeks or months. Because communities grow and change, mapping efforts should be continuous. When conducted within a single congregation, mapping might involve surveying the membership, holding conversations with small groups and religious education classes, talking with ministry leaders, reviewing existing programs, or using time and talent surveys or spiritual gifts inventories.

Map Your Assets   Thoughtfully examine all that your community might be able to offer. The following questions might assist stakeholders in generating a "map" of your community.

- What congregations, agencies, institutions, informal organizations, associations, and networks are already present in our community?

- What do these groups do and why do they do it?

- What congregational resources are already available to their members? To everyone in the community?

- What resources might congregations be willing to offer, if asked?

- What community services and supports are already available to people with disabilities? To everyone in the community?

- What resources might they be willing to offer to congregations, if asked?

- What talents and gifts reside among members of our community?

Compile Your Findings   As you discover what your community has to offer, begin to gather this information in an accessible place. For example, you could create an evolving database to be accessed through a web site, create a printed directory of existing community resources, or develop a brochure listing congregations that are striving to welcome and support people with disabilities. Perhaps a local organization or family resource center would be willing to serve as a central place of referral, connecting people with disabilities and their families with resources and assets identified through the mapping process.

Make Connections   As gifts, talents, services, supports, and opportunities are identified, your next step is to begin fostering relationships and connecting these assets in creative ways. New partnerships can be established among people and groups who share a common vision and recognize that more can be accomplished by working together. This should be a relationship-building process, in which new alliances are formed as capacities found throughout the community are harnessed toward a shared goal. After inventorying your community, you may also discover gaps in supports and services. For example, you might discover that there are no religiously affiliated schools offering special education services for children with autism or few respite programs are currently available. These gaps may suggest areas in which capacities should be further developed.

> "The long-term development of a community rests on its ability to uncover and build on the strengths and assets of its people, institutions, and informal organizations."
> —Lionel Beaulieu (2002, p. 12)

HOSTING A GATHERING ON INCLUSIVE MINISTRY

One additional way of bringing together—and drawing out—members of your community interested in building inclusive faith communities is to host a conference, series of workshops, or weekend retreat. Such gatherings offer people the chance to learn about, wrestle with, and push the boundaries of what it means to be a community that truly welcomes the presence and gifts of people with developmental disabilities. These events can also serve to raise awareness in a community, as well as provide a forum for sharing new resources, successful strategies, creative ideas, innovative solutions, and encouragement.

A variety of different formats exist for undertaking such a gathering. One starting point might be to facilitate a panel discussion or "cracker barrel" session at an upcoming regional or state conference devoted to topics related to religious education, youth programming, family life, faith formation, missions, or congregational leadership. State conferences addressing disabilities, special education, or community supports would also provide an excellent context for these conversations. Congregations, disability organizations, or community networks might also collaborate to sponsor a series of quarterly workshops addressing topics related to ministry with people with disabilities (see Table 7.2). For example, a mental health organization might offer training on depression or schizophrenia to clergy and care ministry leaders, a children's pastor might share steps for starting an inclusive Christian education program, an architect might present low-cost strategies for improving the accessibility of a congregation's facilities, or a group of parents might discuss the joys and struggles of raising a child with disabilities.

Conferences, however, probably offer the most focused opportunity to explore these issues in greater depth and with a bigger crowd. Conferences do not have to be large-scale or expensive. You might decide to arrange a shorter gathering—such as a half- or full-day event—rather than a multi-day conference. They may involve dozens, rather than hundreds, of attendees. The format is limited only by your creativity and available resources. Several resources offer step-by-step guidelines for putting together such a conference (see Allen, 2000; Collins, Epstein, Reiss, & Lowe, 2001; Rife & Thornburgh, 2001; Yee, 2003). The following considerations may be helpful as you plan a gathering.

Planning Team

Begin by forming a planning committee. Your community network might be the right group to take primary responsibility for organizing this event. Or, the team might be comprised of representatives from several congregations and community groups, including rehabilitation programs; independent living centers; parent groups; local, county, and state agencies; disability organizations; or local colleges, universities, and seminaries.

Table 7.2. Sample breakout session and workshop topic ideas

- Models of Ministry: Approaches for Welcoming People with Developmental Disabilities
- Parent and Sibling Perspectives: The Supports We Really Need!
- Creative Partnerships: Bringing Together Congregations and Community Organizations
- Personal Perspectives: Faith Stories of Youth and Adults with Developmental Disabilities
- Disability 101: Promoting Awareness Throughout Your Congregation
- Reflecting on Congregational Practices: Identifying Barriers to Participation
- Everyone Learns: Strategies for Adapting Religious Education Curricula
- Preventing and Addressing Behavioral Challenges
- Extending Invitations: Reaching Out to People with Disabilities in Your Community
- Recruiting and Equipping Teachers, Helpers, Faith Partners, and Other Lay Volunteers
- Disability and Theology: Casting a Vision for Our Work
- Youth Groups: Promoting Participation and Peer Relationships
- Supporting People with Developmental Disabilities to Share Their Gifts with Others
- Implementing a Successful Respite Care Program
- Organizing and Facilitating Support Groups for Parents
- Starting New Conversations: Initiating Disability Ministry in Your Congregation
- Barrier Breakers: Improving Architectural Accessibility
- Nurturing Relationships: Creating Circles of Support
- Spiritual Assessments: Identifying and Honoring People's Preferences
- The Meaning of Hospitality: A Theological Framework
- Establishing a Health Ministry in Your Congregation

Multiple tasks will need to be delegated, including setting a timetable, finding an accessible location, establishing a budget, developing the program, inviting speakers, raising funds, marketing the event, coordinating registration, recruiting volunteers, planning refreshments, addressing technical issues, preparing materials, finalizing arrangements, and coordinating conference wrap-up.

Extending Invitations

Consider who might benefit from attending your conference. Is the program designed to equip a broad range of community members, including clergy, lay leaders, religious education staff, parents, self-advocates, service providers, and community organizations? Will it focus just on welcoming people with disabilities? Or, will it focus more broadly on practicing hospitality with anyone who is living on the fringes of community life? Your program might even focus more narrowly on a particular issue (e.g., inclusive children's ministry, the needs of senior citizens with disabilities, welcoming people with developmental disabilities) or specific faith tradition (e.g., Jewish congregations, evangelical churches). Your conference theme will guide whom you might invite.

Interfaith conferences offer the opportunity to learn from congregations across diverse traditions who are discovering new ways of welcoming and weaving people with disabilities into congregational life. The National Organization on Disability's Religion and Disability Program has already supported communities in organizing more than 250 "That All May Worship" conferences. They provide guidance to groups interested in holding such an event and offer the following principles to guide in planning (Rife & Thornburgh, 2001, pp. 13–14):

1. People with disabilities will be in the forefront of all planning and follow-up activities. Planning meetings, and the conference itself, will be presented in formats and in meeting rooms that are fully accessible to people with disabilities.

2. Religious and disability leaders who come together will be committed to long-term involvement and institutional change. These community "stakeholders" will realize that a successful conference is only a step toward community building.

3. The steering committee in each locality will include clergy and lay representatives from diverse faith traditions, disability groups, and racial and ethnic backgrounds, insofar as this diversity accurately reflects the community.

4. Each conference will include interfaith worship and music.

Whatever your focus, successfully publicizing your event will require you to consider several avenues for dissemination. In addition to contacting the leaders of local congregations and faith-based organizations, consider disseminating conference information through area chapters of various disability-related organizations (see Chapter 3). E-mail listservs, electronic discussion boards, and e-newsletters are all low-cost, effective avenues for spreading word among parents, congregation members, and other community members. Speaking with self-advocacy groups or personally visiting residen- tial facilities helps to extend invitations directly to people with developmental disabilities. Finally, share information about the conference with local newspapers, radio stations, and television news programs, asking them to announce and report on the event. If well publicized, your conference will likely bring new people and partners into your community network.

Program Ideas

Conference programs can reflect a variety of formats. For example, organizers might include time for worship, prayer, keynote speakers, breakout sessions, hands-on workshops, panel discussions, shared community visioning, networking, special music, drama performances, or resource and program exhibits. These activities may be combined in a half- or full-day gathering; two sample program schedules are displayed in Figure 7.1. Session topics should be selected carefully to reflect needs within your community and the availability of speakers. Use the session ideas offered in Table 7.2 to stimulate brainstorming of potential topics

Half-Day Schedule

Times	Activities
8:00–8:30	Registration, refreshments, and networking
8:30–8:45	Welcome message
8:45–9:15	Keynote speaker
9:30–10:20	Choice of breakout sessions
10:30–11:20	Choice of breakout sessions
11:30–12:45	Lunch and panel discussion
12:45–1:00	Closing message and dismissal

Full-Day Schedule

Times	Activities
8:30–9:00	Registration, refreshments, and networking
9:00–9:30	Welcome message and worship activities
9:30–10:00	Keynote speaker
10:15–11:00	Choice of breakout sessions
11:15–12:00	Choice of breakout sessions
12:00–1:00	Lunch and networking
1:00–3:00	Congregational team planning with facilitation
3:00–3:15	Break
3:15–4:15	Panel discussion
4:30–4:45	Closing message and dismissal
4:45–???	Networking and resource sharing

Figure 7.1. Sample half- and full-day conference schedules.

for your own gathering. Holding several sessions concurrently allows conference participants to attend sessions that most closely reflect their interests.

Two additional ideas might be worth incorporating into your conference. First, rather than simply holding informational sessions, consider how you might create a meaningful opportunity for attendees to work together to develop a blueprint for change in their congregations, agencies, or communities. For example, congregations might be asked to form small teams representing different perspectives and programs from within their faith community. Team members would each attend different breakout sessions in the morning and then regroup in the afternoon to share what they have learned and develop an action plan for their congregation. A facilitator and several "experts" in different aspects of disability ministry should be present to guide teams. This approach—sometimes called immersion learning—ensures that attendees leave with the seeds of a plan to take back and flesh out within their respective communities. Second, block out a period of time for conference attendees to gather together to engage in a shared conversation about how to improve their community's capacity to welcome people with disabilities as they ought to. This time could be devoted to creating an overarching vision for the community. Set up small tables and encourage people to sit with new people. Pose several catalyst questions to get small group conversations going, occasionally rearrange group members to promote broader exchange of ideas, and allow time at the end to share themes, lessons, and strategies back with entire group. The World Café process can be helpful for fostering such dialogues (Brown & Isaacs, 2005; http://www.theworldcafe.com).

Reflection and Follow-Up

At the conclusion of the conference, give participants an opportunity to provide feedback on the conference as a whole and on the individual sessions they attended. Ask for their input on the accessibility of the event, as well as their ideas and suggestions for improving the next gathering you might host. You might discover that important topics were overlooked, the day of the conference was inconvenient and thus it limited participation, or important perspectives were not represented. In addition, make sure that attendees know with whom they can follow-up should they want additional information or guidance as they take back lessons to their communities. Finally, ask what steps they are planning to take next as a result of attending the conference.

CONCLUSION

Working together, communities have the ability to completely transform the landscape for people with developmental disabilities and their families. Community networks, asset mapping, and disability gatherings each might serve as a catalyst for bringing scattered efforts to a common focus. Each approach will demand much work and passion, but the community will be stronger for your efforts.

References

Abelson, A.G. (1999). Respite care needs of parents of children with developmental disabilities. *Focus on Autism and Other Developmental Disabilities, 14,* 96–100.

Abery, B., & Ziegler, M. (2003). Supporting social and recreational choice-making by adults with disabilities. *Impact, 16*(3), 13.

Abeson, A., Bosk, E., Timmons, J., & Lazarus, S. (2005). *Impact: Feature issue on meeting transportation needs of youth and young adults with developmental disabilities.* Minneapolis, MN: Institute on Community Integration.

Abrams, J.Z. (1998). *Judaism and disability: Portrayals in ancient texts from the Tanach through the Bavli.* Washington, DC: Gallaudet University Press.

Accessibilities Committee, Unitarian Universalist Association. (1999). *What do I say? What do I do? Interacting with persons who have disabilities.* Boston: Author.

Advisory Committee on Social Witness Policy. (2001). *Harvesting seeds of justice: Ministering in church and society with persons who have disabilities.* (Prospectus for a task force of the Advisory Committee on Social Witness Policy, p. 2). Louisville, KY: Presbyterian Church (USA).

Alban Institute. (2001). *Money and ideas: Creative approaches to congregational access.* Bethesda, MD: Author.

Allen, J. (2000). *Event planning: The ultimate guide to successful meetings, corporate events, fundraising galas, conferences, conventions, incentives, and other special events.* New York: John Wiley & Sons.

American Association on Mental Retardation and The Arc. (2002). *AAMR/The Arc position statement on spirituality.* Washington, DC: Author.

Americans with Disabilities Act (ADA) of 1990, PL 101–336, 42 U.S.C. §§ 12101 et seq.

Ammerman, N.T. (2005). *Pillars of faith: American congregations and their partners.* Berkley, CA: University of California Press.

Anandarajah, G., & Hight, E. (2001). Spirituality and medical practice: Using the HOPE questions as a practical tool for spiritual assessment. *American Family Physician, 63*(1), 81–89.

Anderson, G.C., & Briarwood Task Force for Handicapped Ministries. (1999). *What Christians believe: Confirmation studies for persons with mental retardation and developmental disabilities.* Louisville, KY: Bridge Resources.

Anderson, R.C. (2003). Infusing the graduate theological curriculum with education about disability: Addressing the human experience of disability in the theological context. *Theological Education, 39,* 1–24.

ARCH National Respite Network. (2001). *Program survey report for fiscal 2001.* Chapel Hill, NC: Author.

Arnold, H. (2005, Winter) Using spiritual assessments (continued). *The Religion and Spirituality Division Quarterly, 3.*

Bannerman, D.J., Sheldon, J.B., Sherman, J.A., & Harchik, A.E. (1990). Balancing the right to habilitation with the right to personal liberties: The rights of people with developmental disabilities to eat too many doughnuts and take a nap. *Journal of Applied Behavior Analysis, 23,* 79–89.

Barnes, K. (2005). Winning partnership: Advocate Kelly Barnes speaks out about what's important in choosing a compatible congregation. *Breakthrough, 17*(1), 4.

Bass, S. (2003). *Special children, special needs: Integrating children with disabilities and special needs into your church* (p. 2). London: Church House Publishing.

Beaulieu, L.J. (2002). *Mapping the assets of your community: A key component for building local capacity* (p. 12). Mississippi State: Southern Rural Development Center.

Birch, B.C. (2003). Integrating welcome into the seminary curriculum. *Journal of Religion, Disability, & Health, 7*(3), 23–31.

Black, K. (1996). *A healing homiletic: Preaching and disability.* Nashville: Abingdon Press.

Block, J.W. (2002). *Copious hosting: A theology of access for people with disabilities.* New York: The Continuum International Publishing Group.

Block, M.E. (with invited contributors) (2007). *A teacher's guide to including students with disabilities in general physical education* (3rd ed.). Baltimore: Paul H. Brookes Publishing Co.

Bogdan, R., & Taylor, S.J. (2001). Building stronger communities for all: Thoughts about community participation for individuals with developmental disabilities. In A.J. Tymchuk, K.C. Lakin, & R. Luckasson (Eds.), *The forgotten generation: The status and challenges of adults with mild cognitive limitations* (p. 192). Baltimore: Paul H. Brookes Publishing Co.

Bolduc, K.D. (2001). *A place called acceptance: Ministry with families of children with disabilities.* Louisville, KY: Bridge Resources.

Braddock, D., Hemp, R., Rizzolo, M.C., Coulter, D., Haffer, L., & Thompson, M. (2005). *The state of the states in developmental disabilities: 2005.* Boulder, CO: Coleman Institute for Cognitive Disabilities, University of Colorado.

Brew-Parish, V. (2004). The wrong message—still. *Ragged Edge Online.* Retrieved July 25, 2005, from http://www.raggededgemagazine.com/focus/wrongmessage04.html

Broughman, S.P., & Pugh, K.W. (2004). *Characteristics of private schools in the United States: Results from the 2001–2002 Private School Universe Survey.* Washington, DC: National Center for Education Statistics.

Brown, J., & Isaacs, D. (2005). *The World Café: Shaping our futures through conversations that matter.* San Francisco: Berrett-Koehler.

Butterworth, J., Hagner, D., Heikkinen, B., Faris, S., DeMello, S., &

McDonough, K. (1993). *Whole life planning: A guide for organizers and facilitators*. Boston: Institute for Community Inclusion, Children's Hospital.

Butterworth, J., Hagner, D., Helm, D.T., & Whelley, T.A. (2000). Workplace culture, social interactions, and supports for transition-age young adults. *Mental Retardation, 38*, 342–353.

Carlson, M.C. (2004). *With open hands: Extending hospitality and receiving the gifts of people leaving Northern Wisconsin Center: The Project Homecoming guidebook for faith communities*. Milwaukee, WI: People First Wisconsin.

Carter, E.W., Cushing, L.S., Clark, N.M., & Kennedy, C.H. (2005). Effects of peer support interventions on students' access to the general curriculum and social interactions. *Research and Practice for Persons with Severe Disabilities, 30*, 15–25.

Carter, P. (1999). *Welcome one...welcome all: Inclusive religious education*. Dayton, OH: Institute for Pastoral Initiatives, University of Dayton.

Chaves, M. (2004). *Congregations in America*. Cambridge, MA: Harvard University Press.

Christian Reformed Church in North America. (2004). *Agenda for Synod: 2004*. Grand Rapids, MI: Author.

Cohen, J. (2003). *Disability etiquette: Tips on interacting with people with disabilities* (2nd ed.). Jackson Heights, NY: United Spinal Association.

Collins, B.C., Epstein, A., Reiss, T., & Lowe, V. (2001). Including children with mental retardation in the religious community. *Teaching Exceptional Children, 33*(5), 52–58.

Cook, E. (1998). The role of the church in providing comprehensive services. *National Apostolate Quarterly, 30*(2), pp. 18–19.

Copeland, S.R., Hughes, C., Carter, E.W., Guth, C., Presley, J., Williams, C.R., & Fowler, S.E. (2004). Increasing access to general education: Perspectives of participants in a high school peer support program. *Remedial and Special Education, 26*, 342–352.

Coucouvanis, K., Prouty, R., & Lakin, K.C. (2005). Own home and host family options growing rapidly as more than 70% of residential service recipients with ID/DD in 2004 live in settings of 6 or fewer. *Mental Retardation, 43*, 307–309.

Council on Quality and Leadership. (2005). *Quality measures 2005*. Towson, MD: Author.

Covey, H.C. (2004). Western Christianity's two historical treatments of people with disabilities or mental illness. *The Social Science Journal, 42*, 107–114.

Crane, K., & Skinner, B. (2003). *Community resource mapping: A strategy for promoting successful transition for youth with disabilities*. Minneapolis, MN: National Center on Secondary Education and Transition.

Creamer, D.B. (2003). Toward a theology that includes the human experience of disability, *Journal of Religion, Disability, & Health, 7*, 60.

Davie, A.R., & Thornburgh, G. (2000). *That all may worship: An interfaith welcome to people with disabilities*, pp. 29–30. Washington, DC: National Organization on Disability.

DeYoung, C.P., Emerson, M.O., Yancey, G., & Kim, K.C. (2003). *United by faith: The multiracial congregation as the answer to the problem of race*. New York: Oxford University Press.

Developmental Disabilities Assistance and Bill of Rights Act Amendments of 2000, PL 106–402, 114 42 U.S.C., §§6000 *et seq.*

Dudley, C.S., & Roozen, D.A. (2001). *Faith communities today: A report on religion in the United States today.* Hartford, CT: Hartford Institute for Religion Research.

Dyches, T.T., & Prater, M.A. (2000). *Developmental disability in children's literature: Issues and annotated bibliography.* Reston, VA: Council for Exceptional Children, Division on Developmental Disabilities.

Edwards, J. (1997a). *Celebrating confirmation (Sharing our faith series).* London: Matthew James.

Edwards, J. (1997b). *Celebrating first Eucharist (Sharing our faith series).* London: Matthew James.

Eiesland, N.L., & Saliers, D.E. (1998). *Human disability and the service of God: Reassessing religious practice.* Nashville: Abingdon.

Eigenbrood, R. (2004). IDEA requirements for children with disabilities in faith-based schools: Implications for practice. *Journal of Disability Policy Studies, 15,* 2–8.

Eigenbrood, R. (2005). A survey comparing special education services for students with disabilities in rural faith-based and public school settings. *Remedial and Special Education, 26,* 16–24.

Fewell, R.R. (1986). Supports from religious organizations and personal beliefs. In Fewell, R.R. & Vadasy, P.F. (Eds.), *Families of handicapped children: Needs and supports across the life span* (pp. 297–316). Austin, TX: PRO-ED.

1 Corinthians 12:12, 25–26. *The Message.* Copyright 1993, 1994, 1995, 1996, 2000, 2001, 2002. Used by permission of NavPress Publishing Group.

Fitchett, G. (2002). *Assessing spiritual needs: A guide for caregivers.* Lima, OH: Academic Renewal Press.

Foley, E. (Ed.). (1994). *Developmental disabilities and sacramental access: New paradigms for sacramental encounters.* Collegeville, MN: The Liturgical Press.

Forest, M., & Pearpoint, J. (1997). *Four easy questions.* Toronto: Inclusion Press.

Gallagher, P.A., Powell, T.H., & Rhodes, C.A. (2006). *Brothers and sisters: A special part of exceptional families* (3rd edition). Baltimore: Paul H. Brookes Publishing Co.

Galvin, M. (2001). Bridge Ministries for Disability Concerns: A community ministry model. *Journal of Religion, Disability, & Health, 5*(2/3), 157–172.

Gardner, J.E., & Carran, D.T. (2005). Attainment of personal outcomes by people with developmental disabilities. *Mental Retardation, 43,* 157–174.

Gaventa, B. (2005). Celebrating the sacred in shared meals: Grace and blessing. In K.M. Schwier & E.S. Stewart (Eds.), *Breaking bread, nourishing connections: People with and without disabilities together at mealtime* (p. 115). Baltimore: Paul H. Brookes Publishing Co.

Gaventa, W. (1986). Religious ministries and services with adults with developmental disabilities. In J.A. Summers (Ed.), *The right to grow up: An introduction to adults with developmental disabilities* (pp. 191–226). Baltimore: Paul H. Brookes Publishing Co.

Gaventa, W. (1990). Respite care: An opportunity for the religious community. *Exceptional Parent, 20*(4), 22–26.

Gaventa, W. (1993). Gift and call: Recovering the spiritual foundations of friendships. In A.N. Amado (Ed.), *Friendships and community connections between people with and without developmental disabilities* (pp. 41–66). Baltimore: Paul H. Brookes Publishing Co.

Gaventa, W. (1996). Bring on the church coach! *Disability Solutions, 1*(4), 1, 3.

Gaventa, W. (2003). Why am I? Faith and purpose (Part I). *The Arc Insight, 1*, 8.

Gaventa, W. (2005). A place for ALL of me and ALL of us: Rekindling the spirit in services and supports. *Mental Retardation, 43*, 48–54.

Gaventa, W.C., & Coulter, D.L. (Eds.). (2002). *Spirituality and intellectual disability: International perspectives on the effect of culture and religion on healing body, mind, and soul.* Binghamton, NY: Haworth.

Gaventa, W., & Peters, R.K. (2001). Spirituality and self-actualization: Recognizing spiritual needs and strengths of individuals with cognitive limitations. In A.J. Tymchuk, K.C. Lakin, & R. Luckasson (Eds.), *The forgotten generation: The status and challenges of adults with mild cognitive limitations* (p. 306). Baltimore: Paul H. Brookes Publishing Co.

Getchell, N., & Gagen, L. (2006). Adapting activities for all children: Considering constraints can make planning simple and effective. *Palaestra, 22*, 20–27, 43, 58.

Gleeson, T. (2001/2002). Incorporating spiritual supports into residential services. *Impact, 14*(3), p. 30.

Govig, S.D. (1989). *Strong at the broken places: Persons with disabilities and the church.* Louisville, KY: Westminster/John Knox Press.

Granzen, D. (March, 2005). *Inclusion and reciprocity.* Keynote presentation at the Faith Inclusion Network Conference. Madison, Wisconsin.

Hanson, M.J., & Lynch, E.W. (2004). *Understanding families: Approaches to diversity, disability, and risk.* Baltimore: Paul H. Brookes Publishing Co.

Hatton, C., Turner, S., Shah, R., Rahim, N., & Stansfield, J. (2004a). *Religious expression: A fundamental human right: The report of an action research project on meeting the religious needs of people with learning disabilities.* London: The Foundation for People with Learning Disabilities.

Hatton, C., Turner, S., Shah, R., Rahim, N., & Stansfield, J. (2004b). *What about faith? A good practice guide for services on meeting the religious needs of people with learning disabilities.* London: The Foundation for People with Learning Disabilities.

Hayden, M.F., Lakin, K.C., Hill, B.K., Bruininks, R.H., & Copher, J.I. (1992). Social and leisure integration of people with mental retardation in foster homes and small group homes. *Education and Training in Mental Retardation, 27*, 187–199.

Haythorn, T. (2003). Different bodies, one body: Inclusive religious education and the role of the religious educator. *Religious Education, 98*, 331–347.

Herman, S.E., & Thompson, L. (1995). Families' perceptions of their resources for caring for children with developmental disabilities. *Mental Retardation, 33*, 73–83.

Hingsburger, D., & Tough, S. (2002). Healthy sexuality: Attitudes, systems, and policies. *Journal of the Association for Persons with Severe Handicaps, 27*, 8–17.

Hodge, D.R. (2003). *Spiritual assessment: Handbook for helping professionals.* Botsford, CT: North American Association of Christians in Social Work.

Hoecke, W.C., & Mayfield-Smith, K. (2000). *Respite and the faith community.* Chapel Hill, NC: ARCH National Respite Network and Resource Center.

Hoeksema, T.B. (1995). Supporting the free exercise of religion in the group home context. *Mental Retardation, 33,* 290.

Holburn, S., & Vietze, P.M. (Eds.). (2002). *Person-centered planning: Research, practice, and future directions.* Baltimore: Paul H. Brookes Publishing Co.

Hornstein, B. (1997). How the religious community can support the transition to adulthood: A parent's perspective. *Mental Retardation, 97,* 487.

Individuals with Disabilities Education Improvement Act of 2004, pl 108–446, 20 U.S.C. §§1400 *et seq.*

Janney, R., & Snell, M.E. (2000). *Behavioral support.* Baltimore: Paul H. Brookes Publishing Co.

Jones, L.T. (2004). Case studies: Special needs ministries in real churches. In M. Keefer (Ed.), *Special needs, special ministry: For children's ministry* (p. 50). Loveland, CO: Group Publishing.

Klein, L.L. (2000). *The support group sourcebook: What they are, how you can find one, and how they can help you.* New York: John Wiley & Sons.

Koegel, L.K., Koegel, R.L., & Dunlap, G. (1996). *Positive behavioral support: Including people with difficult behavior in the community.* Baltimore: Paul H. Brookes Publishing Co.

Krajewski, J.J., & Hyde, M.S. (2000). Comparison of teen attitudes toward individuals with mental retardation between 1987 and 1998: Has inclusion made a difference? *Education and Training in Mental Retardation and Developmental Disabilities, 35,* 284–293.

Kregel, J., Wehman, P., Seyfarth, J., & Marshall, K. (1986). Community integration of young adults with mental retardation: Transition from school to adulthood. *Education and Training of the Mentally Retarded, 21,* 35–53.

Kretzmann, J.P., & McKnight, J.L. (1993). *Building communities from the inside out: A path toward finding and mobilizing a community's assets.* Evanston, IL: Institute for Policy Research.

Kruck, K. (2002). *That they may partake* (2nd ed.). Milwaukee, WI: JCM Publications.

Kupper, L. (2001). *A guide to children's literature and disability* (2nd ed.). Washington, DC: National Dissemination Center for Children with Disabilities.

Landes, S.D. (2001/2002). Atlanta's Interfaith Disabilities Network. *Impact: Feature issue on faith communities and persons with developmental disabilities, 14*(3), 28.

LaRocque, M., & Eigenbrood, R. (2005). Community access: A survey of congregational accessibility for people with disabilities. *Journal of Religion, Disability, & Health, 9,* 55–66.

Leichty, P.D. (2003). From exile to inclusion: A community for everyone. *The Mennonite, 6*(4), 9–11.

Leneman, H. (Ed.). (2003). *Bar/bat mitzvah education: A source book.* Denver, CO: ARE Publishing.

Luiselli, J.K. (Ed.) (2006). *Antecedent assessment and intervention: Supporting children and adults with developmental disabilities in community settings.* Baltimore: Paul H. Brookes Publishing Co.

Making rural churches accessible to disabled. (1998). *Christian Century, 115,* 1085.

Marshall, E.S., Olsen, S.F., Madleco, B.L., Dyches, T.T., Allred, K.W., & Sansom, N. (2003). "This is a spiritual experience": Perspectives of Latter-Day Saint families living with a child with disabilities. *Qualitative Health Research, 13,* 57–76.

Maugans, T.A. (1996). The SPIRITual history. *Archives of Family Medicine, 5,* 11–16.

McHugh, M. (2002). *Special siblings: Growing up with someone with a disability* (Rev. ed). Baltimore: Paul H. Brookes Publishing Co.

McKnight, J.L. (1992). Redefining community. *Social Policy, 23*(2), 56–62.

McNair, J. (2000). The local church as a network supporting adults with disabilities in the community: One perspective. *Journal of Religion, Disability, & Health, 4,* 33—56.

McNair, J., & Schwartz, S.L. (1997). Local church support to individuals with developmental disabilities. *Education and Training in Mental Retardation and Developmental Disabilities, 32,* 304–312.

McNair, J., & Smith, H.K. (2000). Church attendance of adults with developmental disabilities. *Education and Training in Mental Retardation and Developmental Disabilities, 35,* 222–225.

McPherson, M.A. (2004). What do families with special needs children need? In M. Keefer (Ed.), *Special needs, special ministry: For children's ministry* (p. 28). Loveland, CO: Group Publishing.

Merrick, L.H. (Ed.). (1993). *And show steadfast love: A theological look at grace, hospitality, disabilities, and the Church.* Louisville, KY: Presbyterian Publishing House.

Merrick, J., Gabbay, Y., & Lifshitz, H. (2001). Judaism and the person with intellectual disability. *Journal of Religion, Disability, & Health, 5,* 49–63.

Meyer, C. (1995). *My confirmation book* (Vols. 1 & 2). Watertown, WI: Bethesda Lutheran Homes and Services.

Meyer, D.J. (Ed.). (2004). *The sibling slam book: What it's really like to have a brother or sister with special needs.* Bethesda, MD: Woodbine House.

Mika, T. (1995). The power of love. *Exceptional Parent, 25*(7), p. 43.

Miles, M. (1995). Disability in an eastern religious context: Historical perspectives. *Disability & Society, 10,* 49–69.

Miller, K.D., Schleien, S.J., Rider, C., Hall, C., Roche, M., & Worsley, J. (2002). Inclusive volunteering: Benefits to participants and community. *Therapeutic Recreation Journal, 36,* 247–259.

Miller, N.B., & Sammons, C.C. (1999). *Everybody's different: Understanding and changing our reactions to disabilities.* Baltimore: Paul H. Brookes Publishing Co.

Miltiades, H.B., & Pruchno, R. (2002). The effect of religious coping on caregiving appraisals of mothers of adults with developmental disabilities. *The Gerontologist, 42,* 82–91.

Minnes, P., Buell, K., Feldman, M.A., McColl, M.A., & McCreary, B. (2002). Community integration as acculturation: Preliminary validation of the AIMS interview. *Journal of Applied Research in Intellectual Disabilities, 15,* 377–387.

Minton, C.A., & Dodder, R.A. (2003). Participation in religious services by people with developmental disabilities. *Mental Retardation, 41,* 430–439.

Morad, M., Nasri, Y., & Merrick, J. (2001). Islam and the person with intellectual disability. *Journal of Religion, Disability, & Health, 5,* 65–71.

Morgan, R.L., & Alexander, M. (2005). The employer's perception: Employment of individuals with developmental disabilities. *Journal of Vocational Rehabilitation, 23,* 39–49.

Mose, J.R. (2001). *Understanding your new student: Steps for planning the spiritual instruction of a student with a developmental disability.* Milwaukee, WI: JCM Ministries.

Mount, B., & Zwernik, K. (1994). *Making futures happen: A manual for facilitators of personal futures planning.* St. Paul: Minnesota's Governor's Planning Council on Developmental Disabilities.

Murdoch, T. (1995). *Children with disability & participation in sacraments: Resource booklet 3.* Brisbane, Australia: Liturgical Commission.

Nangle, K.M. (2001). Transition to employment and community life for youths with visual impairments: Current status and future directions. *Journal of Visual Impairment & Blindness, 95,* 725–738.

National Council of Churches. (1998). *Disabilities, the body of Christ, and the wholeness of society.* Retrieved Oct. 8, 2006, from http://www.nccusa.org. New York: Author.

National Organization on Disability. (2001). *The journey of a congregation.* Washington, DC: Author.

National Organization on Disability/Harris Interactive. (2004). *2004 National Organization on Disability/Harris Survey of Americans with Disabilities.* Washington: Author.

Nerney, T. (2003). *The system of the future.* Ann Arbor, MI: Center for Self-Determination.

Nerney, T., & Vining, V. (2005). Self-determination: Principles for evaluating your system. *TASH Connections, 31*(3/4), 5.

Newman, B. (2001). *Helping kids include kids with disabilities.* Grand Rapids, MI: Faith Alive Christian Resources.

North American Mission Board. (2000). *Providing respite care (support for disabled persons and their families),* p. 1. Retrieved May 8, 2006, from http://www.namb.net

Nouwen, H. (Speaker). (1996). *Open hearts, open minds, open doors: The vulnerable journey* [Video]. Chicago: Pathways Awareness Foundation.

O'Brien, J., & Mount, B. (2005). *Make a difference: A guidebook for person-centered direct support.* Toronto: Inclusion Press.

O'Brien, J., & O'Brien, C.L. (Eds.). (2002). *Implementing person-centered planning: Voices of experience.* Toronto: Inclusion Press.

O'Connell, M. (1988). *The gift of hospitality: Opening the doors of community life to people with disabilities* (p. 8). Evanston, IL: Community Life Project, Center for Urban Affairs and Policy Research, Northwestern University.

O'Connell, M. (1990). *Community building in Logan Square: How a community grew stronger with the contributions of people with disabilities.* Evanston, IL: Community Life Project, Center for Urban Affairs and Policy Research, Northwestern University.

Orsmond, G.I., Krauss, M.W., & Seltzer, M.M. (2004). Peer relationships and social and recreational activities among adolescents and adults with autism. *Journal of Autism and Developmental Disorders, 34,* 245–256.

O'Shannessy, M. (1995a). *Sharing God's love: Preparation for the Eucharist of students with intellectual disability.* Strathfield, Australia: St. Pauls.

O'Shannessy, M. (1995b). *Sharing God's love: Preparation for the confirmation of students with intellectual disability.* Strathfield, Australia: St. Pauls.

Owen, M.J. (1993). The wisdom of human vulnerability. *The Disability Rag & Resource, 14*(5), 19.

Park, J., Turnbull, A.P., & Turnbull, H.R. (2002). Impacts of poverty on quality of life in families of children with disabilities. *Exceptional Children, 68,* 151–170.

Pearpoint, J., O'Brien, J., & Forest, M. (1993). *PATH: Planning Alternative Tomorrows with Hope: A workbook for planning possible positive futures.* Toronto: Inclusion Press.

Perkins, C. (2001/2002). Bridges to faith: Collaborating to connect individuals and congregations. *Impact, 14*(3), 18–19.

Perry, J. (2004). Interviewing people with intellectual disabilities. In E. Emerson, T. Thompson, & T. Parmenter (Eds.), *International handbook of applied research in intellectual disabilities* (pp. 115–132). West Sussex, England: John Wiley & Sons.

Pierson, J. (2002). *Exceptional teaching: A comprehensive guide for including students with disabilities.* Cincinnati, OH: Standard.

Pierson, J. (2004). First steps for launching a children's special needs ministry. In M. Keefer (Ed.), *Special needs, special ministry: For children's ministry* (pp. 51–63). Loveland, CO: Group Publishing.

Plante, T.G., & Sherman, A.C. (Eds.) (2001). *Faith and health: Psychological perspectives.* New York: Guilford Press.

Pohl, C. (1999). Welcoming the stranger: What hospitality teaches us about justice. *Sojourners, 28*(4), 14.

Poston, D.J., & Turnbull, A.P. (2004). Role of spirituality and religion in family quality of life for families of children with disabilities. *Education and Training in Developmental Disabilities, 39,* 95–108.

Preheim-Bartel, D.A., & Neufeldt, A.H. (1986). *Supportive care in the congregation: A congregational care plan for providing a supportive care network for persons who are disabled or dependent.* Goshen, IN: Mennonite Mutual Aid.

Presbyterian Panel. (2004). *Disability issues: The May 2004 survey.* Louisville, KY: Presbyterian Church (USA).

President's Committee for People with Intellectual Disabilities. (2004). *A charge we have to keep: A road map to personal and economic freedom for people with intellectual disabilities in the 21st century.* Washington, DC: Author.

Prouty, R.W., Smith, G., & Lakin, K.C. (Eds.). (2004). *Residential services for persons with developmental disabilities: Status and trends through 2003.* Minneapolis, MN: Research and Training Center on Community Living, Institute on Community Integration.

Puchalski, C.M., & Romer, A.L. (2000). Taking a spiritual history allows clinicians to understand patients more fully. *Journal of Palliative Medicine, 3*, 129–137.

Rabbinowitz, J. (Trans.) (1939). Deuteronomy. In H. Freedman & M. Simon (Series Eds.), *Midrash Rabbah* (p. 92). London: Soncino Press.

Raji, O., Hollins, R., & Drinnan, A. (2003). How far are people with learning disabilities involved in funeral rites? *British Journal of Learning Disabilities, 31*, 42–45.

Rans, S., & Altman, H. (2002). *Asset-based strategies for faith communities.* Evanston, IL: Institute for Policy Research.

Rans, S.A., & Green, M. (2005). *Hidden treasures: Building community connections by engaging the gifts of people on welfare, people with disabilities, people with mental illness, older adults, and young people.* Evanston, IL: Asset Based Community Development Institute.

Renwick, R., Schormans, A.F., & Zekovic, B. (2003). Quality of life for children with developmental disabilities: A new conceptual framework. *Journal of Developmental Disabilities, 10*, 107–114.

Rife, J.M. & Thornburgh, G. (2001). *From barriers to bridges: A community action guide for congregations and people with disabilities.* Washington, DC: National Organization on Disability.

Riordan, J., & Vasa, S.F. (1991). Accommodations for and participation of persons with disabilities in religious practice. *Education and Training in Mental Retardation, 26*, 151–155.

Roker, D., Player, K., & Coleman, J. (1998). Challenging the image: The involvement of young people with disabilities in volunteering and campaigning. *Disability & Society, 13*, 725–741.

Rosenberg, C. (1999). Welcome one, welcome all: Inclusive religious education. *Church & Society, 89*, 75–79.

Rusch, F.R., & Braddock, D. (2004). Adult day programs versus supported employment (1988–2002): Spending and service practices of mental retardation and developmental disabilities state agencies. *Research & Practice for Persons with Severe Disabilities, 29*, 237–242.

Rush, W. (2003). Harvesters with disabilities: A journey testimony. *Journal of Religion, Disability, and Health, 7*, 69–70.

Schalock, R.L., Brown, I., Brown, R., Cummins, R.A., Felce, D., Matikka, L., et al. (2002). Conceptualization, measurement, and application of quality of life for persons with intellectual disabilities: Report of an international panel of experts. *Mental Retardation, 40*, 457–470.

Schulz, E.K. (2005). The meaning of spirituality for individuals with disabilities. *Disability and Rehabilitation, 27*, 1283–1295.

Shogren, K.A., & Rye, M.S. (2005). Religion and individuals with intellectual disabilities: An exploratory study of self-reported perspectives. *Journal of Religion, Disability, & Health, 9*, 29–53.

Sieck, T.F., & Hartvigsen, R. (2001). *How people with developmental disabilities can access the faith community of their choice.* Lakeside, CA: Home of the Guiding Hands.

Silverstein, R. (2000). Emerging disability policy framework: A guidepost for analyzing public policy. *Iowa Law Review, 85,* 1695.

Siperstein, G.N., Romano, N., Mohler, A., & Parker, R. (2006). A national survey of consumer attitudes towards companies that hire people with disabilities. *Journal of Vocational Rehabilitation, 24,* 3–9.

Smietana, B. (2005). Confirming Aaron. *The Covenant Companion, 12.*

Smull, M. (1997). *A blueprint for essential lifestyle planning.* Napa, CA: Allen, Shea & Associates.

Snow, L.K. (2004). *The power of asset mapping: How your congregation can act on its gifts.* Herndon, VA: Alban Institute.

Solomon, M., Pistrang, N., & Barker, C. (2001). The benefits of mutual support groups for parents of children with disabilities. *American Journal of Community Psychology, 29,* 113–132.

Sowers, B.J. (2001/2002). An ecumenical appeal for inclusion: The first U.S. regional initiative. *Impact: Feature issue on faith communities and persons with spencer, 2005 developmental disabilities, 14*(3), 15.

Spencer, S. (2005, May). *Blackhawk Church procedures for kids with special needs.* Madison, WI: Blackhawk Church.

Speraw, S. (2006). Spiritual experiences of parents and caregivers who have children with disabilities or special needs. *Issues in Mental Health Nursing, 27,* 213–230.

Steinmetz, E. (2006). *Americans with disabilities: 2002.* Washington, DC: US Census Bureau.

Stiemke, F.A. (1994). Church-synagogue-temple-mosque advocacy: An avenue for integration in religious and secular communities. *Journal of Religion in Disability & Rehabilitation, 1*(4), 1–11.

Stookey, L.H. (2003). Inclusiveness as hospitality in worship settings. *Journal of Religion, Disability & Health, 7*(3), 95–102.

Swedeen, B. (2002). *Believing, belonging, becoming: Stories of faith inclusion.* Madison, WI: Wisconsin Council on Developmental Disabilities.

Swinton, J. (2001). Building a church for strangers. *Journal of Religion, Disability, & Health, 4,* 56.

Swinton, J. (2002a). *A space to listen: Meeting the spiritual needs of people with learning disabilities.* London: The Foundation for People with Learning Disabilities.

Swinton, J. (2002b). Spirituality and the lives of people with learning disabilities. *Tizard Learning Disability Review, 7*(4), 29–35.

Swinton, J., & Powrie, E. (2004). *Why are we here? Meeting the needs of people with learning disabilities.* London: Foundation for People with Learning Disabilities.

Tada, J.E., & Miller, S. (2002). *Through the roof: A guide to assist churches in developing an effective disability outreach.* Agoura Hills, CA: Joni and Friends.

TASH. (2003). *TASH resolution on spirituality.* Baltimore: Author.

Tassé, M.J., Schalock, R., Thompson, J.R., & Wehmeyer, M. (2005). *Guidelines for interviewing people with disabilities: Supports Intensity Scale.* Washington, DC: American Association on Mental Retardation.

Thompson, J.R., Bryant, B.R., Campbell, E.M., Craig, E.M., Hughes, C.A., Rotholz, D.A., et al. (2004). *Supports Intensity Scale: Users Manual (p. 2)*. Washington, DC: American Association on Mental Retardation.

Turnbull, A., Turnbull, R., Erwin, E.J., & Soodak, L.C. (2006). *Families, professionals, and exceptionality: Positive outcomes through partnership and trust* (5th ed.). Upper Saddle River, NJ: Prentice Hall.

United Nations General Assembly. (1948). *Universal declaration of human rights: Article 18*. Paris: Author. Retrieved from http://www.un.org/overview/rights.html

United States Conference of Catholic Bishops. (2001). *Pastoral statement of U.S. Catholic Bishops on persons with disabilities*, pp. 8–9. Washington, DC: Author.

Vandercook, T., York, J., & Forest, M. (1989). The McGill Action Planning System (MAPS): A strategy for building the vision. *Journal of the Association for Persons with Severe Handicaps, 14*, 205–215.

Van der Klift, E., & Kunc, N. (2002). Beyond benevolence: Supporting genuine friendship in inclusive schools. In J. Thousand, R. Villa, & A. Nevin (Eds.), *Creativity and collaborative learning: A practical guide to empowering students, teachers, and families* (2nd ed., pp. 21–28). Baltimore: Paul H. Brookes Publishing Co.

Van Dyken, B. (1995). Respite care and the religious community. *Exceptional Parent, 25*(7), 41–43.

Vanier, J. (1975). *Be not afraid* (p. 99). Toronto: Griffin House.

Vogel, G., & Reiter, S. (2003). Spiritual dimensions of bar/bat mitzvah ceremonies for Jewish children with developmental disabilities. *Education and Training in Developmental Disabilities, 38*, 319.

Vogel, G., & Reiter, S. (2004). Significance of a bar/bat mitzvah ceremony for Jewish children with developmental disabilities. *Mental Retardation, 42*, 294–303.

Vogel, J., Polloway, E.A., Smith, J.D. (2006). Inclusion of people with mental retardation and other developmental disabilities in communities of faith. *Mental Retardation, 44*, 100–111.

Vredeveld, R.C. (2001). *Caring relationships: Helping people with mental impairments understand God's gift of sexuality*. Grand Rapids, MI: Faith Alive Christian Resources.

Vredeveld, R.C. (2005). *Expressing faith in Jesus: Church membership for people with cognitive impairments*. Grand Rapids, MI: Faith Alive Christian Resources.

Wagner, M., Cadwallader, T.W., & Marder, C. (2003). *Life outside the classroom for youth with disabilities. A report from the National Longitudinal Transition Study-2 (NLTS2)*. Menlo Park, CA: SRI International.

Wagner, M., Cadwallader, T. W., Marder, C., Newman, L., Garza, N., Blackorby, J., & Guzman, A. (2002). *The other 80% of their time: The experiences of elementary and middle school students with disabilities in their nonschool hours*. Menlo Park, CA: SRI International.

Wagner, M., Newman, L., Cameto, R., & Levine, P. (2005). *Changes in time in the early postschool outcomes of youth with disabilities: A report of findings from the National Longitudinal Transition Study (NLTS) and the National Longitudinal Transition Study-2 (NLTS-2)*. Menlo Park, CA: SRI International.

Webb-Mitchell, B. (1993). *God plays piano, too: The spiritual lives of disabled children.* New York: Crossroads.

Webb-Mitchell, B. (1993). Let the children come: Young people with disabilities in church. *Christian Century, 110,* 981.

Wehmeyer, M.L., & Patton, J.R. (Eds.) (2000). *Mental retardation in the 21st century.* Austin, TX: PRO-ED.

Weisner, T.S., Beizer, L., & Stolze, L. (1991). Religion and families of children with developmental delays. *American Journal on Mental Retardation, 95,* p. 650.

White House. (2001). *New Freedom Initiative: Fulfilling America's promise to Americans with disabilities* (p. 23). Washington, DC: Author.

Williamson, P., McLeskey, J., Hoppey, D., & Rentz, T. (2006). Educating students with mental retardation in general education classrooms. *Exceptional Children, 72,* 347–361.

Wolfensberger, W. (1972). *The principle of normalization in human services.* Toronto: National Institute on Mental Retardation.

Wong, Q. (2005). *Disability and American families: 2000.* Washington, DC: U.S. Census Bureau.

Woolever, C., & Bruce, D. (2002). *A field guide to U.S. congregations: Who's going where and why.* Louisville, KY: Westminster John Knox Press.

World Council of Churches. (2003). *A church of all and for all: An interim statement.* Geneva: Ecumenical Disability Advocates Network.

Yee, A. (2003). *The Christian conference planner: Organizing special events, conferences, retreats, seminars, workshops.* Union City, CA: SummitStar Press.

Zhang, D., & Rusch, F.R. (2005). The role of spirituality in living with disabilities. *Journal of Religion, Disability, & Health, 9,* 83–98.

Examples of
Faith Group Statements
Addressing Disability and
Congregational Inclusion

The following list of actions, resolutions, and statements is not exhaustive. Some faith groups leave individual congregations to decide whether or not to take an official position on societal issues; others endorse the statements issued by other denominations and organizations.

Faith group and web addresses	Statement title
American Baptist Churches, USA http://www.abc-usa.org	*Resolution on the Church and Persons with Disabilities* (1978, 1994, 1998) *Resolution on Employment of Persons with Disabilities* (1983, 1994, 1998) *Resolution on Mental Illness* (1991) *Resolution on Ministry to the Handicapped* (1959)
Assemblies of God http://www.ag.org	*Ministry to People with Disabilities: A Biblical Perspective* (2000)
Baha'i http://www.bahai.org	*Human Rights and Disability* (1988)

Catholic Church http://www.usccb.org	*Conclusions of a Vatican Conference on the Family and Integration of the Disabled* (1999) *Welcome and Justice for Persons with Disabilities: A Framework for Access and Inclusion: A Statement of the U.S. Bishops* (1998) *Resolution on the Tenth Anniversary of the Pastoral Statement on Persons with Disabilities* (1988) *Pastoral Statement of U.S. Catholic Bishops on People with Disabilities* (1978)
Central Conference of American Rabbis http://www.ccarnet.org	*Resolution Adopted by CCAR On Persons with Disabilities* (1983)
Christian Church (Disciples of Christ) http://www.disciples.org	*Substitute Resolution Concerning Ministry to Children with Special Needs and Their Families* (1992) *Resolution of Concern for Persons with Conditions of Impairment* (1985) *Resolution Concerning Large Print Hymnals for the Visually Impaired* (1979)
Christian Reformed Church http://www.crcna.net	*Toward Full Compliance with the Provisions of the Americans With Disabilities Act in the Christian Reformed Church of North America* (1993) *Resolution on Disabilities, Acts of Synod* (1985)
Church of England http://www.cofe.anglican.org	*People with Learning Difficulties* (1984)
Church of the Brethren htttp://www.brethren.org	*Conference Resolution: Americans with Disabilities Act* (1994) *Church and Persons with Disabilities* (1981)

Episcopal Church
http://www.episcopalarchives
   .org

Adopt NCC Statement on Disabilities
   (2000)
Re-establish a Resource Center on the
   Disabled (1997)
Authorize Continuation of the Task Force
   on Accessibility (1994)
Commend Passage of the Americans With
   Disabilities Act (1991)
Commend the Task Force on Accessibility
   and Encourage Sensitivity to Persons
   with Disabilities (1988)
Encourage Opportunities Within the
   Church for Persons with Disabilities
   (1985)
Establish a Task Force on Disabled and
   Handicapped Persons (1982)

Evangelical Covenant Church
http://www.covchurch.org

Resolution on Concern for People with
   Disabilities (1997)
Resolutions on Disabilities (1987)

Evangelical Lutheran Church
   in America
http://www.elca.org

Ministry to the Deaf Community (1991)

Ministry with Persons with Disabilities
   (1991)
Accessibility Sunday (1991)

Lutheran Church—Missouri
   Synod
http://www.lcms.org

To Improve Services to Persons with
   Handicaps (1977)

National Council of Churches
http://www.ncccusa.org

Disabilities, the Body of Christ and the
   Wholeness of Society (1998)
No Barriers for Deaf People in Churches
   (1997)

Orthodox Union
http://www.ou.org

Statement on Passage of S.1248,
   Reauthorization of the Individuals with
   Disabilities Education Act (2004)
Commending the House Effort to Improve
   Special Education for America's Children
   (2003)

Presbyterian Church (USA)
http://www.pcusa.org
	Living Into the Body of Christ: Towards
	    Full Inclusion of People with Disabilities
	    (2006)
	Resolution on Disabilities: A Celebration of
	    That All May Enter (2000)
	An Ethical Statement of Care (1985)
	That All May Enter (1977)
	The Church and the Mentally Retarded
	    (1970)

Reformed Church of America http://www.rca.org	*The Reformed Church and the International* *Year of Disabled Persons* (1982) *God's Handicapped Children* (1980) *Rights of the Handicapped* (1975)
Seventh-Day Adventist Church http://www.adventist.org	*Commission for People with Disabilities* (1995)

Southern Baptist Convention
http://www.sbc.net
	Resolution on the Mentally Handicapped
	    (1981)
	Resolution on the Handicapped (1978)
	Resolution on Ministry to the
	    Developmentally Disabled and Mentally
	    Ill (1978)

Union for Reform Judaism http://www.uahc.org	*Transforming Congregations Into Inclusive* *and Caring Jewish Congregations* (1999) *Disabled Persons* (1981) *The Disabled* (1978)

Unitarian Universalist
    Association of
    Congregations
http://www.uua.org
	Accessibility for Persons with Disabilities
	    (1997)
	Persons with Special Needs (1977)

United Church of Christ
http://www.ucc.org
	Called to Wholeness in Christ: Becoming a
	    Church Accessible to All (2005)
	The Calling of Clergy with Disabilities
	    (1999)
	Calling the People of God to Justice for
	    Persons with Serious Mental Illness
	    (1999)

*Concerning the Church and the Americans
with Disabilities Act of 1990* (1995)
*Resolution on the Full Participation of
Persons with Disabilities in the Life of
the Church* (1985)

United Methodist Church
http://www.umc.org

*United Methodist Implementation of
Americans with Disabilities Act* (2004)
Rights of Persons with Disabilities (2000)
Called to Inclusiveness (2000)
Accessibility Grants for Churches (2000)
The Church and Deaf Ministries (2000)
*Abusive Treatment Methods for Persons
with Mental Disabilities* (1996; 2004)
Annual Accessibility Audit (1992, 2004)
*Communication Access for People Who
Have Hearing and Sight Impairment*
(1992, 1996, 2004)
*The Church and People with Mental,
Physical, and/or Psychological
Disabilities* (1984, 1996, 2004)

United Synagogue of
  Conservative Judaism
http://www.uscj.org

Mezuzah Accessibility (1997)
Measures for Persons with Disabilities
(1991)

World Council of Churches
http://www.wcc-coe.org

A Church of All and For All (2003)
*Interim Statement on the Theological and
Empirical Understanding of the Issue of
Disabilities* (1997)
*The Handicapped and the Wholeness of the
Family of God* (1975)

Appendix B

Resources for Service Providers, Families, and Congregations

RESOURCES FOR SERVICE AND SUPPORT PROVIDERS

Amado, A.N., & McBride, M. (2001). *Increasing person-centered thinking: Improving the quality of person-centered planning: A manual for person-centered planning facilitators.* Minneapolis: University of Minnesota, Institute on Community Integration.

Carnaby, S., & Cambridge, P. (2006). *Intimate and personal care with people with learning disabilities.* London: Jessica Kinglsey.

"Community for all" tool kit: Resources for supporting community living. (2004). Syracuse, NY: Human Policy Press. Available on-line at http://thechp.syr.edu/toolkit

Hatton, C., Turner, S., Shah, R., Rahim, N., & Stansfield, J. (2004). *What about faith? A good practice guide for services on meeting the religious needs of people with learning disabilities.* London: Foundation for People with Learning Disabilities.

Holburn, S., & Vietze, P.M. (2002). *Person-centered planning: Research, practice, and future directions.* Baltimore: Paul H. Brookes Publishing Co.

Larson, S.A., & Hewitt, A.S. (2005). *Staff recruitment, retention, and training: Strategies for community human services organizations.* Baltimore: Paul H. Brookes Publishing Co.

McMorrow, M.J. (2003). *Getting ready to help: A primer on interacting in human service.* Baltimore: Paul H. Brookes Publishing Co.

O'Brien, J., & Lyle O'Brien, C. (Eds.). (2002). *Implementing person-centered planning: Voices of experience.* Toronto: Inclusion Press.

O'Brien, J., & Mount, B. (2005). *Make a difference: A guidebook for person-centered direct support.* Toronto: Inclusion Press.

Swinton, J. (2004). *No box to tick: A booklet for carers of people with learning disabilities.* London: Foundation for People with Learning Disabilities.

Swinton, J., & Powrie, E. (2004). *Why are we here? Meeting the spiritual needs of people with learning disabilities.* London: Foundation for People with Learning Disabilities.

RESOURCES FOR FAMILY MEMBERS

Bolduc, K.D. (1999). *His name is Joel: Searching for God in a son's disability.* Louisville, KY: Bridge Resources.

Bolduc, K.D. (2001). *A place called acceptance: Ministry with families of children with disabilities.* Louisville, KY: Bridge Resources.

de Vinck, C. (2002). *The power of the powerless: A brother's legacy of love.* New York: Crossroads.

Fuller, C., & Jones, L.T. (1997). *Extraordinary kids: Nurturing and championing your child with special needs.* Colorado Springs, CO: Focus on the Family.

Gallagher, P.A., Powell, T., & Rhodes, C.A. (2006). *Brothers & sisters: A special part of exceptional families* (3rd ed.). Baltimore: Paul H. Brookes Publishing Co.

Klein, S. D., & Kemp, J. D. (Eds.). (2004). *What adults with disabilities wish all parents knew: Reflections from a different journey.* New York: McGraw-Hill.

Klein, S. D., & Schive, K. (Eds.). (2001). *You will dream new dreams: Inspiring personal stories by parents of children with disabilities.* New York: Kensington Books.

Layman, R. (1988). *My child is different: A guide for Jewish parents of special children.* New York: United Synagogue of American, Commission on Jewish Education.

Osborn, S. T., & Mitchell, J. L. (2004). *A special kind of love: For those who love children with special needs.* Nashville: Broadman & Holman Publishers.

Ransom, J. G. (1994). *The courage to care: Seven families touched by disability and congregational caring.* Nashville, TN: Upper Room Books.

Sharp, M. (2003). *An unexpected joy: The gift of parenting a challenging child.* Colorado Springs, CO: Pinon Press.

Spiegle, J. (1993). *Making changes: Family voices on living with disabilities.* Cambridge, MA: Brookline.

Steere, C. (2005). *Too wise to be mistaken, too good to be unkind: Christian parents contend with autism.* Sand Springs, OK: Grace and Truth Books.

Zurheide, K.J., & Zurheide, J.R. (2000). *In their own way: Accepting your children for who they are.* Minneapolis, MN: Augsburg Fortress.

RESOURCES FOR PEOPLE WITH DEVELOPMENTAL DISABILITIES

Acker-Verney, J., Hattie, B., MacDonald, C., & Lekas, S. (2005). *"More than my disability": A handbook for volunteers with disabilities.* Halifax, NS: Independent Living Resource Center.

Allen, W.T. (2002). *It's my choice.* St. Paul, MN: Minnesota Governor's Council on Developmental Disabilities.

Gritter, R. (1998). *A place for me in God's family.* Colorado Springs, CO: IBS Publishing.

Swinton, J., Powrie, E., & Morgan, H. (2004). *What is important to you: A booklet for people with learning disabilities.* London: Foundation for People with Learning Disabilities.

GENERAL RESOURCES FOR CONGREGATIONS

Balge, E., Koeller, A., & Mose, J. (2000). *Planting the seeds in students with special needs: A guide for including students with special needs in your Sunday school, catechism, or Bible class* (2nd ed.). Milwaukee, WI: JCM Publications.

Bass, S. (2003). *Special children, special needs: Integrating children with disabilities and special needs into your church.* London: Church House Publishing.

Benton, J.L., & Owen, M.J. (1997). *Opening doors to people with disabilities* (Vol.1 and 2). Washington, DC: National Catholic Office for Persons with Disabilities.

Bethesda Lutheran Homes and Services. (1998). *Each one uniquely gifted by God.* Watertown, WI: Author.

Bethesda Lutheran Homes and Services. (2006). *Building a developmental disabilities ministry: A manual for congregations.* Watertown, WI: Author.

Bittner, R. (1994). *Under His wings: Meeting the spiritual needs of the mentally disabled.* Wheaton, IL: Crossway Books.

Bolduc, K.D. (2001). *A place called acceptance: Ministry with families of children with disabilities.* Louisville, KY: Bridge Resources.

Briggs, L.L. (2003). *The art of helping: What to say and do when someone is hurting.* Colorado Springs, CO: RiverOak Publishing.

Brisbane Catholic Education. (2003). *Confidence and capacity: Parish communities knowing and supporting people with disability: A resource book.* Queensland, Australia: Archdiocese of Brisbane.

Browne, E. (1997). *The disabled disciple: Ministering in a church without barriers.* Liguori, MO: Liguori Publications.

Browne, E. (2004). *Creating an inclusive worship community: Accommodating all peoples at God's table.* Liguori, MO: Liguori Publications.

Bureau of Jewish Education of Los Angeles. (1991). *Justice, justice for all: Promoting disability awareness in the Jewish community.* Los Angeles: Author.

Carder, S. (1995). *A committed mercy: You and your church can serve the disabled.* Grand Rapids, MI: Baker Books.

Davie, A.R., & Thornburgh, G. (2000). *That all may worship: An interfaith welcome to people with disabilities.* Washington, DC: National Organization on Disability.

Department of Jewish Family Concerns. (2000). *Al Pi Darco: According to their ways: A special needs resource manual.* New York: Author.

Dicken, P., Young, J., & Baird, S. (2004). *You're welcome: A best practice guide to including disabled people in the life of the church.* Epsom, UK: Through the Roof.

Disabilities in Ministry Committee. (1999). *Ephphatha! Open up!: A children's curriculum for understanding disabilities.* Lima, OH: CSS Publishing Company.

Edwards, J. (1997). *Involving people with learning difficulties* (Sharing our faith series). London: Matthew James.

Gaventa, W. (Ed.). (2005). *Dimensions of faith and congregational ministries with persons with developmental disabilities and their families: A bibliography and address listing of resources for clergy, laypersons, families, and service providers.* New Brunswick, NJ: Elizabeth M. Boggs Center on Developmental Disabilities.

Gaventa, B., & Berk, W. (Eds.). (2001). *Brain injury: When the call comes: A congregational response.* Edison, NJ: Brain Injury Association of New Jersey and The Boggs Center.

Gugel, J.R., & Cleaver, L. (Eds.). (2003). *Toward the goal: A resource for full inclusion of people who are differently-abled into the live of the congregation.*

Chicago: Division for Church in Society, Evangelical Lutheran Church in America.

Harrington, M.T. (1992). *A place for all: Mental retardation, catechesis, and liturgy.* Collegeville, MN: Liturgical Press.

Hoogewind, A.J. (1998). *Parables of hope: Inspiring truths from people with disabilities.* Grand Rapids, MI: Zondervan.

Isaacs, L.W., & Levine, C.N. (1995). *So that all may study Torah: Communal provision of Jewish education for students with special needs.* New York: JESNA.

Kutz-Mellem, S. (Ed.). (1998). *Different members, one body: Welcoming the diversity of abilities in God's family.* Louisville, KY: Witherspoon Press.

McNay, A. (1997). *A place for everyone: A guide for special education Bible teaching-reaching ministry.* Nashville, TN: Convention Press.

Miller, K.C., & Burggrabe, J.L. (1991). *The congregation: A community of care and healing.* San Antonio, TX: Benedictine Resource Center.

Mose, J. (2000). *God's children are differently abled: Classroom activities for disability awareness.* Milwaukee, WI: JCM Publications.

National Catholic Partnership on Disability. (2003). *Opening doors of welcome and justice to parishioners with disabilities: A parish resource guide.* Washington, DC: Author.

Newman, B.J. (2001). *Helping kids include kids with disabilities.* Grand Rapids, MI: Faith Alive Christian Resources.

Newman, B.J. (2006). *Autism and your church: Nurturing the spiritual growth of people with autism spectrum disorders.* Grand Rapids, MI: Faith Alive Christian Resources.

Newman, G., & Tada, J.E. (1993). *All God's children: Ministry with disabled persons.* Grand Rapids, MI: Zondervan.

North West Regional Special Educational Needs Partnership. (2004). *Children with autism: Strategies for accessing the curriculum: Religious education.* England: Author.

Ohsberg, H.O. (1982). *The church and persons with handicaps.* Scottsdale, PA: Herald Press.

Okhuisjen, G., & van Opzeeland, C. (1992). *In heaven there are no thunderstorms: Celebrating the liturgy with developmentally disabled people.* Collegeville, MN: Liturgical Press.

Pathways Awareness Foundation. (updated annually). *Inclusion awareness day workbook.* Chicago: Author.

Patton, S. (2004). *Welcoming children with special needs: A guidebook for faith communities.* Boston: Unitarian Universalist Association.

Pierson, J. (1989). *Reaching out to special people: A resource for ministry with persons who have disabilities.* Cincinnati, OH: Standard Publishing Company.

Pierson, J. (1998). *No disabled souls: How to welcome people with disabilities into your life and church.* Cincinnati, OH: Standard Publishing Company.

Pierson, J. (2002). *Exceptional teaching: A comprehensive guide for including students with disabilities.* Cincinnati, OH: Standard Publishing.

Presbyterians for Disability Concerns. (updated annually). *Access Sunday worship celebration packets.* Louisville, KY: Presbyterian Health, Education, & Welfare Association, Presbyterian Church (USA).

Presbytery of the Cascades, Committee on Congregations. (2002). *Opening doors: A congregational guide for welcoming people with disabilities.* Eugene, OR: Author.

Ramnaraine, B., & Steinhagen, M.J. (1997). *AccessAbility: A manual for churches.* St. Paul: MN: Diocesan Office on Ministry with Persons who are Disabled of the Episcopal Diocese of Minnesota and Office for People with Disabilities, Catholic Charities of the Archdiocese of St. Paul, Minnesota.

Rife, J.M., & Thornburgh, G. (2001). *From barriers to bridges: A community action guide for congregations and people with disabilities.* Washington, DC: National Organization on Disability.

Rosen, H., Address, R., Hochman, M., & Izes, L. (2004). *Becoming a Kehillat Chesed: Creating and sustaining a caring congregation* (Rev. ed.). New York: URJ Press.

Sieck, T.F., & Hartvigsen, R. (2001). *How people with developmental disabilities can access the faith community of their choice.* Lakeside, CA: Home of the Guiding Hands.

Stonebriar Community Church. (2003). *Embracing special-needs families: A church model for ministering to families of children and adults with disabilities.* Plano, TX: Insight for Living.

Tada, J.E. (1999). *Disability ministry Sunday kit.* Agoura Hills, CA: Joni and Friends.

Tada, J.E., & Jensen, S. (1997). *Barrier-free friendships: Bridging the distance between you and friends with disabilities.* Grand Rapids, MI: Zondervan.

Tada, J.E., & Miller, S. (2002). *Through the roof: A guide to assist churches in developing an effective disability outreach.* Agoura Hills, CA: Joni and Friends.

Tada, J.E., & Newman, G. (1998). *All God's children: Ministry with disabled persons.* Grand Rapids: Zondervan.

Toews, J., & Loewen, E. (1995). *No longer alone: Mental health and the Church.* Scottdale, PA: Herald Press.

Trembley, L, & Trembley, D. (1996). *Emmaus eyes: Worship with the mentally challenged.* The Lakes, NV: Eden Publishing.

Verbal, P. (2002). Special ministries for special needs. In M. Keefer (Ed.), *Children's ministry that works: The basics and beyond* (pp. 241–252). Loveland, CO: Group Publishing.

Walker, R.L. (2001). *Breaking the sound barrier in your church.* New York: General Board of Global Ministries, United Methodist Church.

Webb-Mitchell, B. (1993). *God plays piano, too: The spiritual lives of disabled children.* New York: Crossroads.

Webb-Mitchell, B. (1994). *Unexpected guests at God's banquet: Welcoming people with disabilities into the church.* New York: Crossroads.

Webb-Mitchell, B. (1996). *Dancing with disabilities: Opening the church to all God's children.* Cleveland, OH: United Church Press.

Wilke, H.H. (1980). *Creating the caring congregation.* Nashville: Abingdon.

THEOLOGY RESOURCES

Abrams, J.Z. (1998). *Judaism and disability: Portrayals in ancient texts from the Tanach through the Bavli.* Washington, DC: Gallaudet University Press.

Bishop, M.E. (Ed.). (1995). *Religion and disability: Perspectives in scripture, theology, and ethics.* Kansas City: Sheed & Ward.

Black, K. (1996). *A healing homiletic: Preaching and disability.* Nashville, TN: Abingdon.

Block, J.W. (2002). *Copious hosting: A theology of access for people with disabilities.* New York: The Continuum International Publishing Group.

Eiesland, N.L. (1994). *The disabled God: Toward a liberatory understanding of disability.* Nashville: Abingdon.

Eiesland, N.L., & Saliers, D. E. (1998). *Human disability and the service of God: Reassessing religious practice.* Nashville: Abingdon.

Epperly, B.G. (2001). *God's touch: Faith, wholeness and the healing miracles of Jesus*. Louisville, KY: Westminster: John Knox Press.

Foley, E. (Ed.). (1994). *Developmental disabilities and sacramental access: New paradigms for sacramental encounters*. Collegeville, MN: Liturgical Press.

Fritzson, A., & Kabue, S. (2004). *Interpreting disability: A Church of all and for all*. Geneva: WCC Publications.

Gaventa, W.C., & Coulter, D.L. (Eds.). (2001). *The theological voice of Wolf Wolfensberger*. Binghamton, NY: Haworth Press.

Gaventa, W.C., & Coulter, D.L. (Eds.). (2001). *Spirituality and intellectual disability: International perspectives on the effect of culture and religion on healing body, mind, and soul*. Binghamton, NY: Haworth Press.

Govig, S.D. (1989). *Strong at the broken places: Persons with disabilities and the church*. Louisville, KY: Westminster/John Knox Press.

Haeurwas, S. (1986). *Suffering presence: Theological reflections on medicine, the mentally handicapped, and the Church*. Notre Dame, IN: University of Notre Dame Press.

Kelly, B., & McGinley, P. (2000). *Intellectual disability: The response of the church*. Lancashire, England: Lisieux Hall Publications.

Kennedy, S. (Ed.). (1997). *Spiritual journeys: An anthology of writings by people living and working with those on the margins*. Dublin: Veritas.

McCloughty, R., & Morris, W. (2002). *Making a world of difference: Christian reflections on disability*. London: Society for Promoting Christian Knowledge.

Merrick, L.H. (Ed.). (1993). *And show steadfast love: A theological look at grace, hospitality, disabilities, and the Church*. Louisville, KY: Presbyterian Publishing House.

Mitchell, D.T., & Snyder, S.L. (Eds.). (1997). *The body and physical difference: Discourses on disability*. Ann Arbor: University of Michigan Press.

Nouwen, H.J.M. (1972). *The wounded healer*. New York: Image Books Doubleday.

Nouwen, H.J.M. (1988). *The road to daybreak: A spiritual journey*. New York: Doubleday.

Nouwen, H.J.M. (1997). *Adam: God's beloved*. Maryknoll, NY: Orbis Books.

Stolk, J., Boer, T.A., & Seldenrijk, R. (Eds.). (2000). *Meaningful care: A multidisciplinary approach to the meaning of care for people with mental retardation*. Norwell, MA: Kluwer Academic Publishers.

Swinton, J. (Ed.). (2004). *Critical reflections on Stanley Hauerwas' theology of disability: Disabling society, enabling theology*. Binghamton, NY: Haworth Press.

Varnier, J. (1989). *Community and growth*. Mahwah, NJ: Paulist Press.

Varnier, J. (1998). *Becoming human*. Toronto: Anansi.

Varnier, J. (2005). *Befriending the stranger*. Grand Rapids, MI: Eerdmans.

Varnier, J. (2006). *Encountering the 'other'*. Mahwah, NJ: Paulist Press.

Pastoral Care Resources

Collins, G.B., & Culbertson, T. (2003). *Mental illness and psychiatric treatment: A guide for pastoral counselors*. Binghamton, NY: Haworth Pastoral Press.

Friesen, M.F. (2000). *Spiritual care for children living in specialized settings: Breathing underwater*. Binghamton, NY: Haworth Press.

Gaventa, W.C. (2003). Pastoral counseling with individuals with disabilities and their families. In R.J. Wicks, R.D. Parsons, & D. Capps (Eds.), *Clinical handbook of pastoral counseling: Vol. 3* (pp. 120–145). New York: Paulist Press.

Gaventa, W.C., & Coulter, D.L. (Eds.). (2003). *The pastoral voice of Robert Perske*. Binghamton, NY: Haworth Press.

Gaventa, W.C., & Coulter, D.L. (Eds.). (2005). *End-of-life care: Bridging disability and aging with person-centered care*. Binghamton, NY: Haworth Press.

Govig, S.D. (1999). *In the shadow of our steeples: Pastoral presence for families coping with mental illness*. New York: Haworth Pastoral Press.

Kauffman, J. (2004). *Guidebook on helping people with mental retardation mourn*. Amityville, NY: Baywood.

Luchterhand, C., & Murphy, N. (1998). *Helping adults with mental retardation grieve a death loss*. London: Taylor & Francis.

Roukema, R.W. (2003). *Counseling for the soul in distress: What every religious counselor should know about emotional and mental illness* (2nd ed). New York: Haworth Pastoral Press.

Severino, S.K., & Liew, R. (Eds.). (1996). *Pastoral care of the mentally disabled: Advancing care of the whole person*. Binghamton, NY: Haworth Press.

Sussan, K. (2000). Loving the stranger: Accompanying individuals with chronic mental disorders. In D. L. Friedman (Ed.), *Jewish pastoral care: A practical handbook from traditional and contemporary sources* (pp. 325–343). Woodstock, VT: Jewish Lights Publishing.

Van Dyke, L. (2003). *Lessons in grief and death: Supporting people with developmental disabilities in the healing process.* Homewood, IL: High Tide Press.

Walter, K. (1985). *Pastoral ministry with disabled persons.* New York: Alba House.

Weaver, A.J., Revilla, L.A., & Koenig, H.G. (2002). *Counseling families across the stages of life: A handbook for pastors and other helping professionals.* Nashville: Abingdon Press.

Willows, D., & Swinton, J. (Eds.). (2000). *Spiritual dimensions of pastoral care: Practical theology in a multidisciplinary context.* London: Jessica Kinglsey.

ACCESSIBILITY GUIDES

Alban Institute. (2001). *Money and ideas: Creative approaches to congregational access.* Bethesda, MD: Author.

Evangelical Lutheran Church of America (2001). *ECLA accessibility guide: Planning an accessible meeting.* Chicago: Author.

NCCCUSA Committee on Disabilities. (2004). *Equal access guide for meetings, conferences, large assemblies, and worship.* New York: National Council of the Churches of Christ in the USA, Educational and Leadership Ministries Commission, Committee on Disabilities.

Patterson E.A. & Vogel, N.A. (2003). *Accessible faith: A technical guide for accessibility in houses of worship.* Chicago: Retirement Research Foundation.

Reeves, K.N. (Ed.). (1994). *Accessibility audit for churches: Creating access for persons with physically challenging conditions.* New York: General Board of Global Ministries, United Methodist Church.

Thornburgh, G. (Ed.). (1999). *Loving justice: The ADA and the religious community.* Washington, DC: National Organization on Disability.

U.S. Architectural and Transportation Barriers Compliance Board (2002). *Americans with Disabilities Act (ADA): Accessibility Guidelines for Buildings and Facilities.* Washington, DC: Author. Available from http://www.access-board.gov

CURRICULAR RESOURCES

Abiding in Faith: A Resource for Teachers of Adults with Moderate Mental Retardation
Christian Board of Publication
http://www.cbp21.com

Beyond Limits
Vision New England
http://www.visionnewengland.org

Bridges: A Curriculum for Persons with Disabilities
Abingdon Press
http://www.abingdonpress.com

Church words: A Curriculum
Feed All My Sheep: A Guide and Curriculum for Adults with Developmental Disabilities
Geneva Press
http://www.ppcbooks.com

Exploring Faith and Life Bible Study Curriculum Package
Bethesda Lutheran Homes and Services
http://www.blhs.org

Friendship Bible Studies
Friendship Life Studies
Friendship Ministries
http://www.friendship.org

Hearts to Dance: A Time for Everything
Hearts to Dance: Gifts Galore
Hearts to Dance: Old and New
Faith Education Services, Catholic Archdiocese of Brisbane
http://www.bne.catholic.net.au

Living in Faith: A Resource for Teachers of Older Youth and Young Adults Who Are Retarded
Cokesbury
http://www.cokesbury.com

Practical Teaching Methods for Bringing the Gospel to Special Needs Students
Covenant Resource Center
http://www.covenantbookstore.com

The Rose Fitzgerald Kennedy Program to Improve Catholic Religious Education for Children and Adults with Mental Retardation
Silver Burdett Religion
http://www.sbgreligion.com

What Christians Believe: Confirmation Studies for Persons with Mental Retardation and Developmental Disabilities
Bridge Resources
http://www.pcusa.org/bridgeresources

Worship ASAP
Religious education and faith development for children with autism and/or severe and complex learning disabilities.
Church House Publishing
http://www.chpublishing.co.uk

ORGANIZATIONS AND FAITH GROUP OFFICES ADDRESSING CONGREGATIONAL INCLUSION

Anabaptist Disabilities Network
Post Office Box 959
Goshen, Indiana 46527
574-535-7053 (telephone)
877-214-9838 (fax)
http://www.adnetonline.org

Association of Brethren Caregivers
1451 Dundee Avenue
Elgin, Illinois 60120
847-742-5100 (telephone)
847-742-6103 (fax)
http://www.brethren.org/abc

Bethesda Lutheran Homes and Services
600 Hoffman Avenue
Watertown, Wisconsin 53094
800-369-4636 (telephone)
920-261-3050 (fax)
http://www.blhs.org

Causeway Prospects
69 Honey End Lane
Reading, Berks RG30 4EL
United Kingdom
0118-950-8781 (telephone)

0118-939-1683 (fax)
http://www.prospects.org.uk

Center for Religion and Disability
1780 Indian Hill Road
Pelham, Alabama 35124
http://www.religionanddisability.org

Christian Church Foundation for the Handicapped
Post Office Box 9869
Knoxville, Tennessee 37940
865-546-5921 (telephone)
865-525-2282 (fax)
http://www.cchf.org

Christian Council on Persons with Disabilities
301 East Pine Street, Suite 150
Orlando, Florida 32801
407-210-3917 (telephone)
407-385-3601 (fax)
http://www.ccpd.org

Committee on Disabilities of National Council of Churches of Christ USA
National Council of Churches of Christ
475 Riverside Drive, Room 848
New York, New York 10115
212-870-2267 (telephone)
217-870-2030 (fax)
http://www.ncccusa.org

Council for Jews with Special Needs
12701 North Scottsdale Road, Suite 205
Scottsdale, Arizona 85254
480-629-5343 (telephone)
480-629-5365 (fax)
http://www.cjsn.org

CUSA: An Apostolate For People with Chronic Illness or with Disabilities
176 West 8th Street
Bayonne, New Jersey 07002
http://www.cusan.org
ams4@juno.com (e-mail)

Disability Concerns of the Christian Reformed Church
2850 Kalamazoo Avenue SE
Grand Rapids, Michigan 49560-0800
616-224-0801 (telephone)
616-224-0834 (fax)
http://www.crcna.org

**Disability Ministries of the
Evangelical Lutheran Church of America**
8765 West Higgins Road
Chicago, Illinois 60631
800-638-3522 (telephone)
773-380-1465 (fax)
http://www.elca.org/disability

Ecumenical Disability Advocates Network
150 Route de Ferney
Post Office Box 2100
CH-1211 Geneva 2
Switzerland
41 22 791 6026 (telephone)
41 22 791 6409 (fax)
http://www.wcc-coe.org

Episcopal Disability Network
3024 East Minnehaha Parkway
Minneapolis, Minnesota 55406
888-738-3636 (telephone)
http://www.disability99.org

Faith and Light USA
1401 Lawrence Avenue, N.E.
Washington, DC 20017
202-526-3222 telephone
http://www.faithandlight.net

Foundation for People with Learning Disabilities
9th Floor, Sea Containers House
20 Upper Ground
London, SE1 9QB
United Kingdom
020 7803 1100 (telephone)
020 7803 1111 (fax)
http://www.learningdisabilities.org.uk

Friendship Ministries
2850 Kalamazoo Avenue SE

Grand Rapids, Michigan 49560
888-866-8966 (telephone)
616-224-0834 (fax)
http://www.friendship.org or
http://www.ministerioamistad.org

Handi*Vangelism Ministries International
Post Office Box 122
Akron, Pennsylvania 17501
717-859-4777 (telephone)
717-859-4505 (fax)
http://www.hvmi.org

Jesus Cares Ministries
4050 North 95th Street
Milwaukee, Wisconsin 53222
877-505-3675 (telephone)
http://www.jcministries.org

Jewish Guild for the Blind
15 West 65th Street
New York, New York 10023
800-284-4422 (telephone)
http://www.jgb.org

Joni and Friends International Disability Center
Post Office Box 3333
Agoura Hills, California 91376
818-707-5664 (telephone)
818-707-2391 (fax)
http://www.joniandfriends.org

L'Arche USA
H326-19230 Forest Park Drive NE
Seattle, Washington 98155
206-306-1330 (telephone)
206-306-1329 (fax)
http://www.larcheusa.org

Lutheran Special Education Ministries
6861 East Nevada
Detroit, Michigan 48234
888-488-5736 (telephone)
313-368-0159 (fax)
http://www.luthsped.org

National Apostolate for Inclusion Ministry
Post Office Box 218
Riverdale, Maryland 20738
800-736-1280 (telephone)
http://www.nafim.org

National Catholic Partnership on Disability
415 Michigan Avenue NE, Suite 95
Washington, DC 20017-4501
202-529-2933 (telephone)
202-529-4678 (fax)
http://www.ncpd.org

National Jewish Council for Disabilities
11 Broadway, 13th Floor
New York, New York 10004
212-613-8229 (telephone)
http://www.njcd.org

National Jewish Council for the Disabled
333 Seventh Avenue
New York, New York 10001
212-613-8235 (telephone)
212-613-8333 (fax)
http://www.ou.org/ncsy/njcd

North American Mission Board
Disability Awareness Ministry
4200 North Point Parkway
Alpharetta, Georgia 30022
800-634-2462 (telephone)
770-410-6082 (fax)
http://www.namb.net

Pathways to Promise
5400 Arsenal Street
St. Louis, Missouri 63139
314-877-6489 (telephone)
314-644-8834 (fax)
http://www.pathways2promise.org

Pathways Awareness Foundation
150 North Michigan Avenue, Suite 2100
Chicago, Illinois 60601
800-955-2445 (telephone)
888-795-5884 (fax)
http://www.pathwaysawareness.org

Presbyterians for Disabilities Concerns
Presbyterian Church (USA)
100 Witherspoon #4617
Louisville, Kentucky 40202
888-728-7228 (telephone)
http://www.pcusa.org/phewa/pdc

Reformed Church in America
Committee on Disabilities
4500 60th Street SE
Grand Rapids, Michigan 49512
800-968-3943 (telephone)
http://www.rca.org/disciples/disability

Religion and Disability Program
National Organization on Disability
910 Sixteenth Street NW, Suite 600
Washington, DC 20006
202-293-5960 (telephone)
202-293-7999 (fax)
http://www.nod.org

Religion and Spirituality Division
American Association on Intellectual and
Developmental Disabilities
444 North Capitol Street, NW, Suite 846
Washington, DC 20001-1512
800-424-3688 (telephone)
202-387-2193 (fax)
http://www.aaidd.org

Through the Roof
Post Office Box 353
Epsom Surrey KT18 5WS
01372 749955 (telephone)
01372 737040 (fax)
http://www.throughtheroof.org

United Church of Christ
Disabilities Ministries
700 Prospect Avenue
Cleveland, Ohio 44155
866-822-8224 (telephone)
216-736-2237 (fax)
http://www.uccdm.org

United Methodist Church
Disability Concerns
475 Riverside Drive
New York, New York 10115
212-870-3871 (telephone)
212-870-3624 (fax)
http://www.gbgm-umc.org

Unitarian Universalist Association
Accessibilities Committee
25 Beacon Street
Boston, Massachusetts 02108
617-948-6451 (telephone)
http://www.uaa.org

Zachariah's Way
Post Office Box 5565
Gainesville, Georgia 30504
678-643-6781 (telephone)
770-531-0813 (fax)
http://www.zachariahsway.com

NATIONAL ORGANIZATIONS SUPPORTING PEOPLE WITH DEVELOPMENTAL DISABILITIES

American Association for People with Disabilities — http://www.aapd.com

American Association on Intellectual and Developmental Disabilities — http://www.aaidd.org

American Network of Community Options and Resources — http://www.ancor.org

Angelman Syndrome Foundation — http://www.angelman.org

ARCH National Respite Network — http://www.archrespite.org

Association of University Centers on Disabilities — http://www.aucd.org

Autism Society of America   http://www.autism-society.org

Consortium for Citizens with
  Disabilities   http://www.c-c-d.org

Council for Exceptional Children   http://www.cec.sped.org

Disability Info   http://www.disabilityinfo.gov

Easter Seals   http://www.easterseals.org

Institute for Community Inclusion   http://www.communityinclusion.org

Institute on Community
  Integration   http://www.ici.umn.edu

International Rett Syndrome
  Association   http://www.rettsyndrome.org

National Association for
  Christians in Special Education   http://www.nacsped.com

National Association for Down
  Syndrome   http://www.nads.org

National Association for the
  Dually Diagnosed   http://www.thenadd.org

National Association of Councils
  on Developmental Disabilities   http://www.nacdd.org

National Alliance on Mental
  Illness   http://www.nami.org

National Council on Independent
  Living   http://www.ncil.org

National Disability Rights
  Network   http://www.napas.org

National Dissemination Center for
  Children with Disabilities   http://www.nichcy.org

National Down Syndrome
  Congress   http://www.ndsccenter.org

National Down Syndrome Society   http://www.ndss.org

National Family Caregivers
  Association   http://www.thefamilycaregiver.org

National Fragile X Foundation   http://www.nfxf.org

National Organization for Rare
  Disorders   http://www.rarediseases.org

National Organization on Disability	http://www.nod.org
Prader-Willi Syndrome Association	http://www.pwsausa.org
President's Committee for People with Intellectual Disabilities	http://www.acf.hhs.gov/programs/pcpid
Self-Advocates Becoming Empowered	http://www.sabeusa.org
Spina Bifida Association	http://www.sbaa.org
TASH	http://www.tash.org
The Council on Quality and Leadership	http://www.thecouncil.org
The Arc of the United States	http://www.thearc.org
Williams Syndrome Association	http://www.williams-syndrome.org
United Cerebral Palsy	http://www.ucp.org

Index

Page references followed by *b* indicate boxes; those followed by *f* indicate figures; those followed by *t* indicate tables.